Women at Work in
Twenty-First-Century
European Cinema

Women at Work in Twenty-First-Century European Cinema

BARBARA MENNEL

© 2019 by the Board of Trustees
of the University of Illinois
All rights reserved
1 2 3 4 5 C P 5 4 3 2 1
♾ This book is printed on acid-free paper.
Printed and bound in Great Britain by
Marston Book Services Ltd, Oxfordshire

Library of Congress Cataloging-in-Publication Data
Names: Mennel, Barbara Caroline, author.
Title: Women at work in twenty-first-century European cinema / Barbara Mennel.
Description: [Urbana, Illlinois] : University of Illinois Press, [2019] | Includes bibliographical references and indexes.
Identifiers: LCCN 2018032356| ISBN 9780252042225 (cloth : alk. paper) | ISBN 9780252083952 (paperback : alk. paper)
Subjects: LCSH: Working women in motion pictures. | Motion pictures—Europe—History—21st century.
Classification: LCC PN1995.9.W6 M46 2019 | DDC 791.43/6522— dc23 LC record available at https://lccn.loc.gov/2018032356

Ebook ISBN 978-0-252-05096-1

Contents

Acknowledgments vii

Introduction 1

1. The Specter of Domesticity 24
2. Precarious Work in Feminist Film 52
3. Heritage Cinema of Industrial Labor 78
4. Voice in the Cinema of Labor Migration 103
5. Care Work and the Suspicious Gesture 129
6. Reproductive Labor in the Age of Biotechnology 154
7. Crisis Cinema 178

Conclusion 201

Notes 207

References 215

Film Index 233

General Index 237

Acknowledgments

Thinking about invisible emotional labor has made me appreciate the many ways others have sustained me and this project over the years. Several institutions have supported the writing of this book. A two-month research stay as a Paul Mellon Visiting Senior Fellow at the Center for the Advanced Studies of the Visual Arts at the National Gallery in Washington, DC, in 2013 provided me with a unique access to materials and a productive environment for writing. Dean Elizabeth Cropper, associate deans Therese O'Malley and Peter Lukehart, the film department's Margaret Parsons and Joanna Raczynska, senior fellows Arnold Witte and Christine Goettler, and research associate Emily Pugh brought perspectives of art history and visual culture to bear on the project. Based on the early progress I was able to make, the organization Women in German endorsed the book project with a Faculty Research Award in 2015.

As a Marie Skłodowaska Curie FCFP Senior Fellow in 2016–17 at the Freiburg Institute for Advanced Studies I benefited from director Bernd Kortmann's enthusiasm for interdisciplinarity. Carsten Dose, Britta Küst, Petra Fischer, Lena Walter, Kathrin Burkat, and Roland Muntschick made it possible for me to focus on completing a draft of the manuscript. Fellows Martin Bemmann, Todd Carmody, Carolin Duttlinger, Winfried Fluck, Joseph Harris, Lorenzo Kamel, Martin Loughlin, Nicola Piper, Andrea Riemenschnitter, Marie Seong-Hak Kim, and Aude Wirth-Jaillard created community around scholarship.

The University of Florida, especially the College of Liberal Arts and Sciences and the Departments of English and of Languages, Literatures, and Cultures, supported this work generously. I would like to acknowledge the research funding provided by the University of Florida College of Liberal Arts and Sciences. In addition, a one-semester sabbatical, humanities enhancement grants, and a faculty enhancement opportunity grant enabled me to advance the project at its different stages. The Center for European Studies provided summer travel funds and allowed me to participate in a workshop entitled Capitalism in the New Europe with political economist Dorothee Bohle. Collaborating with the center's director, Amie Kreppel, made possible visits by scholars of European cinema, including Anikó Imre, Rosalind Galt, and Karl Schoonover. My former and current chairs, Akíntúndé Akínyemí, Sidney I. Dobrin, Kenneth Kidd, and Ingrid Kleespies, and Associate Deans David Pharies and Mary Watt provided crucial administrative support. My colleagues in German studies, Franz Futterknecht, Will Hasty, Eric Kligermann, and Chris Overstreet, took over the daily grind while I spent a year away from my regular duties. Aida Hozić read parts of the manuscript and watched films with me. More than that, she and Richard Scher opened their home and prepared sumptuous meals for me.

I have been fortunate to present drafts of sections of the book at invited talks and engage in scholarly conversations at several conference panels about cinema and labor. For generous invitations to the Johannes Gutenberg University in Mainz, Johns Hopkins University, Georgetown University, the University of Maryland, College Park, the University of Pittsburgh, and the University of Toronto, I thank Nathan Dize, Angelica Fenner, Uli Linke, John Lyon, Sabine Nessel, Katrin Pahl, Peter Pfeiffer, and Kayla Jean Watson. Emma McGlennen provided me with a thorough and astute response to my talk. I also benefitted from participating on three panels on labor and film at the Society for Cinema and Media Studies. Vinzenz Hediger's excitement for the term "heritage cinema of industrial labor" was an infectious boost! Tamao Nakahara and Daniela Berghahn organized two panels where I tried out initial versions of the ideas included in this book. Daniela also brought key films and readings to my attention. Earlier versions of sections of this book appeared in *Women in German Yearbook* (University of Nebraska Press, 2014) and in *Genre and the (Post)Communist Woman: Analyzing Transformations of the Central and Eastern European Female Ideal*, edited by Florentina C. Andreescu and Michael J. Shapiro (Routledge, 2014). I am grateful for the permission to reuse this material.

Colleagues, friends, and strangers gave time and effort in a myriad of ways. Fellow scholars generously read and commented on individual chapters despite their own writing projects: Monika Shafi, Berna Güneli, and Erica

Fretwell nudged me along with encouragement and critical questions. Erica Carter offered references in more than one important conversation. Ann Manov translated song texts, and world traveler Ada Cruz told me, "You can do it, Professor!" Scholars Hester Baer, Ipek A. Celik, Michael Falser, Elena Gorfinkel, and Jaclyn Kurash generously shared published and unpublished work with me. Filmmakers kindly sent me DVDs or gave me access to their films. Thank you to Ursula Biemann, Clara van Gool, Mako Idemitsu, Ivana Mladenovic, Anja Salomonowitz, and Elke Sasse. Former students, curators, librarians, academics, and cinema directors provided me with film titles: Mary Fessenden, Jodi Greig, Danijela Majstorovic, Erinn Murray, Kerry Oliver-Smith, Amy Ongiri, Katy Ross, and Judy Shoaf. While some of the films and texts ended up on the book's cutting-room floor, watching and reading them informed my thinking.

A handful of continuous collaborators were steadfast supporters from the project's inception to its final incarnation. An enthusiastic advocate, Randall Halle encouraged me throughout the years and staged an important intervention in Paris, no less. Sabine Hake also championed the significance of my undertaking, always with a list of critical questions. Sabine is an important role model and mentor for a generation of scholars—another form of invisible labor. Katrin Sieg's ability to reflect ideas refracted through her own sophisticated thinking left a lasting imprint on the manuscript. Discussing theories, films, and chapters in Gainesville, Washington, DC, Paris, Freiburg, Berlin, Venice, Kassel, and Atlanta maps our shared conversation over the last couple of years. Closer to home, Jeff Adler, historian by training and film scholar by osmosis, has accompanied the project from its infancy through its gestational phases with a critical eye toward detail and a sophisticated understanding of what is at stake in its broader questions. At the University of Illinois Press, Danny Nasset is a dream editor. Two substantive, engaged, and generous manuscript reviews by Hester Baer and Maria Stehle provided rigorous and supportive feedback that identified areas in need of improvement and pushed me to clarify the implications of my argument. I am also grateful to Levy Randolph for helping me with the final preparation of the screen shots. Finally, I thank my family, especially Hans-Dieter Mennel, Mary Mennel, Susan Mennel, Surjo Soekadar, and Bärbel and Werner Stibal, for their patience, care, and unwavering confidence.

Women at Work in Twenty-First-Century European Cinema

Introduction

> Wo Arbeit ist, kann Weiblichkeit nicht sein
> (Where there is work, there can be no femininity).
> —Heide Volkening, "Working Girl—eine Einleitung"
> (Working girl—an introduction), my translation

> The modern assembly-line worker has for some time been
> an outmoded symbol of modern industrial labor.
> —Arlie Russell Hochschild, *The Managed Heart*

> Women [work] double days for love and for money.
> —Jacqui True, "The Global Financial Crisis's Silver Bullet"

Women's work has made a strong appearance in twenty-first-century European cinema. Gone are the sweaty masculine bodies enslaved by heavy machinery in the underground world of Fritz Lang's 1927 film *Metropolis* (Germany). Missing is the collective mass overthrowing the decadent bourgeoisie through a strike, the central trope of labor struggle, as in Sergei M. Eisenstein's 1925 film *Stachka* (*Strike*, Soviet Union). And we will no longer find male French intellectuals discussing Marx while they occupy a factory, as in post-1968 experimental films à la Jean-Luc Godard's *Tout va bien* (*All's Well*; France and Italy, 1974). Instead, hairdressers, typists, and hotel maids populate films made at the beginning of the twenty-first century. Cinema depicts globally mobile managers in female power suits advancing corporate goals as much as it shows us unemployed architects stumbling through European cities. Ranging from the serious to the comedic and from the groundbreaking to the retrograde, these films employ female characters to embody contemporary European fantasies and social realities of the political economy of work. Since 2000 these films have made up a cinema of women's work, the topic of this book.

Women at Work in Twenty-First-Century European Cinema argues that a thematic cluster about female labor in contemporary films captures the tensions between feminist advances and their capitalist appropriations in a continuously transforming Europe. This new and diverse cinema of women's work portrays multiple forms of productive and reproductive labor. Female characters occupy a range of professions and occupations, from traditionally male, such as architect, manager, lawyer, and politician, to conventionally female, such as typist, telephone operator, maid, teacher, and nurse. Female characters populate factories, offices, and homes. They are self-employed or engage in wage labor, including informal and illegal work. Following the imperatives of second-wave feminism, these films make visible domestic labor, for example, mothering and being a housewife, both previously naturalized as female love and care. The films discussed in this book privilege the relationship of one or more female characters to their work. They subordinate plot developments about love, children, or a crime to their primary narratives or aesthetic concerns with labor.

The book's argument that European cinemas share attention to gender and economy relies on discussing films from more than half of the countries that belong to the EU: Austria, Belgium, France, Germany, Greece, Hungary, Italy, the Netherlands, Portugal, Spain, Sweden, and Great Britain until March 2019, as well as Bosnia, Macedonia, and Norway, which are not EU members. The absence of films from cinemas of small nations, for example, Denmark, Scotland, Bulgaria, Malta, and Cyprus, reflects a confluence of a lack of funding and distribution that prevents a cinema from those countries from participating easily in the broader arcs that this book outlines (see Hjort and Petrie 2007).

European cinema's emphasis on women's work pertains to films made in the first decade and a half of the twenty-first century. The book responds to the lack of studies on this period. *Women at Work* discusses films from 2001 to 2016, with the majority in the years 2006 to 2014. The films from this period demonstrate an interest in economics and labor rooted in a material feminism that is not wedded to a Marxist framework. This feminist turn continues the concerns of second-wave feminism but in a theoretical and cinematic language that adapts to different capitalisms across Europe.

The fall of the Wall triggered an outburst of scholarship on European cinema, which has waned as of late. The majority of discussions of film in Europe covers the period of the 1990s, when processes of Europeanization, in instances celebrating an integrated Europe-to-come, were driving research. Katrin Sieg detects an "emergent Euroculture" after the fall of the Wall (2008, 7). In contrast, the economic and cultural refugee crises, populism, right-wing movements, leave campaigns, and Brexit of the first two decades of the twenty-first century threaten the self-understanding and the cohesion of the EU. Yet twenty-first-century cinema in Europe relies on transnational funding infrastructure. Films are regularly cofunded. The first wave of scholarship emphasizing the contrast between past national cinemas and transnational dynamics does not suffice for a comprehensive analysis of twenty-first-century European cinema.

Gendered labor cuts across a wide range of films. Similar to the waning distinction of national cinemas, genre and art cinema are becoming increasingly hybrid. The book covers art film, independent cinema, documentary, political film, and genre cinema, including romantic comedies, action films, thrillers, biopics, and drama. Out of the more than thirty films discussed in this book, the majority belong to independent cinema, many of which would be categorized as "global art cinema" (see Galt and Schoonover 2010). Less than a third belong to genre cinema. Most are evenly distributed across genres, represented by one to three films. Genres provide formulas to offer familiar narratives associated with particular professions. For example, action films narrate stories of human trafficking, which in turn includes migration and sex work. Drama's association with family lends itself to stage the conflict between the drive for paid labor and the charge to care for children. Dystopian science fiction invokes the relationship of biology and technology. The biopic is an increasingly proliferating genre that mainstreams a paradigmatic feminist narrative of women overcoming historical limitations. Yet certain genres also take up professions in new ways, for example, the thriller about central characters who are maids or nannies.

Genre films have traditionally not been representative of European cinema. As a feminist project, particularly one that takes into account economics, this book is committed to discussing independent films, first features, and minor cinemas. But the fact that genre cinema integrates political topics also speaks to the public awareness about work, economy, and gender. The convergence of these issues across the presumed divide between art, political, and genre cinema indicates their prevalence. Film theory tends to privilege the presumed political productivity of the art film, as the latter questions mimetic representation, undermines identification, and creates distance from conventional narratives. The final discussion of the book regarding the weird waves of art films that emerged out of the eurocrisis in Greece, Spain, and Portugal questions such a privileging.

Feminism also manifests itself in the changing significance of the gender of a film's director. Consequently, of the more than thirty films discussed in this book, women directed almost half. During the cinefeminism that developed from second-wave feminism, primarily female filmmakers had explored the topic of women's labor. Now it has proliferated among filmmakers. The essentialist assumption that women will make more progressive and more feminist films about working women does not apply. With the mainstreaming of feminism, the affective appeal of female empowerment has increased across genres and texts. But capitalism has also appropriated and commodified political movements. The book argues that this does not imply that feminism has lost its political impact nor that it is therefore inherently more powerful and accessible.

The selection of films emerged in conjunction with the book's chapter organization. Based on theoretical and social science research about gender and work and the study of European films that address these topics, the chapters examine clusters that integrate theory with aesthetics regarding domesticity, neoliberalism and precarity, industrial and mechanical labor, migration, paid domestic and care work, reproductive biotechnology, and the eurocrisis. As a consequence, the book's organization differs from chapter to chapter. In some instances, chapters include a range of films from across Europe in several genres. In another case, a chapter discusses one genre from one national context. As each chapter reflects a particular intersection of feminist and formal concerns, the readings rely on specific geopolitical histories.

This book asserts that narratives around the figure of the working woman crystallize feminist approaches to the economy. She appears in precarious work environments, in corporations that advance neoliberal capitalism, as a migrant taking care of a child in a home, and as a clone in dystopian fantasies. This observation departs from the argument that several feminist scholars on popular film culture put forth. They propose that we are living in a postfeminist age in which popular television and films advance a retreat from work and instead advocate consumption based on makeover narratives. Films turn to economics because the global financial crisis has brought into sharp relief the processes of finance capitalism, corporatization, austerity, and a transformation of work. Those processes have not affected only women, but women often experience more detrimental effects. At the same time, women's participation has increased in the workforce. This feminist cinema advances neither a position of women as victims of patriarchy nor a utopian notion of an alternative economy. As countries of the EU embrace neoliberal capitalism to different degrees and with a different pace, the access to welfare services diminishes, and the reduced services of the traditional welfare state force care work into the private sphere, where a female labor force that migrates within or into Europe picks up the slack or where women work more hours. The global financial crisis and subsequent austerity programs have exacerbated these trends. Migration into and within Europe corresponds to gendered and racialized sectors that associate subspecialties of work with presumed national or ethnic characteristics (see Anderson 1999). Films portray the export of cheap female labor by countries in the Global South or depict mobile laborers who occupy a border region between two countries marked by economic disparity, as in the German-Polish border towns.

Films do not simply reflect social reality; they also imagine alternatives and offer commentaries on the way we work. Cinema "mediates, rather than simply reflects, history" (Williams 1988, 19). Thus this book employs the contemporary filmic figure of the working woman to investigate the cultural imagination of labor. Female characters often struggle in solitude, in contrast to the traditional iconography of labor, which emphasized the collectivity of the industrial working class. Women lend themselves to embody the neoliberal labor regime because of the association of femininity with flexibility and adaptability. While films depict the increasing participation of women in the labor market, they also criticize the commodification of female professionals in power suits, offered as icons of feminist liberation. Western European films inscribe whiteness when they claim industrial and mechanical labor as national heritage constructed around a female heroine safely tucked away in the past, rewriting postwar history by conjoining industrial advancement with enlightened gender equality. Yet other films emphasize the ways that economic disparity maps onto class, race, and ethnicity.

The category of gender alone does not account for the political economy of labor. Investigating racial, class, and ethnic differences among women matters urgently, as the income gap decreases between men and women marginally while it increases among women and among men because class inequalities are widening (Roberts 2016, 65). The income disparity between men and women is higher in "high-income professions, which includes many jobs in banking and finance, while the smallest pay gap is in the lower paid professions" (65). The book's analyses are therefore attentive to the ways in which film racializes gender or uses a narrative of female advancement of white Western European women to displace historical disparities of class and race. But this book also attends to those instances in which characteristics associated with femininity (e.g., a caring nature) and masculinity (e.g., a competitive nature) do not correlate with the presumably corresponding biological bodies. Some films include caring male and competitive female characters. I probe what political end such characters serve and what kind of formal cinematic features create the gendering of biological bodies on-screen. For example, a film can use soft lighting and warm colors to feminize a male character. As the book demonstrates, such rewritings of gendered characteristics do not always serve progressive goals.

How do we account for this range of representations, which sometimes includes contradictory depictions? Ernst Bloch's notion of the simultaneity of nonsynchronism, developed in the early 1930s in Germany, enables the theorization of the concurrent existence of industrial labor and service work, neoliberal and social democratic economies, feminist advances and antifeminist backlash, and local preindustrial care work and global high-tech management. Or, to put it differently, Bloch's notion makes possible an account of multiple capitalisms, multiple neoliberalisms, and multiple feminisms. Such a view offers an alternative to discourses that posit a totalizing account of neoliberalism as defining economic, social, and intimate lives. Bloch argues that "not all people exist in the same Now. They do so only externally, by virtue of the fact that they may all be seen today. But that does not mean that they are living at the same time with others" (1977, 22).[1] Bloch's model lends itself to the contemporary moment in which transitions, for example, in labor regimes, occur but do not affect all classes, professions, occupations, generations, nations, and regions equally, simultaneously, and to the same extent.

The notion of simultaneity of nonsynchronism illuminates what appears on first sight as contradictory portraits of work in European cinema, since films range from depicting the global managerial class participating in a virtual world of finance to women reduced to local sexual and marital economies. Films idealize industrial labor in the past or capture the daily trials of unemployment in the neoliberal present. A singular film can also capture the simultaneity of nonsynchronism, integrating different forms of economies. Thus the simultaneity of different modes of labor and economy—preindustrial and industrial, domestic and outsourced, collective and hierarchical—does not constitute a contradiction. Bloch also provides a model to account for different temporalities that films express through their pacing of editing and sound, from the acceleration of machines accompanied by rhythmic soundtracks and editing to the slowing down of time in long takes accompanied by elegiac music in the narrative about clones to be harvested in a dystopian future.

This book suggests that the prevalence of the figure of the female worker and the expansion of what comprises work respond to feminism's demands. Countering political philosopher Nancy Fraser's view of feminism as "the handmaiden of neoliberalism" (2013b), this study attends to the productive possibilities inherent in the increase and diversification of the cinematic representation of working women for a discussion of work in the contemporary context. But I also ask what kind of feminist political perspectives a focus on work can open up. Does the "ethics of care"—a concept that emerges in a range of feminist disciplines and discourses—offer a politically productive alternative to the notion of solidarity? Can an ethics of care respond critically and appropriately to a neoliberal labor regime, or is it a weak political perspective rooted in the notion of women's domesticity, available for even more exploitation in times of crisis?

The remainder of the introduction provides an overview of the intersecting academic debates that this book engages and to which it contributes. After a chronicle of the historic role of photography and film in industrialization's efforts toward efficiency, the introduction continues with a survey of the scant treatment of the depiction of labor within film studies and then turns to the burgeoning field of European cinema. A summary of Europe's gendered economy prepares feminist approaches to the representation of women's work in film. The introduction concludes with brief chapter overviews.

Work and Film

Film scholar Elena Gorfinkel evokes the contemporary problem of visually depicting increasingly immaterial labor: "In the wake of post-Fordist, neoliberal policies of flexibilization, casualization, and atomization, the crux of work is made increasingly 'immaterial,' precarious, abstract, and even further alienated" (2012a, 44). Historically, film has played a crucial role in visualizing work processes both in the service of industrial rationalization and as a critical interrogation for a film-viewing public. The cultural imagination of industrial and mechanical labor haunts the contemporary understanding of work, in part because film as a visual medium has emerged "while the classical regime of industrial productions is still in full swing" (Hediger 2009, 130). Visual practices such as photography and film integrally defined the development of scientific management.

However, even before the development of film, capitalist economy and technological inventions of industrialism such as thermodynamics shaped the cultural imagination about gender, for which Mark Seltzer coined the term "body-machine complex" (1992, 65). He argues that in the late nineteenth century the "sexualization of economic relations" projected "economic difference onto sexual difference," defining the "understanding of human nature in terms of the market and the understanding of the market in sensuous terms" (71). The cultural imagination of gendered market economies was already in place when film emerged, and managers used it to advance capitalist efficiency.

The European science of work of the late nineteenth and early twentieth centuries influenced the use of photography and film in the service of mechanical and industrial rationalization (Rabinbach 1990). The concern with labor focused on the economy of the working body. Laboratory investigations measured the rhythm and movement of the human organism in "terms of energy and output" like a machine (183). Efficiency experts mapped the mechanics of the working-class body in industrial production by breaking down and reassembling movements into efficient combinations based on the scientific positivism of Eadweard Muybridge's locomotion studies and Étienne-Jules Marey's chronophotographies (E. Brown 2005, 94). Serial photography and film that visualized movements supported the standardization and rationalization undergirding the second industrial revolution.

Frederick Winslow Taylor ([1911] 2014) established scientific management by disarticulating natural bodies, mapping them onto machines, and standardizing work in the early twentieth century (see also Seltzer 1992, 95; E. Brown 2005, 95). He moved from using the naked eye and a stopwatch to employing photographs to depict steps in a work process, for example, of bricklaying (E. Brown 2005, 8). Elspeth Brown points out that still photographs cannot capture time, which determines efficiency (10). Film—a time-based medium—offers the possibility of documenting and measuring efficiency in time and space.

Industrial consultants Frank and Lillian Gilbreth introduced motion study by filming workers with a clock to record time and a gridded background to measure distance of activities in order to isolate individual movements. They reconfigured established discrete interchangeable motions in the most efficient way to perform given tasks (E. Brown 2005, 21, 77). Whereas Taylor had been concerned with time, the Gilbreths sought to standardize motion (69). As a consequence, work developed from an individual activity to a "national resource threatened by waste and inefficiency" (73). In the same time period, however, movies subverted the clock-scheduled time of work life (83; see also Kuhn 2002). The couple recruited more women into their studies, since female workers were not unionized; they were excluded from trades, and they were at the bottom of the pay scale (Brown 2005, 82, 100). The participants' status increased within the factory in the context of the emerging star system when female workers appeared on-screen. As the Gilbreths successfully advertised and promoted the processes they developed, they made efficiency visible to factory owners, but not for the benefit of the workers. The Gilbreths, however, were less sophisticated than their European colleagues Wilhelm Braune and Otto Fischer (Curtis 2009, 85–86).

Even though Taylorism and Fordism both advance efficiency for production, they also differ. David Nye (2013) explains that while Taylor retrained individual workers to do the same jobs more efficiently, the Fordist assembly line redefined and simplified jobs, pacing the work and thus pushing everyone to move at the same speed. Time, however, is integral to both their approaches. "Taylor maximized efficiency in existing production technologies; Ford transformed the means of production," and thus "Taylor saved time; Ford sped up time" (36). Cinema lends itself to advance and capture Taylorist and Fordist processes, but it also made work a topic in its own right.

The early inventors of cinema—for example, the Edison laboratory staff and the Lumière brothers—also turned to capturing work in their very first films. In 1893 two members of Edison's laboratory staff, William Kennedy Laurie Dickson and William Heise, staged and shot one of their demonstration films, *Blacksmithing Scene* (United States), after concluding the experimental process of developing the new medium but before beginning commercial production of film. Shot in their Black Maria studio in West Orange, New Jersey, the one-minute film was later shown in kinetoscopes (a peep-hole machine used by one individual viewer at a time). In *Blacksmithing Scene*, three men act as blacksmiths working together, rhythmically taking turns hammering iron in the center of the shot and then passing around a bottle of beer. The background is unadorned, and the tools (an anvil, a hammer, and a forge), costumes (leather aprons), and acting define the scene as a workplace. Film historian Charles Musser calls the integration of "work, pleasure and socializing" "nostalgic," as labor and leisure were already separated (2004, 16). His insightful analysis of the early integration of film and labor points to a key issue in its representation: the difficulty of imagining work beyond what is familiar from the past.

The staged *Blacksmithing Scene* contrasts with *La sortie de l'usine Lumière à Lyon* (*Workers Leaving the Lumière Factory in Lyon*; France, 1895) by Auguste and Louis Lumière, which shows their employees, mostly women, leaving their factory. Crossing the threshold from both "the space of work (the factory)" to "the space of leisure (the space outside)," the film focuses on "the boundary between work and play" (Musser 2004, 18). Musser compares Edison's homosocial "bastion of masculinist culture" with the heterosocial world that the Lumières created. The brothers, Musser points out, were trained in the middle-class convention of bourgeois photographs, which included the "feminine in its emphasis on the domestic sphere" (21–23). Musser correctly emphasizes the distinguishing features between these two earliest examples of films about work and importantly links their convergent gendering to the two dissimilar modes of production of the American Edison versus the French Lumière studios. But despite their crucial divergence, both films invoke the verisimilitude of labor, albeit through different means: one on a set and the other on location.

Film critically reflects on capitalist exploitation with the same tools that the medium uses to promote efficiency, namely, through pacing. A slow pace can create a feeling of boredom, while a fast pace can effect a sensation of speed. In a critique of Fordist capitalist production, films most commonly project speed through movement, camera position, editing, and sound. The opening sequence of Charlie Chaplin's *Modern Times* (United States, 1936) famously employs standardization of movement on a conveyer belt in the factory to critique the privileging of machines over humans. Chaplin's trademark character, the little tramp, is unable to synch his movements with the assembly line, which is speeding up as per the commands of the factory director; consequently, the machine swallows him. Michael North suggests that this scene enacts "[Walter] Benjamin's notion that film might offer a means of transforming modern regimentation into play" (2009, 190). We should keep in mind that Hollywood itself functions according to a division of labor, and so, according to North, Chaplin resisted "the dreaded command 'More speed'" in Hollywood (190). These early examples illustrate how film, even though put in the service of industrial efficiency, was also the medium par excellence to critique capitalism's demand for ever-expanding rationalization in order to increase profit.

Despite this intimate connection between film and work, film studies scholarship throughout the twentieth century has marginalized the topic of labor in part by reducing the scope and limiting the methodological approach. Peter Stead's authoritative survey, *Film and the Working Class: The Feature Film*

FIGURE 0.1. *Modern Times* (Charlie Chaplin, 1936)

in British and American Society (1989), represents both a lone book publication and the canonical framing of the topic. Presumably unintended, it performs a history of "the classic pathos of the male industrial worker" (Moitra 2009, 337). In Stead's volume, the accuracy of representation becomes the standard for assessing individual films about labor. He measures the veracity of the depiction according to its distance from or proximity to realism. Certain key tropes and settings emerge from his study, such as the strike and the coal-mining and steel industry (Stead 1989; in regard to Hollywood, see 66, 74; in regard to British cinema, see 105, 113). Stead's critique of the 1940s British government films for showing "people at work in factories, shipyards, and mines but never on their own terms" reveals the underlying presumed link between the working class and authenticity (126). He views the producer-director team of Tony Garnett and Ken Loach as emblematic of the early 1960s "new British realism" and its "fascination with the working class" in the "industrial North" (195–197). Social realism was reduced to a style when it moved into television, which replaced national cinema (206–208). The depiction of the postindustrial world of unemployed and casually employed workers engendered a move away from realism to light comedy (214–217). Stead's discerning history of English-language films about the working class reveals that filmmakers, critics, and scholars share an understanding of what constitutes labor that prevents other forms of work (e.g., domestic) or other forms of style (e.g., experimental) from appearing in cinematic, journalistic, or scholarly discourse.

In contrast to the scarcity of twentieth-century scholarship on labor in film, the early twenty-first century experienced an upsurge of creative and academic interest in visual culture and work, including the success at film festivals of such films as *Deux jours, une nuit* (*Two Days, One Night*; Belgium, France, Italy; Jean-Pierre and Luc Dardenne, 2014), *Toni Erdmann* (Germany, Austria, Switzerland, Romania; Maren Ade, 2016) (both discussed in chapter 2), and *I, Daniel Blake* (UK, France, Belgium; Ken Loach, 2016). Representative contemporary publications continue the focus on working-class masculinity defined by industrial labor, not surprisingly privileging male auteurs. For example, for her book-length study, Ewa Mazierska explicitly "chose Marx" as her theoretical framework for a reading of work in cinema and "privileged texts . . . and films that enjoyed significant critical or popular acclaim"; thus a "large part . . . belong to a canon of European cinema and auteurist tradition" (2015, 1–3). Without doubt, the twelve male directors that she lists represent the canon of a twentieth-century cinema of labor, but the absence of any female director also reflects the circularity of this approach, as a methodology that relies on a Marxist premise valorizes auteurs indebted to Marx.

Derek Nystrom complicates the cinematic prevalence of white, blue-collar men to which American films of the 1970s "continually returned" by proposing that they represent a product of a "middle-class fantasy about class" (2009, x). He thus reveals that these depictions tell us more about the development of the "professional-managerial class (PMC) during this period," which experienced a "disproportionate growth and concomitant strength" vis-à-vis "a triumphant, mobile capital and a weakened working class" (4–5). Even though his book title, *Hard Hats, Rednecks, and Macho Men: Class in 1970s American Cinema*, traffics in the stereotypical notions of working-class masculinity, his argument complicates the presumed link of said configuration to authenticity that defines Stead's approach (1989).

A few current approaches to the topic have moved away from the singular emphasis on working-class masculinity. Mazierska's edited collection (2013) indicates a current paradigm shift in its three-part structure of "neoliberal work," "national and transnational cinemas," and "genre" and with important essays initiating an analysis of a new European cinema of precarity (Bardan 2013) and the depiction of affective labor (Fraser 2013). In a special issue of *Framework*, "The Work of the Image: Cinema, Labor, Aesthetics," Gorfinkel expands our understanding of the relationship of labor and cinema by emphasizing the labor of aesthetics: "The image is the product of work and does a certain kind of work, but also makes the spectator work" (2012a, 44). The fact that she highlights the cinema as "a spectacularized product of a labor that remains consistently off-scene—be it the labor behind the camera, be it the bodies placed before it"—challenges us to consider the ways in which films deny or reflect on the labor of their own production (43).

During the last decade, Vinzenz Hediger and Patrick Vonderau (2009a) have defined a new field of study that centers on industrial films, an area that had previously garnered hardly any attention and that demanded a different contextual approach. Major corporations started their in-house production units in the early twentieth century (Krupp in Germany in 1913 and Ford in 1914), making films with an "organizational functionality" (Hediger and Vonderau 2009b, 37, 39). Corporate films provide "institutional memory," "share the company's stated goals," improve "organization performance on all levels," and project a "corporate identity" (40–42). The depiction of work on film creates certain similarities across genres, even if their goals differ.

Corporate and narrative feature films about work share conventions and mutually influence each other. For example, Hediger and Vonderau discuss a corporate film "with a modernist score and visually stunning travelling shots" (2009b, 44). Industrial films, Martin Loiperdinger shows, rely on the "human body" as the "reference point" (2009, 71). They anthropomorphize, for example, a car in a film about its production (Vonderau 2009, 159). Feature films about industrial labor also compress time (Loiperdinger 2009, 69). Industrial films and feature films about work share formal conventions and key tropes, such as the "agile and effective gestures of the workers," the "travelling shot of the factory," and the "factory as well-oiled machine" (Hatzfeld, Rot, and Michel 2009, 199).[2] These tropes characterize cinema about labor from its early history, and twenty-first-century films reference such tropes to evoke their accumulated tradition.[3]

With the rise of immaterial, digital, and electronic labor, technological innovations have obscured the components of the work process. As film has historically depended on visibility, this poses a problem for filmmaking. Hediger discusses the computer as an agent of rationalization in the twentieth century, as the machine "eliminates input, particularly in terms of physical labor" (2009, 127). He argues that information technology created "a crisis of visibility" that affected "the regime of knowledge" (128). This dilemma extends to narrative film and in instances produces a return to obsolete tools, for example, the typewriter, in an attempt to visualize work processes on-screen (see chapter 3).

If film studies scholarship has marginalized labor as a topic, it has given even less attention to women's work. Those discussions focus primarily on domesticity in Hollywood cinema and female heroes of the labor struggle. Consistent with the general emphasis on the working class and the strike, scholarly books celebrate labor activists and female strikers (Borda 2011; Enstad 1999), focus on the cinematic representation of domesticity (McHugh 1999), or excavate the labor that goes into creating a star, particularly her body (McLean 2004), and all of these books do so in relation to the United States.

In regard to European cinema, scholars rarely pay attention to women and work. One exception concerns a group of scholars who elaborate on the figure of the white-collar office worker associated with modernity to illuminate the relationship of economies of love and labor (Biebl, Mund, and Volkening 2007). In the collection's introduction, Heide Volkening explains the volume's intention to trace the status of the working girl in the structuration of gender and work, which includes the construction of the figure in literary, artistic, filmic, and musical representations, as well as her presence in the social practices of the everyday (2007, 9). According to Volkening, the working girl emerged in late nineteenth-century mass culture and populated spaces, such as the store, the office, the street, and the movie theater (10–11). Importantly, the volume emphasizes the economization of feeling, on the one hand, and the romanticizing of labor relations on the other, a structure that continues to define narrative organizations in contemporary films (17).

Among the handful of book-length studies on the topic, Anca Parvulescu's forceful theoretical account of the filmic "traffic of women" in Europe stands out. According to Parvulescu, European films reflect that women from Eastern European countries migrate west "so that they can do a lot of the physical household work and the immaterial, caring labor traditionally performed by a wife within the institution of marriage" (2014, 2). Parvulescu points out that the "countries of East Europe have a history of needing to either *prove* their Europeanness or actively *produce* it" (3, italics in the original). In other words, to participate in Europe, Eastern Europe has to perform femininity. The relative lack of analytical attention to the narrativization of women's work in European cinema not only contrasts with the many films about working women and the films' success, for example, the awards won by *Toni Erdmann* and *Two Days, One Night*, but also comes into stark relief in contrast to the academic output on European cinema since the fall of the Wall in 1989, the topic of the next section.

European Cinema in Film Studies after the Fall of the Wall

The collapse of the Eastern Bloc and the process of Europeanization after 1989 have fundamentally altered European cinema. During the Cold War, the term "European cinema" signaled distinct national cinemas grouped into Western European art cinema versus Eastern European socialist realism. For much of the conception of European cinema, Hollywood functions as the reference point (see also Elsaesser 2005). Such repeated emphasis on the categorical difference of European cinema from Hollywood reifies the latter's dominance. At the end of the Cold War and coinciding with the fall of the Wall, film scholars Richard Dyer and Ginette Vincendeau initiated a discourse on European cinema. They sum up the attitude toward European cinema in 1989: "There is America, which is Hollywood, which is popular entertainment, and there is Europe, which is art" (1992, 1). Since the early 1990s, scholars have asked whether a European cinema exists beyond "the sum of the cultures of its nation states" (5; see also Petrie 1992; Sorlin 1991).

The first decade of the twenty-first century saw an unprecedented scholarly output on European cinema in response to the post-1989 European expansion process: conferences, research groups, and academic publications proliferated (Forbes and Street 2000; Konstantarakos 2000; Aitken 2001; Fowler 2002; Ezra 2004; Elsaesser 2005; Galt 2006; Mazierska and Rascaroli 2006; Kovács 2007; Halle 2008, 2014; Sieg 2008; Betz 2009). These books collect authoritative essays in chronological order (Ezra 2004), survey canonical periods and films (Forbes and Street 2000), or reprint and combine earlier essays with newly written materials (Elsaesser 2005). The paradigm of successive national waves, such as Italian neorealism, the French New Wave, and New German Cinema, still organizes post-Wall surveys on European cinema, reinforcing the dominance of Western European cinema. For example, Elizabeth Ezra's *European Cinema* (2004) addresses canonical periods of Western Europe in fourteen out of sixteen chapters. The fact that Eastern European film constitutes a distinct field of research indicates that it has not acquired the status to stand in for European cinema (see, e.g., Imre 2005).[4]

Only a few volumes radically rethink the conception of European cinema beyond an assemblage of national cinemas (Galt 2006; Halle 2008, 2014; Sieg 2008; Betz 2009). Instead, innovative methodological approaches flourish in the discourses about individual European national cinemas, presumably because the processes of transnationalization have brought the nation as analytical category into sharper relief after its long previous existence as a naturalized entity.[5] Reflecting the self-definition of Europe as enabling internal mobility but reinforcing external borders, much scholarly discussion of European cinema focuses on migration, mobility, and space (Konstantarakos 2000; Mazierska and Rascaroli 2006; Brown, Iordanova, and Torchin 2010; Loshitzky 2010; Verstraete 2010). These volumes offer important and accurate descriptions of European films but fall short in regard to theorizing conceptions of European cinema beyond the thematic cluster of migration and mobility.

Similarly, feminist approaches proliferate in regard to national film cultures but not concerning transnational European cinema (see, e.g., Frieden et al., 1993a, 1993b; Flitterman-Lewis 1996; Hughes and Williams 2001; Marsh and Nair 2004).[6] Presumably, scholars have honed their feminist approaches during the long disciplinary histories of national cinemas. Rosalind Galt's (2006) and Mark Betz's (2009) volumes on European film stand out among the publications. They both offer important revisions to the historiography of European cinema: Betz by providing an archaeology of the international coproduction of omnibus films in the 1960s and Galt by analyzing European films from the late 1980s to the mid-1990s that return to the immediate postwar period, a historical moment that, according to her, presented a political opening. Both of their books depart from the presentism of the notion of European film by articulating alternative genealogies of parallel but distinct national art cinemas. They mobilize feminist theory for their revision of European cinema, particularly rethinking Laura Mulvey's influential notion of the female spectacle: Betz analyzes how the auteurs of the French New Wave's turned their female lovers into stars, while Galt questions Andrew Higson's critique of the spectacular landscape in heritage films. In their critical engagement with the history of European cinema and its accompanying theoretical paradigms, they make feminist theory do important and innovative work, but not in the service of articulating a feminist conception of European cinema.

Approaches that attempt to elucidate both differences and confluences in twenty-first-century European cinema have tended to focus on accounts of funding and distribution of the underlying economics of European culture in general and film in particular. Since the EU economically supports films to enhance European visual culture, first with the Eurimages program and then with the follow-up, Creative Europe, scholars emphasize the relationship between economic infrastructure and film production and distribution (Jäckel 2003; Halle 2008).[7] By creating funding structures for films that imagine transgressing national boundaries within Europe, the EU attempts to generate feelings of belonging and foster cultural imagination beyond nation-states. Twenty-eight countries participated when the European-Mediterranean (EUROMED) partnership was established in 2006 (Halle 2014, 140). Randall Halle explains how the EU's integrated funding schemes organize film festivals and fund films that circulate as "national-appearing," relying on essentializing narratives about distinct cultures (2014, 135). In contrast to films funded by the EU that represent national cinemas while circulating globally, internally funded or market-driven films address a national audience with titles that are often unknown outside the internal distribution circuit. Instead of a linear development from national to transnational cinema, the cinemas of Europe rely on simultaneous and overlapping regional, national, and transnational dynamics.

This book relies on the findings by Halle and Anne Jäckel but puts its emphasis on how films reflect gendered economics narratively, sometimes self-reflexively gesturing to the conditions of their own financing. Research that privileges the funding structure has tended to subordinate the formal-aesthetic concerns of films to the conditions of their production. By contrast, my analyses foreground medium-specific categories, such as sound, gesture, and genre. Those aesthetic categories express social realities of women's work in contemporary Europe. This methodology acknowledges films' potential to exceed the conditions of their production and highlights the ability of filmic aesthetics to contribute to the discourse on women's labor.

Europe's Gendered Economy and Feminist Theory

The aim of gender equality has changed throughout the unification process in the treaties of the EU. It originally experienced "momentous landmarks, beginning with equal pay in the Treaty of Rome," explain Diane Perrons and Ania

Plomien; the "pursuit of gender equality" continued until the global financial crisis, after which policies subordinated social to economic objectives and marginalized concerns about women (2014, 301). Paola Villa and Mark Smith explain that following the Lisbon process "the female employment target had been surpassed in a number of countries and the EU rate was relatively close" (2014, 281). The crisis reversed such gains and influenced the European Employment Strategy, revealing that the institutionalization of gender mainstreaming had been superficial. In 2008 the European Economic Recovery Plan did not mention gender, women, or equality (281). When in 2010, at the height of the crisis, the EU initiated the follow-up program, Europe 2020, gender equality goals were sidelined (282). Short-term responses to the crisis and a focus on male unemployment led to excluding "previously established gender equality priorities" (282).

Villa and Smith offer an additional explanation for the receding commitment to women's economic equality: when the EU members established the European Employment Strategy in 1997, the EU consisted of fifteen countries, including social-democratic Sweden and Finland, with a predominance of center-leftist governments committed to gender equality. By 2010, when the Europe 2020 growth strategy began, the twenty-seven member states included postsocialist countries with neoliberal market politics and socially conservative values (with the exception of Slovenia) (Villa and Smith 2014, 283). Villa and Smith conclude that at that point, instead of gender equality, "a competition-based neoliberalism dominated political aspiration amongst much of the EU member states" (383). Thus Bloch's concept of simultaneity of nonsynchronism also captures the national, regional, and historical differences among EU countries.

The recent feminist interest in the economy and materialism rearticulates key topics from second-wave feminism—labor, reproduction, and economy—as part of Europeanization, globalization, neoliberalism, and biotechnological developments. In that process, feminist scholars have revised materialist approaches to labor in the context of global capitalism, while queer and transgender studies have transformed the understanding of feminism's foundational category, "woman." Feminist scholars in the social sciences, such as economics, political science, and sociology, are returning to and updating academic advancements from the 1970s and 1980s regarding economy and labor, for example, Marilyn Waring's (1988) classic critique of national and international accounting systems as obscuring subsistence labor primarily performed by women (Bjørnholt and McKay 2014). Feminist sociologists (Adkins and Dever 2016) have updated Carole Pateman's 1988 model of the sexual contract to the current post-Fordist context. Pateman had revised Jean-Jacques Rousseau's model of the social contract, proposing that the marriage contract historically accorded the husband his wife's labor power. Other feminist sociologists (e.g., Coontz 2011) have revisited the emphasis on the housewife in Betty Friedan's classic *The Feminine Mystique* ([1963] 2013), while political theorist Kathi Weeks (2011) has returned to the demand for "Wages against Housework" (Federici 2012a), and radical second-wave feminist Shulamith Firestone's "infamous call to seize control over the means of reproduction" (Weeks 2011, 182).

The notion of postfeminism—a neoliberal backlash against feminism that takes place in popular visual culture, especially in mainstream Hollywood film and television in the United States and Great Britain—dominates contemporary scholarship on women and work in visual culture. Yvonne Tasker (1998) has captured postfeminist female characters as "working girls," intentionally invoking the proximity of the term's meaning to the prostitute and the diminutive, immature woman, which she shares with Diane Negra's *What a Girl Wants?* (2009) and the discourse on chick lit and chick flicks (see Ferris and Young 2007). Negra, Tasker, and Elizabeth Nathanson (2013) claim that films and television, primarily those from the 1990s, portray women in a retreat from wage labor, where competitive masculinity reigns supreme. They suggest that postfeminist films and television series emphasize an entrepreneurial self-improvement in which the self becomes the project of betterment (see also McRobbie 2009). Television makeover shows in particular place a burden on women to take personal responsibility for their happiness. According to these scholars, neoliberalism asserts itself through technologies of the self and offers consumption as a mode of self-reclamation.

Representative of a trend among scholars who analyze Hollywood films and television in the 1990s, Negra posits a postfeminist retreat of American middle-class women that ignores their counterparts among the working class. According to her, postfeminist culture in film narratives responds to the economic insecurity of the 1990s, gives expression to women's dissatisfaction with a masculine definition of careers, and offers a formula of personal happiness through a retreat to home and consumption. Postfeminist discourse may vilify individual feminist characters, but it maintains and rewrites the feminist notion of choice as individual prerogative, suggesting that equality has been achieved and feminism is therefore obsolete.

This book asserts that diverse feminist cinemas exist. These include postfeminist films and television series, as well as a range of independent films from different regions and countries in Europe that engage in diverse feminist aesthetics. The scholars who frame the cinematic representation of women's work—most often a creative job in the city—through the lens of postfeminism suggest that the films only offer the promise of the good life to white middle-class characters (see also Berlant 2011). Yet the main characters in films of the heritage cinema of industrial labor do not belong to the middle class. These female characters signify working-class identity, no matter how flawed their depiction.

As female migrants who work in the domestic sphere enable middle- and upper-class European women to advance professionally, films project traditional femininity, such as sacrificial maternal love, onto migrants from the Global South. Films that purport a progressive stance idealize such racialized and feminized characters as saviors. Other films create phobic narratives that portray female labor migrants in Europe as a destabilizing presence. Such films interpellate spectators into anxiety about outsourcing intimate care work. The fact that films imagine the relationships among women who are employers and employees, native-born and migrants, and from different European countries indicates an awareness about the gendered and racialized political economy of labor. The mainstream films at the core of the postfeminist argument do not entertain such concerns. Bloch's notion of the simultanety of nonsynchronism captures the coexistence of concurrent postfeminisms and feminisms.

The central figures in the films discussed in this book engage in productive labor or creative work instead of enjoying leisure, in contrast to Negra's, Tasker's, Nathanson's, and Angela McRobbie's analysis of mainstream film and popular culture in the 1990s in the United States and Great Britain. The precarization of work after 2000, particularly after the global financial crisis in 2008, has ushered in a new understanding of women's roles in the economy. Instead of a predominance of female middle-class identity historically associated with the role of the housewife, often caricatured as leisure, films portray women caught in the precarity of insecure jobs. Repeatedly, films reveal unemployed workers, professionals in a conflict with their presumed maternal role, or characters participating in illegal and insecure economies. None of these characters is solidly middle class. Films expose the difficulty of obtaining the fantasies of a secure middle-class existence through taking up a profession by repeatedly emphasizing the fragility of class belonging, played out in films about female managers. None of the films discussed in this book depicts the good life as easily attainable for its main female characters: they are haunted by demands of feminine domesticity or threatened by the loss of what they have achieved through their own labor. In the rare films that promise "the good life"—through marriage or self-determined work—that life will take place after the narrative has concluded. The films assembled here collectively show characters desperately struggling toward goals, even if those consist of retaining a low-paying job without a promise for its attainability. Thus, a general sense of instability pervades many of these films, which does not prevent them from offering both analysis and gestures of resistance.

The centrality of women in the cinematic representation of labor goes beyond a postfeminist abdication of work and retreat into the private sphere, a contemporary misguided feminist celebration of wage labor, or neoliberal emphases on technologies of self and consumption. But this cinema's feminist intervention can only come into view if we move beyond mainstream television series and blockbusters and attend to the diverse films from a range of production values, geographic sites, and genres in a synthetic view.

"The sign 'Woman,'" to use Katrin Sieg's term (2008, 14), is of particular interest for the imagination of Europe either as an idealized space (Rifkin 2005) or as a site of crisis (Hozić and True 2016) and austerity (Blyth 2013; Karamessini and Rubery 2014). Sieg shows that the "sign 'Woman' has long circulated in cultural fantasies of international relations" (2008, 14). Films and plays, she explains, dismantle "narratives of desire for the global that are organized around the sign of woman" and "call into question the fiction of European gender equality by bringing into view the international, ethnic division of feminine care work and the growth of a low-paid service sector of immigrant women of color" (3). A legacy of cultural representation attaches to the sign "woman" while it responds to recent social, economic, and cultural transformations.

This book maintains that the many female characters who embody labor function as sites for critical negotiation over gender roles, agency, and subjectivity in the present. The framework of this argument links contemporary social theory to the emphasis of labor in second-wave feminism. The central female figures function thus as a seismograph of the transformed context of labor in the aftermath of deindustrialization, globalization, mass migration, and neoliberalization. Importantly, however, the attention to earlier models of feminist theory prevents the readings from assuming that the neoliberal economy produces absolutely new labor conditions. Instead, the subsequent readings trace how new dimensions of migration, biotechnology, and flexible workplaces also continue structures of racist, classist, or sexist dynamics. This book's attention to work implies that bodies are laboring productively and reproductively. Somebody is still setting and clearing the tables, cleaning the hallways, washing the sick, inputting the data, and answering the phones. Cinema captures, aestheticizes, and accords value to those acts of work. Importantly, upper- and middle-class women profit from the invisible labor of others—and cinema advances a critique of women who participate in and benefit from the structures of exploitation.

Contemporary feminist cinemas employ a range of aesthetics and narrative strategies. They engage in a materialist turn, paying attention to the ways in which female subjects are implicated in the economic structures and how they can resist their imbrication. In some instances this takes the form of minor gestures, including those of care and solidarity. However, at the same time, the films do not endorse master theories or ideologies. Instead of emphasizing gender as a category of oppression, they trace the ways in which capitalism enables women to participate in its structures of capital accumulation through outsourcing or reduces them to the precarious life in search of work. Contemporary European feminist cinemas depart from the 1970s cinefeminism by not advancing a coherent style and investment in the liberation through access to equality and through professional identity. Instead, contemporary feminist films engage in a range of narrative strategies and aesthetic styles. The extreme and sometimes weird waves respond to the invisible processes of financialization and resist appropriation of mainstream media and the naturalizing processes of neoliberalism.

Chapter Summaries

The first chapter returns to foundational feminist theories about women's work as they emerge from the second women's movement and emphasize the private unwaged sphere to account for the value of unpaid labor. Contemporary films rewrite the understanding of the gendered private sphere of invisible labor inhabited by women—but, as I show, the specter of domesticity haunts the representation of women who work for pay outside the home. The opening chapter thus charts women's work in contemporary European cinema organized around the axis of private and public, as well as domestic and wage labor. Chapter 2 outlines diverse feminist films that respond to neoliberalism's appropriation of qualities considered feminine for its labor regime. Female characters embody precarious labor conditions in films by political filmmakers who emphasize social realism as the aesthetic frame for the depiction of work. Films from the former Eastern Bloc critique the past socialist privileging of proletarian labor as much as they criticize capitalism's commodification of women. I then turn to films that represent a feminist cinema.

In response to the outsourcing of heavy industries from Western Europe to Eastern Europe and the Global South, films in France, Germany, and Great Britain have produced a heritage cinema of industrial and mechanical labor organized around central female figures, the topic of chapter 3. This cinema claims industrial heritage for a nation seemingly devoid of a migratory and minority labor force. The chapter's readings analyze how the heritage cinema of industrial labor represses multicultural identity into the musical soundtrack. The celebration of the female heroines of a historic strike revises the history of both labor activism and feminism. The chapter contrasts such narrative strategies with a film from the former Eastern Bloc that does not idealize factory work in the past but depicts it as copresent with an emergent capitalism.

The next two chapters focus on women's labor migration. Chapter 4 highlights voice in films about women migrating for work. Based on its intimate link to the female body, voice claims authenticity, and its use in voice-overs endows female characters with agency. The chapter traces different configurations of voice in narrative, documentary, and art films. It emphasizes the separation of sound and image in films about women migrating into Europe that link the voice to melancholic memories of a mythical homeland, while the image connects the destination country to the rationality of ocular perception. A reading of a documentary film about capital harnessing the surplus of affective labor in call centers and of an art film that experiments with ventriloquizing voices concludes the chapter.

Connecting migration to reproductive labor, chapter 5 focuses on gestures as the site of ambivalence in the context of paid domestic labor and care work in the home. In this context, genres come to the fore, as the chapter demonstrates how romantic comedy contains the ambivalence surrounding the gestural language of the maid who functions simultaneously as a worker and as the object of romance. The chapter then compares two thrillers that exploit the ambivalence surrounding the gesture of the domestic worker in the private sphere of the home to question the cognitive ability of the spectator. Chapter 6 continues the discussion of reproductive labor in the context of organ harvesting and biotechnology in films that situate biopolitics among refugees and clones. In a discussion of three dystopian films, the chapter distinguishes between the different critiques they advance against biotechnology, arguing that a humanistic critique necessitates a recourse to women's biology that displaces the emphasis on labor.

The final chapter discusses the role of women and work in the unexpected art cinema that emerged during the global financial crisis in Greece, Portugal, and Spain, but it also includes two films from Germany and the Netherlands that confront the dominance of white masculinity in the financial profession. The films that respond to the crisis are diverse and unconventional in their aesthetics, ranging from a six-hour retelling of *The Arabian Nights* to dancers performing interviews of bankers in London's financial district. The extreme aesthetics captures the rupture of the familiar social world but also constitutes a search for a cinematic language to express the immaterial processes of finance and the economic global collapse.

The representation of female heroines at work weaves throughout the different chapters. However, more often than not, these characters function as metacommentary on the political economy in the overlapping frames of local, regional, national, transnational, and global contexts. They embody a new materialist and feminist cinema in Europe.

CHAPTER 1

The Specter of Domesticity

> The private realm of the household was the sphere where the necessities of life, of individual survival as well as of continuity of the species, were taken care of and guaranteed.
> —Hannah Arendt, *The Human Condition*

> The sturdy figure of the "worker" ... in clean overalls, with a bag of tools and lunch-box, is always accompanied by the ghostly figure of his wife.
> —Carole Pateman, *The Sexual Contract*

> To want wages for housework means to refuse that work as the expression of our nature.
> —Silvia Federici, "Wages against Housework"

This chapter returns to the central role of housework in second-wave feminist theory to consider the relevance of femininity and domesticity for twenty-first-century European films about women engaged in wage labor. Second-wave feminism mapped unpaid housework and paid labor onto the private and public spheres. Historically, dominant ideology considered the private home to be "the proper sphere of activity for women ... outside and beyond the public domain of citizenship" (Carter 1997, 77). Domesticity characterizes the home, where maternal care tends to its inhabitants, particularly children. Intimately "linked to the history of the bourgeois family," the domestic sphere evokes privacy, safety, comfort, and warmth in the cultural imagination (Shafi 2012, 4).

Feminism employed the term "housework" as an organizing metaphor for women's economic role. The figure of the housewife embodies the patriarchal ideology of women's caring nature that serves to deny their work in the private sphere. In the labor market, this dynamic manifests itself in discriminatory unequal pay and gender segregation into the care and service professions. The presumption of women's caring nature haunts cinematic narratives about working women as they enter the paid labor force. Twenty-first-century European films depict working women as the norm in an enlightened, modern Europe based on equality. Yet the specter of domesticity—the notion of women's innate maternal and domestic nature—characterizes either the mise-en-scène or the narrative development. Similarly, the imaginary of the nuclear family with the breadwinner father and the caring mother haunts depictions of contemporary families as narratives imply working mothers' deficiencies and contextualize female professionals in settings defined by cold colors that evoke alienation from their domestic abilities.

This chapter highlights the theoretical legacy from second-wave feminism as gender, class, and race continue to organize the social reality and cultural imagination of work in neoliberal capitalism. Gone is the male breadwinner model, while employers, including the state, contract and subcontract women into precarious working conditions. Key terms and paradigms from second-wave feminism have been adapted to neoliberal economic, social, and cultural environments. Yet the emphasis on the continuity of feminist theory contrasts to scholarship that posits an absolute break that supposedly defines postfeminism, postsocialism, and an all-encompassing neoliberalism. Even though second-wave feminists originally established their central terms on the basis of the nuclear family in postwar Keynesian economics, the critique of national and global accounting and the model of the (hetero)sexual contract still provide theoretical frames through which to account for the neoliberal and post-Fordist transformations of labor. Feminist theory of the 1970s and its continuation in social science scholarship offer an alternative to the totalizing account of neoliberal transformation of labor and economics in twenty-first-century Europe. Returning to earlier debates about women's labor allows these transformations of work, women's roles, public discourse, and cinematic representation to come to the fore.

European films of the twenty-first century seemingly fulfill the feminist demands of the second women's movement. They validate domestic labor and portray female characters participating in the paid labor market, previously associated with masculinity. Rarely do twenty-first-century European films organize a narrative around a housewife or set a story entirely in the domestic sphere. Those exceptional films with housewives as central characters validate domestic labor. The housewife as icon of middle-class domestic femininity disappears and reemerges as an idealized figure of the past. Films project narratives about domestic labor into a preindustrial history, a postwar period, or outside of any identifiable historical moment. In these visions of exceptional moments, domestic labor mobilizes work's utopian potential, the flip side of the image of laborious drudgery. A utopian possibility inheres in housework as nonalienated labor beyond exchange on the capitalist market. In some instances, then, domestic labor enables a vision of an alternative economy based on care and collaboration. Such a model differs from "economic man's" self-interest, which defines Adam Smith's participants in the market economy.

Migration within and into Europe has also affected the gendered organization of work. As female migrants enter the market for domestic labor, they enable European middle-class women to leave the home. The nuclear heterosexual family transforms. What happens to the figure of the housewife when contemporary narratives depict women in the paid labor market as the European middle-class norm? The specter of domesticity inflects narratives by racializing maternity. Discredited as an inept native European, such a character necessitates a migrant onto whom films project caring femininity but who remains in the margin of the narrative. The splitting of maternity onto deficient white Northern European women and essentialized migrants from outside of Europe or its Eastern countries calls for an intersectional analysis. Such an account of the imbrication of race, gender, and class points to the limitations of Western Europe's second-wave feminism, which posited gender as the primary analytical category. The specter of domesticity occurs in the tactile, haptic, and olfactory sensorium of the film's visual vocabulary. Domesticity's historical entanglement with femininity still shapes the understanding of gender. European films demonstrate the difficulty of validating an economy based on care without reproducing essentialist notions of gender and race.

While the explicit presence of the figure of the housewife is waning, a lingering subtext of the naturalization of feminine care influences narratives about professional women in the twenty-first century. Stories about women entering into masculine professions produce heterosexual character configurations that show male partners shouldering domestic and maternal care, serving to indict the female characters for their deficiencies. Films express the legacy of the naturalization of domestic labor in women's lack of domestic abilities by using harsh lighting and cold colors, shot compositions of lone female characters in empty spaces, melodramatic narratives of "too late," and character composition. The specter of domesticity haunts these supposedly progressive depictions of working women. Essentialist notions of caring femininity assert themselves not only in melodramatic narratives of maternal failure but also in the cold colors that frame female professionals.

Contemporary Western feminism marginalizes the experience of women in postwar communist and socialist countries. There, feminism had a different relationship to paid labor because "in former socialist states, gender equality and wage labor were mandated" (Suchland 2011, 851). Postsocialist feminism does not idealize labor as the path to liberation because that ideology failed under the past communist and socialist political systems. Even though dogmatic Marxism sees gender discrimination as a secondary contradiction and wage labor in the public sphere presumably liberated women in the former Soviet Bloc, in reality working women under communism and real-existing socialism still faced the double burden of paid and domestic labor. Jennifer Suchland claims that wage labor "is part of the dynamic of domination and not just a solution," implying that "work can neither promise liberation nor equality," which should caution women in Europe's twenty-first-century neoliberal labor regime (851). Thus, while this chapter critically focuses on the spectral presence of women's naturalized domestic ability embodied in the figure of the housewife, it does not advocate for a celebration of wage labor as access to the public sphere and citizenship. On the contrary, this chapter demonstrates how for women such an illusionary path is paved with contradictions.

Is Female to Male as Labor to Work as Private to Public?[1]

Prior to second-wave feminists theorizing invisible labor, Hannah Arendt's differentiation between public work and private labor described a model that obscured housework but also developed theoretical tools that could validate the uncounted work that women perform. Arendt provides an account of the classical Greek distinction between free men's work in the demos and women's and slaves' labor in the oikos and its development into industrial labor and the mass market. She maps the binary of gender onto public versus private, democratic equality versus patriarchal inequality, and work versus labor. She criticizes the transformation of the public sphere into the all-pervasive capitalist market of mass production and consumption. Her critique of Marx's emphasis on labor as revolutionary force and the validation of work offers a potential tool to conceptualize women's contributions and their value beyond the capitalist market. But in order for the value of women's work to come into view, her model's deeply ingrained gendering of the private/public split needs rethinking.

Arendt reacts to the dominance of labor in the theories and the social reality of modernity. As the Industrial Revolution replaced workmanship with labor, its division characterizes modern processes that enable mass production (Arendt 1998, 124). Labor, which in her understanding is a repetitive response to necessity, reproduces its power but leaves no permanent trace (90). She locates a contradiction in Marx's claim that man distinguishes himself from animals through labor and his view that the communist revolution promises its abolition (98–99, 105). Labor's ability to produce a surplus accelerates production and consumption so that products lose their use-value and become objects of consumption. Work, in contrast to labor, creates durable artifacts distinct from nature (7–8).

The household carries a paradoxical legacy: it exists outside the public sphere of democratic politics, but it also serves as the prime metaphor for national economies. Greek thought saw the polis as a democratic space for free men and the home as a place of unequal relations where the paterfamilias ruled over his wife, children, and slaves (Arendt 1998, 32). Freedom defines the political realm, whereas force characterizes private households (31). This social and political formation differs from the emergence of the modern nation-state, as a national economy requires collective housekeeping, which blurs the line between the private and public. Even though Arendt was not critical of the gendering of private and public, her differentiation between oikos and polis enables a rethinking of seemingly unproductive activity, such as women's domestic work, precisely because it is not part of the industrial labor process.

Theorizing Invisible and Unpaid Domestic Work

Feminist scholars of the second women's movement responded to the invisibility and lack of value accorded to women's work with particular attention to housework. Domestic labor achieved an emblematic status in feminist activism and theory because it was simultaneously invisible and integral to femininity and the (hetero)sexual contract. The work that creates domesticity maintains a continuous hold on the cultural imagination of femininity. Current feminist scholars rely on key concepts that the second women's movement put in circulation while adapting them to the transformation of the economy.

The validation of housework in feminist theory asserts that women contribute productively and reproductively to society. Sociologist Ann Oakley interviewed forty housewives in 1971 London on "housework as *work*" to make "visible the invisible," because domestic labor defines the feminine role and serves as barrier to equality (1974, 2–3, 29–30, italics in the original). Based on her definition of work (expenditure of energy, contribution to the production of goods or services, pattern of social interaction, social status for the worker, and payment), housework only differs in its lack of pay (26). Housework consists of heterogeneous tasks demanding different skills that are in instances monotonous, boring, and never finished but that reward housewives with autonomy (41–60). In sum, the significant difference of housework from other forms of labor does not inhere in the characteristics of the activities but in their defining tie to femininity, which, in turn, determines the lack of pay.

Silvia Federici extends Oakley's argument by proposing that the attributes of femininity are the "*work functions*" of naturalized and unwaged domestic labor (2012b, 8, italics in the original). These work functions pertain to professions in the female sector: nurses, maids, teachers, and secretaries. Federici's slogan "Wages for Housework" makes visible that women's free reproductive labor contains and reduces costs for capitalism and is therefore central to its functioning (8). The Keynesian Western European postwar model of reproduction assumed the male wage, but in the 1970s the female labor force expanded dramatically, coinciding with the explosion of the service sector. Since then, the international division of labor harnesses the labor of women from the Global South for the reproduction of the European workforce. These women produce cheap commodities for export, including the service of care work, for example, in the international adoption market, surrogacy motherhood, and the sex industry (66–107). The definition of the metaphor of housework has expanded from signaling the site of the exploitation of housewives to indexing a complex dynamic of women's labor on a transnational scale, in which European women benefit from the cheap labor of women in the Global South whether they migrate to Europe or not. European women can rely on the domestic work of migrants in their homes and the long-distance reproductive labor of women in the Global South. Domestic labor has thus become detached from domesticity and marriage, deterritorialized from the home in Europe, and dispersed around the globe. A mobile female workforce reterritorializes reproductive labor in different configurations in Europe and elsewhere.

Whereas Oakley documented housewives' own work experience to describe the labor that inheres in housework, and Federici invented a radical slogan to capture structural inequality, Marilyn Waring (1988, 2) approached the invisibility of women's work from the perspective of national and global accounting. She demonstrated that the United Nations System of National Accounts (UNSNA), the precursor to the gross domestic product (GDP), records subsistence and domestic work as nonproductive activity. This accounting system considers housework and child care productive when a paid domestic worker—a nanny or maid—performs them but otherwise nonproductive (31). Reproductive labor, Waring explains, biologically reproduces the labor force and the relations of production (e.g., lower pay and lower status), as well as those of reproduction (e.g., through marriage) and the social relations between women and men (e.g., through religious, legal, and cultural beliefs and practices) (188). Waring demonstrates that national and global accounting systems define labor merely as those activities that produce profit on the market and consumption only as results from purchases on the market (27, 61). The relation between unpaid labor and accounting systems still skews economics when women enter the wage-labor market, as the next generation of feminist economists pointed out.

In the same year, Carole Pateman added a legal dimension to the discussion of women's work to argue that a sexual contract established men's freedom and women's subjection. Patriarchal society privileges the public sphere, where the social contract refers to civil freedom, deeming the sexual and marriage contract to be natural and thus politically irrelevant (Pateman 1988, 3–6). In contrast, Pateman claims that sexual difference is political because it distinguishes between freedom and subjection (6). The fact that wives are not paid for their housework indicates women's unequal position in the marriage contract. The sexual contract does not apply only to the private sphere, because patriarchy extends across both spheres (12). Men, as breadwinners, support and protect housewives with their family wages (136–137). As man and woman replicate the contract every day through the sexual division of labor, the marriage contract is also a form of labor contract (115). She asks: "What kind of laborer is a (house)wife?" (116–117). Becoming a wage laborer presupposes that an individual owns their labor power and can contract it out, but the housewife lacks jurisdiction over her own labor (135–136). Pateman aptly captures the iconography of gendered labor: "The sturdy figure of the 'worker,' the artisan, in clean overalls, with a bag of tools and lunch-box, is always accompanied by the ghostly figure of his wife" (131). But if women enter the market, what ghostly figure accompanies them? The specter of the housewife haunts the woman on the market as her uncanny double.

The second women's movement had envisioned that the economy would adapt to the needs of women and families. Instead, "gender mainstreaming" produced higher incomes and economic independence for some women and increased inequality among women (Aslaksen, Bragstad, and Ås 2014, 25–26). Contemporary feminist economists criticize how women's unpaid care work functions to absorb the costs of the global financial crisis.[2] A quarter century after the publication of Waring's influential book, they consider the economic outlook for women to be "gloomy" (Bjørnholt and McKay 2014, 8). Women bear the brunt of austerity measures through their double role in the labor market and as users of public services (8). Neoliberalism's transfer of responsibility for care from the public to the private realm exponentially affects women. Women more so than men make up for the contraction of the welfare state in the private sphere. In the public sector, gender-based occupational segregation exposes women to unemployment and underemployment (9). "Feminization of poverty" denotes women's vulnerability to the risk of being poor, while unpaid and invisible labor continue to be "crucial to the efficient functioning of market based economics" (24, 14). Acknowledging unpaid labor in the home also corrects accounting in national economies (Aslaksen and Koren 2014, 63–65).

In Sweden, Norway, and Finland, awareness about women's unpaid labor predates the second women's movement, having occurred as early as 1892 in Norway (Aslaksen and Koren 2014; Varjonen and Kirjavainen 2014). Both the Norwegian and the Finnish histories are instructive: Norway stopped accounting for unpaid housework in its national budgets in the 1950s so that it could compare its national economy to that of other countries (Aslaksen and Koren 2014, 60). The story of a Finnish task force on household production from the late 1990s to 2006 expresses how the topic of domestic unpaid labor falls between the cracks of economists, the public, and feminists (Varjonen and Kirjavainen 2014, 73). According to members of the task force in 2006, unpaid productive activities in households added 39 percent to the GDP (76, 77). However, when the task force presented its results to the public, journalists failed to understand the statistical language, economists were undeterred in their approach, and scholars in women's studies were not interested (81–82). The authors ask whether the need for making unpaid domestic labor visible had passed (82). This indifference might result from the rarity of the figure of the housewife, but as Federici has shown, the effects of the notion of unpaid and naturalized feminine care work with roots in the domestic sphere pervade the national and global division of labor and thus should continue to concern feminists.

But what happens to the sexual contract when the heteronormative nuclear family with the male breadwinner with a family wage no longer constitutes the European norm? How does a post-Fordist sexual contract erode collective bargaining, life-long employment, and contractual labor rights (Adkins 2016, 13)? Lisa Adkins argues that post-Fordist capitalism has restructured labor as capital without the regulatory constraints of Fordism. A worker "*is* human capital," she claims (20, italics in the original). Yet this reorganization of labor also includes the continuation of traditional associations of femininity with domesticity and maternity in the private sphere. Mommy blogs, for example, offer a "palimpsest of both new and old labor, home and work, production and consumption" (111). Such new forms of traditional labor, clarifies Jessica Taylor, reflect "the shifting boundaries between home and work, enabled in this case by the material conditions of new media, where sites of income generation (the internet) can be accessed from anywhere" (2016, 111). Home-based entrepreneurism promises a path to middle-class respectability through the compatibility of work with motherhood, domesticity, and intimacy while it extends financial capitalism into the domestic sphere, which becomes the place for capital accumulation.

The women working at home who appear in feature films are a far cry from those women Oakley interviewed in the early 1970s. Yet key terms established on the basis of the nuclear family in postwar Keynesian economics, such as Waring's critique of national and global accounting and Pateman's sexual contract, still provide a theoretical frame through which to account for the neoliberal and post-Fordist transformations of labor. Gone is the male breadwinner model, while employers, including the state, contract and subcontract women into precarious working conditions. The presumption of women's natural ability to care still haunts cinematic narratives about working women, even if female characters have left the home and entered the paid workforce.

Beautiful Drudgery

As the popular European imagination casts women as independent working professionals in the public sphere, European cinema in the twenty-first century rarely focuses on housewives, and contemporary feminist arguments do not pivot on unwaged labor in the domestic sphere. As Oakley anticipated and Federici made explicit, housework becomes visible at the moment when European women enter the labor market in increased numbers and outsource domestic work to other women, often migrants. Subsequently, contemporary European films that focus on domestic or subsistence work are set in the past or presuppose a crisis, such as the aftermath of war.

Veteran Swedish filmmaker Jan Troell's *Maria Larssons eviga ögonblick* (*Everlasting Moments*, 2008) emphasizes the physical labor of housework among the Swedish working class of the early twentieth century, before household mechanization. The film tells the story of Troell's distant relative Maria Larsson, mother of seven children and married to Sigfrid (Siggi) Larsson, an abusive and drunken dock worker who advances to owning a hauling business after he has spent some time in jail because he threatened to kill Maria with a razor blade.[3]

Maria constantly works for her own and other families, while she develops a love for photography after she has won a Contessa camera at a fair.

Everlasting Moments validates and aestheticizes domestic labor, emphasizing the porous boundary between housework and creative activity. Narratively, the film contrasts taking photographs to the drudgery of physical labor in the home. Maria's practice of taking photographs conflicts with her household demands, including being a mother, but it also enables her to experience a different temporality. The film shows how Maria photographs the everyday—her children, a butterfly, a dead girl—in her surroundings, while keeping the camera hidden. Instead of depicting artistic production and the domestic as mutually exclusive, the film celebrates Maria's creative practice as it emerges from her home and work environment.

Maria's photography links private to public. Her first two photographs capture her cat and her four children, reminding us of the long history of women developing wage labor and art out of the domestic space. Maria works on a continuum of paid and unpaid labor. She scrubs, sews, washes, and irons for her family for free and for others for pay. It is thus that Troell situates his film in the past without creating nostalgia for physical labor and poverty. She takes photos of her family for pleasure and for others for a fee. Maria stages a setting to bring forth a beauty that inheres in her subjects. Roland Barthes explains that in a photograph "the loved body is immortalized" (2010, 81).

The film emphasizes Maria's domestic work through shot composition, camera distance, and editing. Repeatedly, scenes begin with close-ups of her working hands in the process of sewing, ironing, or scrubbing. Instead of using establishing shots to orient the viewer in time and place, scenes open with the camera capturing Maria working close to the ground. For example, early in the film, a shot begins with a close-up of Maria pinning the dress hem of Ernestine Fagerdal, an upper-class wigmaker. The low camera position aligns the audience with Maria and inscribes the societal hierarchy into the next visual composition, when a medium long shot shows Maria cowering behind the stately woman who stands upright, framed by a doorway and heavy drapery that make up the mise-en-scène of the bourgeoisie.

The subsequent scene begins again with a close-up of Maria's laboring hands: this time the hands are scrubbing a wooden floor. When the camera pulls back, the shot shows Maria working in a different, formal setting, and the audio track reveals men discussing her husband Siggi's drunken appearance in public. The narrator, Maria's daughter, Maja, provides a voice-over that explains that the family belongs to the local temperance society. As the camera reverses the previous direction, the male members of the temperance society appear in the foreground, dressed in formal attire and stiffly sitting around a table debating Siggi's public behavior, while an open door in the background frames Maria working on her hands and knees.

The shot captures the problem of the simultaneous visibility and invisibility of domestic labor: according to the narrative, the men are unaware of Maria's presence. Their eyelines look away from her, but she works in the center of the perspectival lines of the shot—a distant focal point for spectators. When the men realize that she can hear them, they close the door but still do not acknowledge her presence. Even though Maria's figure in the background plane can escape an audience because the conversation in the foreground dominates, she occupies the center of carefully composed lighting that illuminates her figure and gives the shot a painterly quality.

The validation of Maria's physical domestic labor relies on the distinction between male and female sectors. Siggi first works on the docks and later in a limestone quarry before he launches a hauling business. The film crosscuts between scenes showing Siggi performing dangerous physical labor and those depicting Maria washing, ironing, sewing, and scrubbing. The crosscutting of scenes in the different spheres inscribes their spatial segregation, but the parallelism also validates Maria's domestic labor by comparison. Shots of Siggi and Maria working emphasize the physical nature that defines working-class labor in the early twentieth century. Maria transgresses class and gender boundaries when she embraces the modern technology of photography with the help of Sebastian Pedersen, a kind owner of a photography store who takes a liking to Maria and recognizes her talent. Yet this transgression is possible because photography is not defined exclusively as masculine labor; it is also a leisure pastime associated with bourgeois culture.

The narrative contrasts the drudgery of labor with the artistry of taking photographs, but the film's overarching aesthetics, evocative of early twentieth-century photography, endows both daily physical labor and photography

FIGURE 1.1. *Everlasting Moments* (Jan Troell, 2008)

with a beautiful sensibility that transcends their difference. The film's warm sepia tones evoke the tinted effect of early black-and-white film and faded photographs. Shots emphasize the play of light, which serves as a leitmotif. The film shifts from black and white to color midway but retains a muted and pale color palette for the rest of the film, evoking faded memories.

Everlasting Moments tells a story deeply embedded in Swedish history but does not claim labor in the service of reifying the nation. Armond White suggests that Troell's style recalls "the documentary realism of the vérité movement" and a "naturalism" with a "tension between the spiritual and the sensual that hails from his Scandinavian heritage, and directly from such masters of human conflict as August Strindberg and Ingmar Bergman" (2008, n.p.). Housework as labor becomes visible when it takes place in the past among the working class, where men and women physically toiled in segregated sectors. Troell emphasizes domestic labor's physicality and materiality through camera distance, shot compositions, and editing and endows it with an aesthetic sensibility of cinephilia.

Subsistence Labor in the Shadow of Trauma

The validation of domestic labor based on gender segregation similarly defines Bosnian filmmaker Aida Begić's small-budget film *Snijeg* (*Snow*, 2008). It also emphasizes close-ups of the women's hands when they are working and aestheticizes their labor and its products. Like *Everlasting Moments*, *Snow*'s action occurs in the past, after the Bosnian war. It advances an alternative vision of a market economy that emerges from the care inherent in domestic and subsistence labor.

The film's action takes place in a village in eastern Bosnia outside of Zvornik, now part of Bosnia-Herzegovina, in 1997. Through its narrative and aesthetics, it poses fundamental questions about the role of productive and reproductive labor for creating a future for women and children following war trauma. The men in the village have been killed; only a grandfather and a traumatized young boy have survived. The women in the village—the protagonist, Alma, her mother-in-law, Safija, Nadija, Jasmina, old Mrs. Fatima, and Sabrina—engage in subsistence labor propelled by Alma's dream of expanding their economy to feed the country. The narrative covers the events of one week and ends with a brief vignette a decade later. Two outsiders, Miro and Marc, arrive and offer to purchase the land for development. While the women consider the offer, the two visitors are stuck in the village because of car trouble. The boy's memory reveals Miro to be the murderer of the missing village men, and Miro's confession about the location of their dead bodies provides narrative closure. The film's emphasis lies with the women's work of harvesting, preparing, and selling fruits and vegetables from their land.

The majority of shots emphasize the daily labor the women perform collectively and communally with mechanical tools, following the rhythm of the seasons and days of the week. Repeatedly, shots focus on the individual movements of the women's physical labor as they turn, push, grind, and stir, for example, while making plum jam. The absence of men reflects the social reality of killed Muslim men after the Balkan war, but it also creates a narrative conceit of a female collective. A division of labor emerges among the women, as they do not live in a (hetero)sexual contract, per Pateman. They envision their subsistence work as contributing to an emerging market economy but have difficulty accessing it.

The film's narrative arch intertwines two strands, one that brings closure to its violent past and another that concerns the region's economic future. At their intersection lies the role that the land value plays in differently gendered political economies: the women perform physical labor that turns fruit into products that they bring to the market, whereas the men represent global capitalism, which sees the village as an object for financial speculation. "Economic woman" Alma embodies an alternative to Adam Smith's understanding of *Homo economicus*. In order to advance the village, she calculates investments to increase production and distribution. However, her motivation differs fundamentally from the supposed rational makeup of the male archetype as Katrine Marçal describes the figure: "Emotion, altruism, thoughtfulness, solidarity are not part of his character in the standard economic theories" (2016, 26). As Alma imagines that her village can feed the nation and beyond, a utopian hope integrates regional pride with an altruistic concern. Her highly symbolic figure thus offers an alternative to the historical construction of the gendered split into economic man and innately caring woman incapable of "maximizing her own gain" (29). By emphasizing Alma's economic success as the film's happy ending, the narrative implies that care and economic calculation are not mutually exclusive. The women's domestic labor does not locate them outside the market. Instead, the film envisions a different kind of economy altogether that emerges from the collapse of the former Yugoslavian nation-state and its ideological underpinning of communism.

The spectacle of labor in repeated long takes with a static camera emphasizes the processes of domestic and agricultural tasks and thus provides a metacommentary on women's domestic work. Children play in the frame, for example, while the women focus on their individual tasks, invoking Oakley's description of housework as multiple chores overlapping with continuously ongoing childcare. While the characters in *Snow* cook, core, shred, and can, the children's play creates a parallel soundtrack of repetitive rhymes and actions, socializing them into the future roles of women—a point in Oakley's analysis.

When Alma understands that the other women, with the exception of her mother-in-law, have signed the contract to sell the land, their different attitudes about their economic options in the postwar period come to the fore. The other women argue that they want to sell their land so that they can move into the city, because their lifestyle does not reflect the living standards of the twentieth century. Their concerns reflect on the danger of participating in a rhetorical and perceptual strategy that Dipesh Chakrabarty (2000) has identified with Orientalist projections, which propose that Eastern Europe's supposedly outdated economic structures position it in the feminine role vis-à-vis a masculine, advanced West. The film imagines a market economy that resists global finance capitalism, embodied by men whose characters collapse past violent enemies and future economic seducers. This alternative vision of a capitalist market economy integrates productive and reproductive labor after the ideological collapse of the communist state, in which women's liberation was based on industrial labor while the state partially took over reproductive labor. *Snow* presents a model of sustaining and sustainable capitalism while it self-reflexively expresses an awareness that its tools and organization of labor are anachronistic.

The film does not presuppose a linear temporal development in which the women inhabit an outdated past from which they will move to a modern future. Instead, they are aware of the simultaneity of different forms of capitalisms. Mrs. Fatima recycles consumer goods that appear in their village in the form of mass-produced American clothing, turning them into traditional craft. Their life in the village is neither part of a capitalist teleology nor located in an entirely different temporality. Diverse models of femininity include Alma's embrace of physical labor but also the other women's fantasies of leisure, consumption, and profit.

Snow aestheticizes the women's work and their products, moving beyond the social realist depictions of labor that emphasizes drudgery, repetition, and exhaustion. Instead, sunlight repeatedly shines through the glasses of fruits and jams in different colors, shapes, and textures that emphasize the sensuality and materiality of processing fruits and vegetables. The close-ups of hands touching, weaving, and kneading different materials such as fabrics and jam approximate a sense of tactility and create spectatorial intimacy. The women's work mirrors the "*artisanal modes of production*," which, according to Thomas Elsaesser, define European cinema in contrast to Hollywood, which relies on "an *industrial mode of production*" (2005, 492, italics in the original). But *Snow* does not evoke competition with Hollywood; the overdetermining binary maps Serbs and Bosnians onto men and women. Instead of an anxiety about Hollywood, *Snow* expresses concern about the violent past continuing in the form of new global economic power that would reign over regional culture. Miro and Marc are local stand-ins of an absent company that in turn symbolizes transnational corporations. *Snow* references a European context for its images of economy produced by and with women, endowing the self-reliance of a local economy and the artisanal mode of production with a momentum for a future to come.

Suffocating Domesticity

Whereas *Everlasting Moments* is set in a distant past in a small harbor town in Sweden, and *Snow* depicts life in a village in war-torn Bosnia, *Home* (2008), an enchanting, symbolic, and entertaining film by independent award-winning French-Swiss director Ursula Meier, takes place in an unspecified geographic location in an equally undefined present tense. European women's increased participation in the workforce makes a playful drama about the meaning of home possible. *Home*'s fantasy of self-reliance tells the story of the eccentric nuclear family of Marthe and Michel and their three teenage children, Judith, Marion, and Julien. They live in a house next to an abandoned highway, which they cross liberally and use as an extension of their yard. They watch television on a sofa on their lawn and play hockey on the highway. Marthe's clothes and the family's division of labor evoke a 1950s nuclear family, as Michel drives to work every day while Marthe stays home to take care of the household and the children. The narrative hints that a trauma in Marthe's past makes it impossible for her to leave the home when traffic takes over the highway and interferes with the family's idyllic life. The family accommodates the infringement of the traffic in ever more absurd ways. In sleepless desperation, they isolate the house against the noise with bricks and cement. They lack oxygen, and the interior deteriorates. At the final turning point, the mother takes a hammer and destroys the wall they had built that filled in the front door. The concluding traveling shot shows the family members liberated and walking through fields away from their former home and the highway.

The film simultaneously acknowledges domestic and care work and critiques domesticity's inward-looking limitation that can turn into neurotic attachment. *Home*'s style forgoes any claim to realism. The fantastic setting extends the home into the garden and the yard into the highway. The family claims and uses the highway as their space for play and leisure, ignoring the boundaries between private and public. Asking what home, family, and parenting mean, the film opens with a passionate game of hockey on the empty highway and repeatedly returns to the motif of play. When the trucks arrive, the camera angle shoots them from below so that they appear as a threatening invasion.

The film employs an ironic tone in the depiction of Marthe's care for her children and her home. Evoking traditions of French cinema, the film recycles iconographic motifs in pastiches of style from the postwar period. Marthe's call that she will "do whites" punctuates the action with the structuring repetition of domestic upkeep, even when the narrative has entered the deteriorating downward spiral. Anachronisms do not place the narrative in an earlier historical period but establish the family's eccentricity. Means of electronic communication such as computers and cell phones are lacking, but Marthe receives items she purchases through the mail. The playful acts of domesticity change as the highway reopens. When Marthe hangs her laundry in her yard and the trucks honk, she realizes that they are reacting to her lacy underwear blowing in the wind. Understanding that the truck drivers have sexualized her domestic activity, she takes down her laundry, which appears inside the home throughout the remainder of the film, when the domestic setting folds in on itself. Marthe ultimately cannot stem the destructive forces from the outside as they invade not only the home but also her sensibilities and physical abilities, including her ability to uphold the domestic fantasy of creating comfort and pleasure outside of time and place.

With the reopening of the highway, the domestic interior deteriorates as Marthe loses her upkeep abilities, including her physical strength. The family turns the house into a fortress against noise and exhaust fumes, the children eat out of cans, and cigarette butts litter the house. With the insulation on the walls, the domestic interior resembles an exterior construction site. Marthe continues her domestic chores like an automaton entering the realm of the absurd. In the end, the family members are literally and metaphorically suffocating. With the development from playful eccentricity to asphyxiating domesticity, the film manages a rare feat, opening with a utopian notion of domesticity, acknowledging the invisible labor that goes into it, and then pointing to the danger inherent in a turn away from the public sphere. As the family members walk away from their home in the final shot, the moving traveling shot emphasizes their liberation from the cultural conventions of domesticity and the division of labor that undergirds it.

Cool Labor

The previous section discussed the filmic depiction of housework in the early twenty-first century, when the housewife appears as an anachronism. The films are set either prior to household mechanization, in the aftermath of war, or in an undefined time and place. These three films acknowledge labor in the home while they critique the limitations of the domestic sphere. The next two sections address how films stage the movement out of the home and into the labor market. The specter of domesticity—often in the form of demands for maternal care—shapes narratives and aesthetics of films about women who take up paid work. The departure from classical roles puts pressure on character configurations in films, masculinizing women, feminizing men, and racializing maternal care. The setting of the illegal and informal economies of the first two films discussed here, *Miele* (*Honey*; Italy, France; Valeria Golino, 2013), set in Italy, and *Biutiful* (Mexico, Spain; Alejandro González Iñárritu, 2010), set in Spain, seems to allow characters to transgress gender roles and to participate in global and local economies; but as this section demonstrates, gendered and racialized assumptions about care work determine the narratives.

In *If Women Counted* Waring points out that national and transnational accounting systems estimate the gray economy. Films tend to represent women as objects and not subjects in films about human or sexual trafficking, evoking voyeurism and exploiting sex and violence. *Honey*, the only feature-length film by successful Italian actress Valeria Golino, reverses this paradigmatic gendering. Protagonist Irene works as a clandestine procurer of drugs available legally in Mexico to assist sick and old people in Italy with suicide. Believing that assisted suicide should be legal, she follows a precise procedure. Irene appears emotionally detached, while the procedures are heart-wrenching for the siblings and spouses who attend to their loved ones while Irene administers the deadly drugs. Irene lives alone in a beach house, runs and surfs, and has a sexual relationship with a married man. A turning point occurs when she meets the older architect Mr. Garibaldi, who wants to commit suicide without disclosing any life-threatening disease. She feels that she has to prevent him from killing himself, and when she is unable to do so, she abandons her illegal work and resumes her medical studies.

Throughout the film the emphasis shifts from noirish conventions of Irene as a solitary, masculinized protagonist to a melodramatic mode as the specter of feminine care increasingly determines the narrative. The many shots of Irene's detached solitude, when she jogs on the beach, swims in the ocean, or travels to Mexico, reflect the conventions of cool thrillers associated with assassins, such as the classics *Le samouraï* (Jean-Pierre Melville, 1967), *Léon* (*Léon: The Professional*; Luc Besson, 1994), and *Nikita* (Luc Besson, 1990). The film evokes the cool stylization that defined 1980s French *cinéma du look*. Yet in *Honey*, Irene's hard-boiled facade crumbles and her detachment dissipates when she confronts the unexpected effect of her lethal actions. After setting up the cool aesthetics of the solitary, clandestine global worker trafficking drugs, the film concludes with a melodramatic moment of "too late," when Irene rushes toward Mr. Garibaldi's house only to arrive after he has jumped to his death. Irene cannot maintain her detached persona and illegal economic activity because she cares too much. The film highlights her solitary existence with many shots of her moving through crowds without making eye contact or standing alone in shot compositions surrounded by expansive space in repeated shots at the airport. When she spends time with Mr. Garibaldi, their presence in shared two-shots with limited conversations watching others in solitary activity, for example, on treadmills at the gym, implies that the two relate despite their solitary existence.

The cool effect of the masculine thriller includes the erotic charge of detached sex acts in contrast to familiar sexual intimacy. Early sex scenes emphasize Irene's skinny, boyish figure and her lack of interest in accoutrements of femininity. During her travels to procure drugs, she masquerades in the global boyish thug attire, consisting of baseball hat, hoodie, backpack, and headphones, to isolate herself from her surroundings. Most of her travel occurs in the anonymous global nonspaces of airports and hotel rooms. This is work, after all, and its repetition marks the temporal organization of the film, when Irene repeatedly looks up at information screens at international airports. As she begins to care about Mr. Garibaldi, she gives up the unattached sex with her married lover. The double life that is part of many plots that take place in the underground economy relies on emotional detachment, which Irene is losing as the narrative progresses.

By yoking Irene's participation to an ethical understanding of end-of-life decisions and by reversing her position when she cares about one of her clients, the film connects women's presumed nature to an ethics of care. Virginia Held, among others, summarizes an "ethics of care as a moral theory,"

FIGURE 1.2. *Honey* (Valeria Golino, 2013)

proposing "normative perspectives" "from the outlines of egalitarian families and workplaces, to the moral responsibilities of parents and citizens, to the ethical evaluations of governmental and foreign policies" (2006, 3). She sees the ethics of care as practice and value that define justice and economics and limit markets. An ethics of care centers on others, often those who are in need, such as children, in contrast to moralities based on "the image of the independent, autonomous, rational individual" (10). The ethics of care, according to her, also values emotion, such as "sympathy, empathy, sensitivity, and responsiveness," and even anger when it occurs in response to an unjust situation (10).

Held proposes that this feminist ethics requires a "radical transformation of society": "It demands not only just equality for women in existing structures of society but equal consideration for the experience that reveals the values, importance, and moral significance of caring" (2006, 12). Held's assumption of family and the individual differs from those feminists who view the family as limiting to women. She contrasts her notion of "persons as relational and interdependent, morally and epistemologically" to liberal feminist morality (13). In the films in this chapter, characters repeatedly move from a pragmatic to an ethical stance. Held's notion of an ethics of care offers a theoretical approach that elevates care work and moves beyond the naturalization of women's domestic labor. Held is aware that her model runs the danger of imbuing underpaid and invisible work outside of wage labor with moral superiority.

Honey indicates the challenge of imagining an ethics of care within a socioeconomic and legal context not based on its values. In the end, Irene understands that she cannot guarantee the outcome of her intentions in an unregulated market and returns to her study of medicine. We presume that she will continue to pursue the possibilities of humane death, but the film eclipses her future. *Honey* articulates a critique based on the ethics of care, but in order to do so, it relies on and thus reproduces essentialist notions of femininity.

European Precarity and African Maternity

Mexican-born director of global art cinema Alejandro González Iñárritu's internationally successful film *Biutiful*, set in Barcelona, shares the setting of the gray economy. The male protagonist takes care of his young children, but the film projects caring femininity onto a female migrant from the Global South who remains a minor character. The precondition for the film to claim her innate maternal ability lies with the domestic failure of the European woman.

The film takes place among the urban lower class of cosmopolitan Barcelona in the twenty-first century and centers on the male character, Uxbal, who struggles to care for his two children, Ana and Mateo, while he is dying. Focusing on his moves through the city, *Biutiful* strikingly and affectively captures precarious life in Barcelona around the time of the financial crisis. Uxbal works as a go-between among different participants of the underground economy: Chinese undocumented laborers who pirate DVDs and brand-name handbags; their Chinese boss, Hai, who runs an illegal sweatshop; a group of undocumented African street vendors; and members of the police force, whom Uxbal pays off. He is separated from his bipolar wife, Marambra, who takes drugs and has a sexual relationship with his brother, Tito. The African Ige begins to assume responsibility for Uxbal's children as he is dying.

Uxbal belongs to what Guy Standing defines as the precariat, "the class-in-the-making," which experiences "temporary laboring status," "part-time employment," and "flexibility" (2011, vii, 9, 15, 24). Melodrama appears as an apt narrative form for the cinematic representation of the precariat. Lacking class consciousness, the precariat does not access the rational discourse of social realism. Erratic close-ups emphasize the grittiness of the interior of Uxbal's apartment and of the exterior of the streets as he shares the precarious life in the shadow economy with undocumented migrants. He desperately saves cash because he does not have access to health care, retirement, and life insurance. Precarious work in the illegal or semilegal sphere operates in the high-risk zone of death and deportation.

The film's melodrama derives its force from the repeated disastrous results of Uxbal's well-intended actions. He buys used heaters for the Chinese workers that turn out to be defective and kill the migrants who are locked and trapped in a basement. The police arrest and deport the African migrants, including his friend Ekweme. After a night in a bar, Uxbal discovers that Marambra left their son, Mateo, alone while she went on a trip with Ana. The melodramatic narrative accumulates excessive devastating outcomes of Uxbal's good intentions. He embodies the moral suffering traditionally associated with female characters. Steve Neale explains in his classic text, "Melodrama and Tears" (1986), that such a construction situates the spectator in a position of dramatic irony, knowing or anticipating more than the character does. The film combines the gritty realism of on-location shooting in the streets of Barcelona with the melodramatic narrative structure that aligns spectators with the morally superior character at the center of the film. The film shifts melodrama's gendered economy: traditionally, the central figure of the melodramatic narrative is a white woman whose suffering produces tears in the female spectator, particularly in its subgenres, the domestic and maternal melodrama. Uxbal's spiritual ability to talk to the dead also feminizes his character.

The film's progressive imagination of a desperate and economically disadvantaged father relies on the presence of destructive white femininity and of selfless maternal care by a black female migrant. Medium close-ups show in loving detail Uxbal's care of his children: he cooks, brushes their hair, helps them with their homework, and puts them to bed. Ige appears as savior at the end of the film. Her husband, Ekweme, hopes to return to Spain after he is deported, but she wants to settle in their homeland. When she decides to stay in Spain to care for Uxbal's two children, she sacrifices her desire for her own home. The night before he dies, she packs her bags and takes the money he gave her. We see her depart for the train station. Her return occurs in an ellipsis so that it appears in an unexpected and magical melodramatic "nick of time" (see Neale 1986). The film narrativizes and naturalizes Ige's sacrificial maternity. Shots constantly frame her in domestic environments quietly engaged in maternal tasks in the background, such as feeding her baby, doing the laundry, taking Uxbal's children to school, or picking them up. The shot compositions do not emphasize her labor, as in the depictions of Uxbal; thus the film essentializes her caretaking ability.

The film codes Uxbal's ex-wife, Marambra, as an unfit mother lacking heterosexual commitment as she has sex with his brother, Tito. Marambra's irresponsible behavior serves to emphasize the natural ability of the woman from the Global South to care for Uxbal's household and children. The first night that Ige stays at Uxbal's apartment, he wakes up late the next morning and asks Ige about the children. She tells him that she took them to school. Ige's ability to care for the children without Uxbal's instructions evokes the classic domestic melodrama *Imitation of Life* (United States; Douglas Sirk, 1959). In it, the white aspiring actress, Lora Meredith, picks up homeless African American Annie and her light-skinned daughter, Sarah Jane, at the beach and offers to let them stay at her apartment. The next day, while Lora is out, Annie impersonates a maid, completes all household tasks, and thus enables Lora's success by creating the illusion that she belongs to the upper class.

Scholars and film critics have labeled such a character "the magical negro," such as, for example, Whoopi Goldberg's character, Oda Mae Brown, in *Ghost* (United States; Jerry Zucker, 1990). Cultural theorist Kwame Anthony Appiah suggests that the "saint is a crucial type" for blacks in films with an otherwise primarily white cast, which he connects to "the tradition of the superior virtue of the oppressed" (1993, 83). Heather J. Hicks applies his argument to the economics of the late twentieth and early twenty-first centuries, suggesting that "films reflect contemporary upheavals at the nexus of masculinity and economics" (2003, 29). Hicks relies on Donna Haraway's discussion of "the homework economy," which makes white men "newly vulnerable to permanent job loss" (1991, 166). Work is "feminized, whether performed by men or women," with characteristics "formerly ascribed to female jobs, jobs literally done only by women" (66). The underlying new time arrangements of deskilled workers do not follow regular work days. As the film depicts Uxbal's permanent hustle at all hours of the day and night, the female African migrant, Ige, emerges as a quiet and magical presence in his home. Such a division of labor invokes the traditional split between private and public projected onto not only gendered but also racialized workers. Uxbal and Ige emerge as the film's final couple as a result of Marambra's domestic failure and Ekweme's deportation.

Ige's function as savior transcends her role in the diegesis as it allows the audience to focus empathy on Uxbal in his role as precarious and caring subject who transgresses the traditional limitations of masculinity. The film explicitly critiques the economies in which Uxbal traffics among the corrupt police and the network that exploits undocumented workers. It uncritically projects care work onto a woman from the Global South. Like much contemporary theory, the film frames precarity onto a continuum of small-time criminality of the locally underemployed to life-threatening survival strategies of undocumented migrants. Whereas the social realist cinema of labor centered on the nuclear family of the industrial laborer, this example of global art cinema captures new formations of kinship, albeit organized around the male native subject. The specter of domesticity racializes maternity and divides the female figures into the binary of sexual whore and maternal saint, which the seemingly progressive critique of precarious life maps onto native versus migrant women.

Cold Labor

Maternal failure also applies to professional women in other seemingly progressive films. This section analyzes two films that depict female characters who have left domesticity behind and taken up masculine professions. The legacy of domesticity manifests itself in the feminization of the male characters in heterosexual relationships. *1001 Gram* (*1001 Grams;* Norway, Germany, 2014), by independent Norwegian director Bent Hamer, depicts its protagonist, Marie, in charge of maintaining the official Norwegian weight of the kilo, including checking its accuracy at businesses and institutions. At a convention in Paris, she meets Pi, a former physicist who works as a gardener. During the course of the narrative, Marie loses her father, has a car accident, returns to Paris, falls in love with Pi, and leaves Norway to be with him. The final sequence depicts them together in Paris, leaving open whether she will return to Norway.

Notions of domesticity manifest themselves cinematographically in the color palette. The film aligns North and South, women and men, work and leisure on an axis of cold versus warm colors. It associates Marie with blue and green colors, bare environments, and empty spaces and Pi with warm colors, a lush mise-en-scène, social activity, and vibrant nature. The cinematography reverses gendered conventions of lighting, color, and mise-en-scène as a result of Marie's presence in a workplace concerned with accurate measurements. The film opens with shots of the lab in light blue. A close-up of a machine announces the film's narrative investment in labor associated with science and objectivity, none of which is traditionally associated with femininity. Such an opening shot has become a signature for films about work, from Fritz Lang's classic silent film *Metropolis* (1927) to the industrial films that Vinzenz Hediger and Patrick Vonderau discuss in their edited volume, *Films That Work* (2009a). Accordingly, the first shot of the protagonist introduces Marie dressed in a white lab coat, with her hair sternly tied back and an expressionless face.

Marie's house is indistinguishable from other houses in her monotonous neighborhood. The cinematography portrays Marie's home as equally barren and institutional as her workplace, obscuring the difference between work and leisure. Cold colors and harsh, dark lighting define the interior of her house. Long takes of a long shot show her in a bathrobe smoking in the undecorated house surrounded by unopened boxes. A shot from above emphasizes the planned nature of the community, and a shot from the front registers the modernist geometry and the absence of decorative and living elements, such as flowers. The mise-en-scène suggests that Marie is happy neither at home nor at work. The film consistently casts Marie in harsh light and surrounded by cold colors such as blue. For example, a sequence in a hospital crosscuts her with her father's male, older doctor. Soft lighting envelops the doctor, who is seated in front of a window that looks out on greenery. The shot of Marie positions her in

FIGURE 1.3. *1001 Grams* (Bent Hamer, 2014)

harsh light in front of a cold blue wall, reversing the gendered film conventions of associating femininity with soft and masculinity with harsh lighting.

The camera's distance from Marie in her home discourages an audience's possible intimate relation to her character, implying, in turn, her alienation from her surroundings. She does not perform any domestic chores. Instead, the unopened boxes in her living room indicate her refusal to make a home out of her house. A man in a pilot uniform enters the house and takes individual items, for example, a painting, implying a past failed relationship. The narrative does not provide us any information about a break-up or previous marriage, employing instead a minimalist style used by Scandinavian and Icelandic auteurs that teeters between tragedy and comedy. Marie's association with objectivity and rationality goes hand in glove with failed domesticity. Yet its exaggerated absence defines the mise-en-scène, the narrative, and the characters, which allows Pi to fulfill the missing characteristics in a reversal of the traditionally gendered romance. *1001 Grams* appears to depict the normalcy of working women, but the coldness that it associates with Marie's workplace, home, and character implies that wage labor undermines women's domestic abilities, including for marriage and the sexual contract.

When Marie takes leave from her work to move to Paris to be with Pi, the cinematography shifts. Marie and Pi appear in two-shots at his house, bathed in warm colors with a golden hue and soft lighting. The film ends with them sharing a bath in an intimate and sensual space. The stereotypes of the warm South and the cold North define the nonnormative gender characteristics. The film validates emotional connection and intimacy through the figure of Pi, who performs caring masculinity. Framed by domestic settings and immediately expressing intimacy, Pi transforms Marie in a gendered reversal of the romance plot. While the film does not question women's competence for work coded as rational and masculinity, it nevertheless implies that such labor turns them into cold and detached beings. In sum, an old anxiety undergirds the egalitarian narrative, the specter that women will lose their femininity and ability to create domesticity when they leave the private sphere and engage in paid labor.

Dangerous Work and the Failure of Maternity

Tusen ganger god natt (*1,000 Times Good Night*; Norway, Ireland, Sweden, 2013), by successful Norwegian director Erik Poppe, similarly asks about the consequences of women entering a male profession, in this case, war photography. The narrative depicts the seduction of the dangerous thrill combined with social commitment. It stages a conflict between the engagement with the

FIGURE 1.4. *1,000 Times Good Night* (Erik Poppe, 2013)

global, dangerous world of Afghanistan and Kenya and the safe domesticity of the family's home in Ireland. Marcus, the husband of the female protagonist, Rebecca, criticizes his wife's lack of concern for the well-being of her children when she repeatedly puts her life in danger. Inhabited by terrorists, refugees, militants, and inept aid workers, the Global South produces a social instability that affects the main character, her family, and their domesticity. The (hetero)sexual contract cannot prevent such an onslaught of dangerous violence. The specter of domesticity not only haunts this film but comes crashing down on it. The construction of sympathetic and caring male characters in *Biutiful*, *1001 Grams*, and *1,000 Times Good Night* responds to the independent female wage earner who has abandoned her role as the housewife.

In *1,000 Times Good Night*, Rebecca is a war and crisis photographer who lives with her husband, Marcus, and their two daughters in a large house in Ireland. After she returns home from a photo shoot in Afghanistan of young female suicide bombers during which she was injured, her husband confronts her about the effects of her professional risk-taking. She promises to stop working in dangerous regions but takes her daughter Steph to a supposedly safe assignment in a refugee camp in Kenya, where her daughter accidentally videotapes an attack by armed guerrillas. After their return, a melodramatic crisis engulfs the family because Rebecca has put the life of her daughter at risk. The film closes with Rebecca leaving her family to continue photographing female suicide bombers.

Rebecca is not without maternal and domestic qualities. Smell constitutes one way in which the film negotiates her domesticity, a sensual counterpoint to the emphasis on visuality associated with photography. Marcus claims that Rebecca's equipment smells of death and throws it out of the house, foreshadowing her expulsion from the domestic sphere. When Rebecca is home, she enjoys domestic activities like tidying her children's rooms. In a sensual relationship to her daughters, she smells their clothes while she folds and puts them away. Smell in the domestic bourgeois sphere has a long history of combining the "labor-saving qualities and the aesthetic benefits" (e.g., of soap) that served to erase "the traces of strenuous labor" (Carter 1997, 68). As women engage in professional work, cultural representation rearticulates domestic work as leisure.

Throughout the film, the emphasis of the narrative shifts from the conflict-ridden Global South and Middle East to the crisis within the family in the northern hemisphere, where a desperate father demands with increasing violence what has been promised to him via the (hetero)sexual familial contract: the mother's love for his children. The fact that he cares about his children and not himself conjures up a selfless masculinity that nevertheless demands what was customarily contracted to him. Increasingly, the adrenaline-pumping dramatic action moves north, where the couple's fights mirror the deadly violence in the Global South.

The leitmotif of the female suicide bomber frames the narrative as shots of ceremonial preparation bookend the film. The film aligns Rebecca's embrace of the deadly risk with young female suicide bombers who choose death over life, destruction over creation, and religion over education. The film opens with a young woman's enigmatic ceremonial preparations, only to reveal that she is a suicide bomber. The first shots invoke voyeurism and suspense through the presence of Rebecca as Western photographer. The figure of the female suicide bomber indexes Rebecca's conflict between maternal concerns for these ideologically and geographically distant girls and the professional demand that she does not save them so that she can get the photo shoot. The crisis abroad becomes a foil for the deterioration of the Western nuclear family. Rebecca's profession as a war photographer mediates the global crisis diegetically for a magazine audience, but her actions as photographer also mediate dramatic events extradiegetically as the film interpellates its audience members as witnesses of a hidden and secret ceremony. The presence of Rebecca's documentary camera and the long, silent sequence give the scene an ethnographic quality that serves to authenticate the rituals.

With her phallic camera, Rebecca assumes the masculine position. Such a role is a far cry from feminist film theory that suggests that traditional film structures the gendering of its characters such that women appear as spectacle and men propel the action along (see Mulvey 1988). Rebecca's agency occurs primarily with women as spectacle—young female suicide bombers and refugees—on the other side of the lens. As Rebecca's editor is also a woman, the professional world of circulating images becomes entirely female. The spectacle here is not one of eroticized or spectacularized middle-class femininity but one of despair in the Global South that invites a look of horror.

In twenty-first-century European film, global economic differences structure looking relations and not sexual and psychoanalytic ones. The didactic speech that Rebecca's daughter Steph gives to her classmates about the necessity of her mother's professional activity for global humanity, equality, and information underscores this argument. This rational humanist vision contrasts with Rebecca's final failure. When she returns to Afghanistan after she has left her family behind, she is horrified to witness a teenage girl the same age as her daughters being prepared as a suicide bomber. Trying to repress her tears, she now has difficulty taking the photos for the assignment. Now, sudden maternal care—not for her own children but for global girls—challenges her professionalism. In other words, the filmic narrative implies that women are at the mercy of their maternal instincts, while a professional career also confuses their proper expression. Whereas previously the violence of the Global South has infected her persona so that she carried "death" home, now Rebecca has brought the value of caring for the life of girls with her. In contrast to her earlier risk-taking behavior, she now falls to her knees in despair. Thus the ending invalidates her professional role to inform and educate the public.

The film's liberal portrait of a modern middle-class European family with two professionals in a comfortable home in Ireland includes a wife in a dangerous, masculine profession and a husband who is the primary caretaker of the children. Yet underneath this progressive veneer, the film discredits the dangerous commitment of the female professional as seduction and addiction to risk. At the end, Rebecca is left with nothing. The proximity to the suicide bomber envelops her, as if her destructive force spreads virus-like among women. Ultimately, the cypher of the girl suicide bomber is a transgression of gender far beyond Rebecca. With its lack of any political, geographical, or social, including familial, context, the girl suicide bomber associates political and gender subversion with destructive violence in the world at large, which the thrill of the masculine profession might bring home. And since the home is reminiscent of the bourgeois sanctuary, war photography and the presence of Rebecca's computer function as a metaphor for the ways in which global instability enters middle-class homes. *1,000 Times Good Night* allegorizes the inability of retaining the domestic space as hermetically sealed from the world at large once mothers and wives leave the private sphere.

Conclusion

This chapter began with Arendt's account of the classic Greek differentiation between work and labor, which located labor in the domestic sphere undertaken by women and slaves. Throughout the 1970s and 1980s, feminist scholars accounted for the domestic sphere's missing value in national and international economies and contextualized it in the (hetero)sexual contract. With women entering the paid labor market and its neoliberal reorganization, feminist scholars have adapted those models to women's work across the porous border of the private and the public. Films about housework are rare in the early twenty-first century, and the few that exist situate domestic labor in the past or in unknown locations. *Everlasting Moments*, *Snow*, and *Home* cinematically capture the labor inherent in housework. The films aestheticize domestic work and foreground its affective, sensual, and tactile dimensions. *Snow* suggests an alternative market economy based on collective domestic and subsistence work.

By contrast, in films that depict women entering the paid labor market, the specter of domesticity inflects characters, the narrative, and the mise-en-scène. *Honey*, a film that takes place in the illegal economy, frames its main character, Irene, in a cool aesthetic that unravels when she unexpectedly cares about one of her customers. In *Biutiful* the inability of the European woman to nurture her children produces the female African migrant as deus ex machina. The feminization of the film's main character, Uxbal, finds its echo in other male characters with caring attitudes: Marie's lover, Pi, and Rebecca's husband, Marcus. In films such as *Honey* and *1001 Grams*, cinematography accompanies women in masculine professions. The ghostly presence of the specter of domesticity shapes the films' haptic, sensory, and emotional realms. Cinema traditionally subordinates those feminine dimensions of film to the primacy of the image linked to cognition, rationality, and thus masculinity. In sum, the collapsing ideal of the nuclear family with the male breadwinner who has a housewife by his side haunts the working women in twenty-first-century European films.

CHAPTER 2

Precarious Work in Feminist Film

> That's the glass ceiling we are fighting against....
> I don't want to represent *the* female gaze.
> —Barbara Albert quoted in Sophia Charlotte Rieger,
> "Interview with Barbara Albert"

> In other countries there are more women working in the business world; it doesn't suit the picture of Germany. Though we have a female chancellor... but she has to be masculine to succeed.
> —Maren Ade quoted in Mark Peranson, "A Battle of Humor"

> Flexible global capitalism does not exclude or discriminate against women as it did in the last century. It cannot afford to do this because it needs them as flexible workers and as loyal consumers.
> —Tatjana Turanskyj, "Vom Leben in der Scheinemanzipation"

If the ghostly figure of the housewife haunts the representation of female professionals, how do feminist films articulate women's work in the context of the neoliberal emphasis on flexibility, the postindustrial rise of service labor, and transnational outsourcing to the Global South? How do films from the former Eastern Bloc position themselves vis-à-vis the communist past of collective industrial labor and the capitalist promise of consumption? To answer these questions, the chapter begins by addressing films by left-wing directors who have moved from their postwar emphasis on solidarity among the industrial working class to a focus on solitary female figures who struggle under conditions of post-Fordism and neoliberalism. Western European political filmmakers Ken Loach—associated with the postindustrial North of England—and the Dardenne brothers—of the Seraing region of Belgium—depict harried solitary female heroines. Their films indicate a transformation of the leftist gendered imagination of labor. In contrast, postsocialist films from the Eastern European countries capture working women after the collapse of communism that celebrated the worker hero, both male and female. These films question the communist legacy of privileging the proletariat, as well as capitalism's promise to women that the heterosexual contract with the Western victor will provide access to consumption.

Relying on alternative, collaborative structures of production, feminist filmmaking in the new millennium responds to the neoliberal labor regime. It tells stories of precarity that affect under- and unemployed women, as well as those who exploit others through outsourcing and downsizing. Contemporary feminist cinema accounts for the loss of past left-wing and feminist utopias of solidarity, deconstructs the notion of freedom, and delineates the limitations of feminism's promise. Neither sexual liberation nor collective solidarity offers a singular response to European neoliberal labor regimes that threaten women with precarious working conditions, on the one hand, and implicates them in structures of global exploitation, on the other. Nevertheless, these European films, I argue in this book in general and in this chapter in particular, constitute an alternative to the postfeminist films and television shows that have appropriated feminist concepts of choice and empowerment. In contrast, European independent feminist cinema critiques the gendered economies of labor. The films discussed here not only recount neoliberalism's effects on the precariat but also critically depict those middle- and upper-class women who advance in neoliberal economies.

The neoliberal restructuring of work pertains to women in specific ways. Instead of capital's social contract with collective labor, post-Fordist subcontracting transforms workers into self-employed entrepreneurs who assume risks and costs by investing in their own human capital (Adkins 2016, 2). The sexual contract of the twenty-first century occurs "in a context of precarity, wage repression, increasing unemployment, ongoing financialization and pervasive debt" that applies particularly to historically feminized professions associated with welfare, such as social work, nursing, and education (14). In subcontracted services, women typically work part-time and have little access to training, union representation, occupational pensions, or employment protection (21).

Outsourced social service jobs result in "deteriorating job quality for women" and "low job quality," which decrease women's "chances of becoming part of the standard labor force" (Benjamin 2016, 166). For women, traditional forms of discriminatory labor practices intersect with neoliberal structures of flexibility.

Political theorists expand the understanding of neoliberalism from its roots in the value of the free market to an all-encompassing political and societal structure that not only changes the organization of work but also shapes subjectivities. For example, Wendy Brown accuses neoliberalism of converting "every human need or desire into a profitable enterprise," producing rising inequality, commercializing human life, approximating corporate and finance capital, and leading to crises and austerity (2015, 28). She calls neoliberalism "an order of normative reason" that disseminates the "*model of the market* to all domains and activities" (31, italics in the original). Brown extends the logic of the neoliberal economy to the sum of human activity. The subsequent readings of the films support her analysis of the ways in which neoliberal labor regimes manifest in women's daily lives, but they also counter such a totalizing view as they capture the incompleteness and inconsistency of the neoliberal project. The films offer modes of resistance, including in the form of refusal, for example, of femininity. Feminist cinema in Europe models solidarity and mutual support while working through the loss of the utopian promise of the social movements of the 1970s. While a neoliberal ideology aims to reorganize social life according to capitalist market principles, this does not mean that subjects internalize and accommodate such a transformation. These films employ aesthetics for a discourse that makes visible and critiques what Brown calls "normative reason" (31).

Several scholars emphasize neoliberalism's appropriation of feminism, particularly in popular visual culture such as television and blockbusters (see, e.g., McRobbie 2009, 1). Rosalind Gill and Christina Scharff (2011), Elizabeth Nathanson (2013), Hilary Radner (2011), and Diane Negra and Yvonne Tasker (2007) analyze how second-wave feminism's vocabulary of "empowerment" and "choice" now functions as an "individualistic discourse" in media, popular culture, and institutions of the state (McRobbie 2009, 2). Their analyses rely primarily on mainstream blockbusters such as *Bridget Jones's Diary* (Sharon Maguire, 2001) and *Sex and the City* (Michael Patrick King, 2008) and television makeover (*Queer Eye for the Straight Guy*, Bravo TV, 2003–2007, and *What Not to Wear*, TLC, 2003–2013), cooking, and cleaning (*Clean Sweep*, TLC, 2003–2007) shows (8). Angela McRobbie claims that popular culture offers a "promise of freedom and independence... through wage-earning capacity" in a "new form of sexual contract" (2).[1] McRobbie believes that "a new feminist political imaginary [is] increasingly inconceivable," as the very discourse of empowerment disempowers women (26, 49). While *Women at Work* relies on these scholars' insights about postfeminist rhetoric in popular culture, it nevertheless departs from them by arguing that a feminist independent cinema in Europe articulates an important critique of the gendered economies of labor. While these scholars forcefully analyze mainstream popular culture, they overlook precisely those forms of independent, political, and marginal cultural production that articulate feminist visions. In an unintended consequence, their claims that emphasize postfeminist media obscure explicitly feminist films.

Political theorists such as Nancy Fraser and Kathi Weeks return to second-wave feminism from the contemporary vantage point of the neoliberal economy. Fraser emphasizes the parallel development of second-wave feminism and neoliberalism and then accuses the former of enabling the latter. She argues that even though second-wave feminism began with a radical challenge to "male domination," it turned into "identity politics" that emphasized "recognition" instead of "redistribution" precisely at the moment that "a rising neoliberalism declared war on social equality" (2013a, 1). Fraser accuses feminism of "a dangerous liaison with neoliberal efforts to build a free-market society" as "the handmaiden" of a new capitalism (2013b). Yet neither did feminism support neoliberal restructuring, nor did the free-market ideology rely on feminism. Historical accounts of the rise of economic theories in the think-tanks leading up to the 1980s "counterrevolution" outline anticommunism, antiunionism, and a fundamental belief in the free market—but the advocates of neoliberalism did not reference feminism or even demonstrate familiarity with its tenets (see, e.g., Cockett 1994).

Weeks contrasts a positive reevaluation of second-wave autonomous Marxist feminism to mainstream liberal feminism in her study that claims the centrality of work for an analysis of capitalism. She accuses both liberal feminists and Marxists of naturalizing and idealizing work (2011, 5). Arguing against a work ethic that disciplines subjects into docile classed and gendered subjects, Weeks calls for a political "refusal of work" to expose labor as "the primary basis of capitalist relations" (8–9, 97). Such a strategy, however, runs counter to the political efforts and theoretical emphasis of feminists who validate the unacknowledged labor that inheres in emotional, care, intimate, and body work (see Kang 2010). The films I discuss in this chapter neither fetishize labor for women, as Weeks accuses liberal feminism of doing, nor advocate a refusal to work, as she proposes.

Lauren Berlant's phrase "cruel optimism" carries important theoretical currency in the discussion about the cultural manifestation of neoliberalism. Berlant defines cruel optimism as a relation that exists "when something you desire is actually an obstacle to your flourishing," such as "food, . . . a kind of love[,] . . . a fantasy of the good life, or a political project" (2011, 1). In her understanding, "optimistic relations" become cruel "when the object that draws your attachment actively impedes the aim that brought you to it initially" (1). Berlant proposes that fantasies of "upward mobility, job security, political and social equality, and lively, durable intimacy" are "fraying" because the postwar social-democratic promise has faltered (3). Precarity, according to her, cuts across class and constitutes the dominant experience of the present (192). Even though Berlant argues against the precariat as a "global class" (192), she reads French filmmaker Laurent Cantet's *Ressources humaines* (*Human Resources*; France, UK, 1999) as demonstrating the "precarious universal of the neoliberal moment" (222).

The notion of universality turns precarity into an all-encompassing condition and obscures the social and economic differentiation that exists in neoliberal economies. Free-market capitalism does not decrease but increases economic cleavages not only between men and women but also among men and among women. Berlant (2011, 222) reads *Human Resources* as depicting the failure of transmitting the hope for upward mobility from a working-class father to his manager son. However, when relying on gender as the category of analysis, historical continuity comes into sharp relief, as the working-class daughter was never the heir to her father's aspirations. In its idealization of a past solidarity, Cantet's film falls back on the patriarchal organization of the heterosexually gendered working-class family. Such depiction and criticism of contemporary labor regimes run the danger of nostalgically venerating the past industrial labor conditions and in the process of such idealization equating the working-class family with patriarchy.

In sum, this chapter's readings rely on contemporary criticism by feminist scholars in political theory and film studies that focus on neoliberalism's precarious working conditions. The films reflect the daily manifestations and effects of precarious working conditions. At the same time, they do not represent a precarious universal (Berlant 2011), a postfeminist appropriation of feminism (McRobbie 2009), an all-encompassing neoliberalism (Brown 2015), or the refusal to work (Weeks 2011), and they have not become the handmaiden of neoliberalism (Fraser 2013b). Importantly, however, precarious work defines twenty-first-century feminist cinema in Europe. Precarity does not characterize the shared embodiment of a victimized class offered for identification, as was the case with left-wing social or socialist realist standard strike narratives, for example. Instead, precarity constitutes a pervasive everyday experience that evokes reactions from antagonism, shame, and resistance to an avenue for individual advancement. If chapter 1 outlined films that appear feminist on the surface but that were haunted by the specter of domesticity, then chapter 2 delineates the proliferation of films that focus on women's participation in a precarious labor market without reducing their presence to victims.

Precarious Management and the Legacy of Social Realism

Feminization and casualization characterize labor's global transformation and its attendant conditions of flexibility and precarity. The increase of immaterial, affective, and emotional work accompanies a decrease of industrial labor. British director Ken Loach's 2007 film *It's a Free World...* captures this new reality but comes to it from a longtime commitment to Marxist analysis of labor under capitalism, an important influence on his filmmaking. The transformation of work has produced a shift in the cinematic embodiment of labor along lines of gender from male to female. The collective of masculine proletarians no longer embodies contemporary labor. Instead, young solitary women, mobile and flexible but also harried and entrepreneurial, become emblematic of the neoliberal labor regime. The female embodiment of the cultural imaginary of work in turn shapes narrative structures and the affective address of the audience. Thus, Loach's *It's a Free World...* continues and departs from his directorial signature. The film asks how working-class women can become entrepreneurs without access to capital, on the one hand, but also shows how Western European women profit from labor exploitation made possible by transnational migration, on the other.

From the twenty-first-century perspective, Loach appears as a representative of the classic vernacular of the social realist depiction of labor. However, his films, according to George McKnight, "have been controversial" in their time (1997, 1). Both the Left and the Right attacked Loach. While the Left, particularly in the film studies journal *Screen*, saw him as naive and not politically sophisticated in a Godardian sense, the Right and the mainstream press, according to Deborah Knight, viewed his films as "didactic, overwritten, too raw and too political" (1997, 60). Over time, however, Loach has emerged as a symbol for the committed filmmaking associated with the English industrial and postindustrial North.

Labor centrally defines Loach's oeuvre with an emphasis on the "workplace, on the locations and circumstances of waged or unwaged labor" (Knight 1997, 62). After Margaret Thatcher's creation of enterprise culture, Loach focused on "widespread unemployment" and "the casualization of labor; the growth of the black economy" (Laing 1997, 26). Accordingly, *It's a Free World...* tells the story of London roommates Angie and Rose, who set up an agency that recruits undocumented migrants and makes a profit from exploiting them through low and unpaid wages, as well as overpriced housing. When Angie does not pay their wages, they kidnap her son, Jaimie, and demand the money that she owes them. The film concludes with Angie continuing her recruitment of workers from Eastern Europe.

The depiction of the ways in which globalization and Europeanization open possibilities for working-class women through entrepreneurism continues and departs from Loach's cinematic and political conventions. During his long career, Loach portrayed "ordinary people, frequently working-class individuals and their families . . . tak[ing] collective action" (McKnight 1997, 2). Angie's exploitation of migrant workers actively negates collective solidarity. The film departs from Loach's previous focus on conflicts between organized labor and management, often depicted in strikes. In the past, McKnight explains, Loach's characters aimed to improve "working conditions or . . . the relationship between labor and management" (3). *It's a Free World . . .* does not present precarity and management as mutually exclusive as they appear in much critical discourse about neoliberalism. Although the film foregrounds the profits available through flexibility and entrepreneurism to Western Europeans, Angie's work, despite her role as manager, remains precarious. Angie and Rose come from lower-class backgrounds, indicated by their living conditions, their personal styles, and their previous jobs at a call center and at a recruitment agency. As Angie exploits institutional loopholes to advance her own capitalist interests, she provides a contrast to Loach's central characters in his past films who came "into direct conflict with dominant social institutions or political organizations" (2). Instead, Loach constructs an ambivalent main character.

Conflict over collectivity and solidarity characterizes the relation between Angie and her father in their intergenerational conversations. He admonishes her for not paying the migrants a minimum wage. The film questions the motivation of his position as well: he cares more about his grandson, Jaimie, than about her. Her parents judge her not only because she exploits migrant workers in an illegal activity but also because they consider her an unreliable and unfit mother. Her father frames his political ethics in the context of national and kinship interests, particularly for his grandson's future chances to get a decent job when migrants undercut hourly wages. The narrative implies poor parenting when the undocumented workers kidnap Jaimie after Angie sends him to open the door for a pizza delivery while she does not tear herself away from a violent movie inappropriate for a young boy.

Leaving behind the paradigmatic representation of the male working class as iconography for labor opens up productive possibilities because the gendering of masculine labor and feminine home never fully captured the nature of work. The centrality of the female character marks a stark contrast to Loach's past oeuvre. In the late 1990s, according to McKnight, "male central characters dominate" in Loach's films, while his past female characters are "traditionally identified with home and family" (1997, 5, 6).[2] Yet Loach's entrepreneurial flexible female worker also embodies the characteristics of the class traitor who undermines international solidarity.

Angie and Rose's relationship captures the fluidity between friendship and profession as they launch their agency in their apartment and outside a bar, reflecting what Melissa Gregg has labeled "work's intimacy" (2011). While Gregg sees this development as a result of computerization, the porous boundary between private and public, work and leisure, and friendship and professional collaboration had always shaped the working lives of women. Particularly, Angie's job of managing people would seem to demand interpersonal communication skills coded as feminine. But the illegality of her endeavor produces risk and violence, which erupt and escalate repeatedly and cyclically. Angie constantly takes high risks and asserts herself among the men around her by shouting and cursing. The many shots of her riding her motorbike in full gear visually obscure her female body and evoke masculine notions of freedom and mobility. McRobbie calls such a figure "the phallic girl," who adopts the habits of masculinity, such as heavy drinking, swearing, smoking, getting into fights, and having casual sex, without her representation advancing a "critique of masculine hegemony" (2009, 83). Loach highlights Angie's working-class roots in her attempts at performing masculinity at the workplaces, such as construction sites, and the reversal of the sexual contract when she makes advances to migrant men.

FIGURE 2.1. *It's a Free World . . .* (Ken Loach, 2007)

The centrality of the female characters has aesthetic consequences. The film creates a painful intimacy as the camera employs extreme close-ups, for example, in a sequence that depicts Rose quitting her work relationship with Angie. Throughout the narrative, Angie's actions repeatedly shock Rose, who nevertheless remains in their partnership because of the profits they reap. After a couple of successful months, they look at an office space, and Rose hopes that they will begin hiring documented migrant workers. When Angie proposes to contract illegal Ukrainians in order to pay off the office, the women search for housing for them at a caravan site where undocumented migrants live. When they find out that the site has no space available, Angie alerts immigration services so that the migrants living there will be deported and she can house workers there herself. This incident marks the breaking point for Rose. During the subsequent car ride, the camera remains extremely close, making it uncomfortable for the audience because of Angie's horrific acts and the ensuing conflict between the two women in the small space. The tightness of the composition does not allow the audience to gain distance from Angie. As she turns her head away from Rose, we do not see her face—a refusal of the conventional shot reverse shot. This strategy contrasts with Loach's early films set in factories, such as *The Price of Coal* (1977), when he employed a distant camera in a documentary style typical of social realism. In *It's a Free World...* the camera vacillates between tight compositions that create intimacy and distant shots of Angie's mobility in the city while she is riding her bike. Different from distant social realist depictions of union activists that ask spectators to reflect on political demands, the composition in *It's a Free World...* traps an audience with Angie in raw emotionality without suggesting a political alternative or offering an emotional release.

This intimacy goes hand in glove with an emotional push-pull that concludes in a circular narrative trajectory. The film begins with shots of Angie recruiting workers in Poland and ends with a similar sequence of her in Ukraine. We are pulled close into alignment with Angie in the film's opening, when her male colleagues harass her sexually, and midway, when the Youth Council questions her about her job in order to assess whether Jaimie may live with her. Shots of Angie riding the motorbike offer kinetic pleasure to the audience. When she takes home an Iranian family, the film evokes sentimentality. The emotional push occurs immediately after such scenes, when she manipulates the workers by providing them with false passports and imploring them to be subservient, when she and Rose invite two young migrant men to their house because the women are "horny," and when she lies to the workers that she is paying taxes and hence cannot pay their wages.

Loach's depiction of a female entrepreneur who exploits undocumented migrant workers responds to the neoliberal emphasis on the free market and new inequalities brought about by Europeanization. Loach expands the notion of work to include transnational and sexual economies across legal and illegal frames with the trained eye of the filmmaker who has attended to the changing role of labor under post–World War II capitalism. He depicts the ways in which management and precarity are not mutually exclusive and demonstrates the pernicious nature of a thoroughly neoliberalized subject who commodifies friendship and sex. While the shift from collective male to solitary female character responds to the development from Fordist labor to post-Fordist work practices, the female character also comes to stand in for the abandoning of traditional working-class values.

Precarious Labor and Elusive Solidarity

Similarly committed to a cinema of labor in the postindustrial and neoliberal context, the Dardenne brothers have long focused on the precariat made up of migrants, women, and children. Born in 1951 (Jean-Pierre) and 1954 (Luc), they are about two decades younger than Ken Loach, who was born in 1936. They share a dedication to filming the marginal in documentaries and feature narrative films that derive from their early interest in labor politics. Their independent films have been successful at film festivals, particularly at Cannes.[3] A body of substantive scholarship and critical reception covers the ethics and aesthetics of their oeuvre, something that does not apply to the majority of filmmakers covered in this book, particularly the female filmmakers.

With two scholarly monographs and a lively scholarly debate about their films, they have garnered a status as ethical observers of the postindustrial condition and the neoliberal effects on the precarious class in formerly industrialized Western Europe (see Cooper 2007; Mai 2010; Frölich 2011; Mosley 2013; Rushton 2014). Philip Mosley (2013, 1) situates their films in the context of "new French Realism," which includes Cantet, whose *L'emploi du temps* (*Time Out*; France, 2001), *Human Resources*, *Entre les murs* (*The Class*; France, 2008), and *Vers le sud* (*Heading South*; France, Canada, 2005) concern unemployment, labor conditions, and multiculturalism in France and its global contexts. Mosley proposes that these directors share "a preoccupation with the lives of working-class individuals struggling to survive with a measure of dignity in a new world order that for them is mainly one of poverty, unemployment, and social disintegration and environmental ruin" (1). The Dardenne brothers' oeuvre has shifted from political documentaries about factory strikes to fictionalized narratives about precarious existence.

As the Dardenne brothers belong to the contemporary canon of cinema about labor, scholarly discourse, particularly in the two monographs by Joseph Mai (2010) and Mosley (2013), emphasizes the biographical connection to Seraing, a former industrial region in Belgium. From 1974 to 1983 the Dardenne brothers documented workers during deindustrialization. Their first forays into narrative fiction film occurred from 1986 to 1992, and since 1996 they have become successful feature-length filmmakers. They also produce the work of other filmmakers with their production company Les Films du Fleuve, which in 2016 led to four coproduced films at Cannes, including their own *La fille inconnue* (*The Unknown Girl*; Belgium, France, 2016) and Loach's *I, Daniel Blake* (UK, France, Belgium, 2016), which won the Palme d'Or.

The Dardenne brothers tell stories about female characters in a realist style that departs from an earlier tradition of leftist emphasis on strikes and masculine industrial labor. They retain the documentary impetus with narratives that take place in the regional landscape affected by new labor laws, neoliberalism, and migration. Their training in social realism has attuned them to the vicissitudes and conditions of the contemporary economic context of labor. The Dardenne brothers trace political and aesthetic continuity in the economic transformation. Their work thus offers an important corrective to scholarship that emphasizes only the distinct nature and newness of neoliberalism.

Their award-winning feature film *Deux jours, une nuit* (*Two Days, One Night*; Belgium, France, Italy, 2014) tells the story of Sandra, who gets fired from a solar-panel company when she returns to work after a medical leave. During her absence, management gave employees the choice either to receive their individual 1,000-euro annual bonus (and Sandra would be fired) or to give up their bonus (and she could keep her job). The manager offers to let the employees vote a second time, and in preparation for that vote, Sandra visits her fifteen coworkers over one weekend and tries to convince them to let her keep her job. The film depicts Sandra moving through the city, sometimes alone, sometimes with her husband, Manu, and her colleague Anne. At the ending, after a tie vote, the manager suggests to Sandra that she can keep her job if he fires one of the short-term workers. Sandra rejects the offer. Her political act enhances her well-being.

The Dardennes' oeuvre associates postindustrial labor with drudgery, disaffection, and the desperation of the homeless, jobless, and migrants circulating through decaying cities looking for money, semilegal work, or illegal business activities (Mosley 2013; Mai 2010). In contrast to many of the Dardenne brothers' other films that depict the under- and unemployed, *Two Days, One Night* takes place in the lower middle class, whose members are dependent on a dual income but are surrounded by the accoutrements of the modern happy family. Consequently, the mise-en-scène differs strikingly from the brothers' other films, an important factor for filmmakers whose style results from the "*mise-en-scène* rather than from their editing" (Mosley 2013, 85). This film contrasts the harrowing narrative with a colorful and bright contemporary home, where Sandra and Manu live with their two children. Their home's interior includes blue wallpaper with big gray flowers and red curtains in the bedroom. Sandra tidies the children's bedrooms, with their cheery wallpaper, lovingly setting stuffed animals on their colorful bedding. Repeatedly, the play with sunlight and its shadow sheds a warm glow on the family's togetherness at home or on Sandra's skin as she walks through the city in desperation. In this film, the precarious labor condition is invisible, hidden by a veneer of supposed nonhierarchical teams at work and seemingly stable living conditions at home. Technology has changed from coal to solar energy sold by companies that have displaced the political collectives of the 1970s. The film thus thrives on the contrast between the happiness that the surrounding objects signify and the characters' emotional despair. The workplace relies on networks and teams, seemingly democratic and collaborative, as the vote asks workers to make an impossible choice. Short-term contracts and the informal process of negotiating the conditions that affect Sandra create her and her colleagues' precarious situation.

The Dardenne brothers make haptic and kinetic films through a focus on bodies (Mai 2010; Mosley 2013). A mobile camera accompanies Sandra as she moves through the city on foot and by bus and car. *Two Days, One Night* continues the cinematic style that other scholars have identified as typical for the Dardenne brothers: individual scenes begin in medias res without narrative exposition or establishing shots. This strategy conveys the feeling of mobility as the camera moves from one location to the next in a consistent pattern of

FIGURE 2.2. *Two Days, One Night* (Jean-Pierre Dardenne and Luc Dardenne, 2014)

cuts (see Mosley 2013; Mai 2010). Other characters are peripatetic too, which increases Sandra's walking distances as she attempts to find her colleagues and is repeatedly sent somewhere else by their relatives. Thus, her movement physically maps the network among her colleagues. Following her, we gain insight into the workers' activities during their leisure time. Some have second jobs to make ends meet, others coach soccer, work on their own homes, or undertake domestic chores.

Scholars highlight the "ethical encounter," described by Emmanuel Levinas, in the Dardennes' films in general and in *Two Days, One Night* in particular. The ending of Sandra's ethical choice to forgo employment in order not to betray her colleague extends her action into the political realm. When Sandra meets her colleague Timur, he starts crying, ashamed that he voted for her termination. Timur reveals how when he was new to the company, Sandra had pretended that one of his mistakes was hers in order to protect him. He commits his vote to her and offers to call another colleague. Like Timur, Sandra repeatedly cries, which she tries to hide from her children. Shame of weakness but also the possibility of redemption pervade those moments.

Sandra's final act of solidarity transforms her. When she calls her husband, she says, "We put up a good fight." Only spectators witness Sandra's gesture of resistance and her subsequent transformation. The audience is privy to the act of solidarity in the boss's office, which differs from the traditional depiction of the strike as icon of the collective. On the DVD extra materials, the Dardenne brothers explain that they wanted to ask what solidarity could look like in the context of contemporary neoliberalism.

Two Days, One Night suggests that if we look for the working class as a collective of white masculine industrial workers with dirty faces and heavy tools, we might search in vain. But if we look for a dispersed workforce with a range of time-limited contracts, of diverse genders and ethnicities, and in aspirational middle-class settings, we find precarious working conditions. Precarity is pervasive but not always dramatic. *Two Days, One Night* models a gesture of resistance.

The Industrial Ruins of Communism

The two films discussed so far both belong to Western European leftist auteur cinema in the tradition of social realism. They foreground solitary women moving through the urban environment in search of a surplus or retaining their jobs. The film discussed in this section, Macedonian director Teona Strugar Mitevska's *Jas sum od Titov Veles* (*I Am from Titov Veles*; Republic of Macedonia,

Belgium, France, Slovenia, 2007), focuses on women's limited access to work and subsequent movement through a city in the former Eastern Bloc. The film aestheticizes precarity as postsocialist normalcy. Its strikingly beautiful images create a composite of a feminine-feminist vision critical of the communist past and the capitalist present.

Capitalism in postsocialist countries did not fulfill the fantasies of those living under past socialist dictatorships, argues Jennifer Suchland (2011). As Eastern European women's response differs from the understanding of inequality in the United States, Western feminists ignore the fact that women in postsocialist countries criticize the "gendered impact of the triple transition" in economics, politics, and the social sphere, particularly regarding the market "as a sphere where only men could play the rough-and-tumble game of capitalism" (846, 850). *I Am from Titov Veles* captures one such feminist response to the transition period, encapsulating a critical perspective on the legacy of past communism and on the newly arrived stagnant capitalism.

In the film, three grown sisters—Slavica, Sapho, and Afrodita—share a home in Titov Veles, Macedonia, after the collapse of communist Yugoslavia, where the town's main steel factory has poisoned the environment. Afrodita endows the postindustrial and decaying landscape with striking fantasies of a virginal pregnancy. Her voice-over reveals that the sisters' parents met in former Yugoslavia when they were displaced from Greece. When their mother received a visa to travel to Greece, she disappeared, and their father died. Slavica, who is a methadone addict, works in the factory. Sapho procures visas for the sisters and an Albanian husband for Slavica through sex work. Sapho and Slavica finally leave, but Afrodita is unable to depart, fantasizing a love story with the sexually abusive methadone nurse Aco. The film concludes with Afrodita and Slavica trapped inside their burning house after Slavica returns in search of methadone.

The young nation of Macedonia, landlocked on the European continent, does not belong to the EU. A nation centrally located inside Europe, it lies outside the political and economic structures of the EU. Mirroring Randall Halle's (2014) observation that coproductions fund films that appear as national cinema, *I Am from Titov Veles*'s opening credit sequence lists an extensive lineup of coproducers, including regional, national, transnational, and global funding sources, individual producers and coproducers, film festivals, and diplomatic and cultural national institutions from France, Belgium, the Netherlands, and Slovenia. These European funding sources shape a film outside of the EU that presents an allegory of a nation that lies paradoxically within Europe.

Production and diegesis echo each other's sibling structure. The director, Teona Strugar Mitevska; her actress and producer sister, Labina Mitevska, who plays Afrodita; and their set-designer brother, Vuc Mitevska, who created the setting together form the production company Sisters and Brother Mitevska, which by 2017 had produced four films. Sibling ties constitute a kinship configuration different from the heterosexual romance of male director and female star that Mark Betz (2009) has analyzed in postwar European art cinema. On another level, however, the mode of production and diegetic world contrast. As Halle (2014) points out, money flows more easily across the borders of Europe than people. The film's long list of European funding sources diverges from its narrative about the sisters' desperate desire and frustrated attempts to leave Macedonia. While the Iron Curtain restricted their parents' mobility, the EU limits the sisters' movement.

This beautiful film, set in the mise-en-scène of the ruins of state socialism, depicts the social entrapment of women in a place marked by a transition into an uncharted future. Tito's socialist past, captured in faded murals, a poisoned environment, and a dilapidated factory, overshadows the daily life of the sisters. Aesthetically and narratively, the film belongs to what Rosalind Galt and Karl Schoonover have labeled "global art cinema," which includes "overtly artistic textuality, art-house theatre exhibition, and the international circulation of foreign films" (2010, 4).[4] *I Am from Titov Veles* also references socialist realist cinematic conventions, not least through the centrality of the factory that organizes the town of Titov Veles and the filmic narrative.

Post-1989 films of East-Central Europe have embraced magical realism, realist fiction in which magical things happen without any seeming contradiction, in contrast to the mandated socialist realism of the communist past (Skrodzka 2012). *I Am from Titov Veles* reimagines femininity transcending the social reality of the postcommunist transition with an emphasis on dream-like scenes. Magical realism's "investment in visualizing metamorphosis" determines its affinity for transition and transformation (xii). *I Am from Titov Veles*

FIGURE 2.3. *I Am from Titov Veles* (Teona Strugar Mitevska, 2007)

applies the metaphorical language of magical realism to the changing understanding of femininity and labor to inscribe fantasies of mythical reproduction into the postcommunist and postindustrial landscape.[5]

The palimpsest of cultural references portrays postsocialism not as a linear development from socialism to capitalism but instead as a present moment haunted by the traumatic past without a clear path toward the future. The fantasy-inflected depiction of femininity, however, creates a cinematic language that criticizes the former conventions of socialist realism, which negated femininity and disavowed women's double burden, as well as current capitalism, which reduces women to their sexual exchange value. Afrodita gives birth from her mouth in visually stunning scenes that take place in a lake. The film later returns to those fantasies when she steals a baby and escapes in a boat through the reeds dressed in a striking green gown. The scenes invoke the Greek myth of Aphrodite taking the infant Adonis to Hades so that Persephone can take care of him. Names and mythological references create a cultural-geographical landscape, with Macedonia between the West, symbolized by Greek mythology, and the East, represented by Anton Chekhov's play *Three Sisters*, in which the eponymous heroines long to be in Moscow instead of in a small town, the same way these three sisters desire to leave Macedonia for Greece.

The references to myth, Afrodita's fantasies, and the accounts of capitalist circulation and exchange of women together integrate different temporalities. "Modern time," explains Bliss Cua Lim, "so universal and so empty," controls work and leisure, obscures cultural differences, and excludes the "primitive" and the "anachronistic" (2009, 33, 12). Through her fantasies Afrodita moves in and out of modern time. Thus, the film critiques the illusion of capitalist linear development of progress, offering simultaneous different temporalities.

The film associates the ruins of postsocialism with faded colors, from the opening shot of a mural on which Afrodita walks, to the muted green colors in the factory at night, when Slavica and Victor meet in the empty building, and the rusted metal in the locker room of the basketball team. Individual strong, vibrant colors—red, green, blue, and gold—define the women's clothes in fabric that enhances sensuality, sexuality, and femininity. The composition of the characters sets stark visual accents in the monochromatic barren landscape of the postindustrial aesthetics of rust. Monika Lorber's costumes create a color palette that contrasts the mise-en-scène of the deteriorating factory backdrop. The dresses' glamorous sartorial quality, traditionally associated with film stars, the ultimate commodification of female bodies in the studio system, seems out of place in the postindustrial and postsocialist setting. The disjuncture between the fantasy of femininity and the reality of postcommunism counters the past disavowal of femininity as the precondition for communism's ideology of gender equality. The dresses' evocative colors and flowing softness contrast to the steel factory. While the film criticizes capitalism's reduction of women to their sexual use and exchange value, the excess of the beautiful costumes set in the decaying workplaces also captures capitalism's material possibilities. This showcasing of the commodity fetish in light of its absence during years of cognitive poverty constitutes an ironic difference between postcommunist and Western feminism.

I Am from Titov Veles invokes past communist ideologies that privilege industrial labor with the central site of the dilapidated factory—a multivalent signifier. While working in the factory, Slavica appears in gender-neutral overalls with a hard hat and protective glasses that she wears while melting steel. A shot montage shows her silhouette walking across a corridor and up the stairs in the factory, a shot that is reminiscent of Sergei M. Eisenstein's *Stachka* (*Strike*; Soviet Union, 1925). *I Am from Titov Veles*, however, does not dynamically move toward strike, rebellion, or revolution as do the classic political films about labor. Slavica does not identify with the factory or her brigade, as many socialist realist narratives would have it. Nor does she serendipitously excel at her career, as in a postfeminist narrative. Work provides neither liberation nor equality; as Suchland points out, "Work is not unproblematically or universally liberatory" (2011, 852).

The film critiques the limited possibilities for women under capitalism, as prostitution offers the most lucrative activity for the sisters. But it does not show Sapho in a sex act, as is typical of films that portray prostitution; instead, we see her getting up early and putting on her elegant red dress and matching high-heeled shoes before leaving the house. After a temporal ellipsis, we witness the good-bye to the customer in the car. When Sapho returns, she reveals that the new owner of the factory is going to marry Slavica and provide a visa for her to leave. Sapho's commodification achieved her strategic goals. Slavica's new husband, Victor, purchases the factory. Such a clear inscription of the Western masculine subject taking over the Eastern site of production and body for reproduction demarcates the limited parameters of the women's agency. Suchland concludes, "The terms of their personal economic advancement do not tend to propel them, or their countries, beyond the structural constraints of economic globalization" (2011, 851). *I Am from Titov Veles* captures a rogue capitalism in which the women sell their bodies, as the town sells its factory for scrap metal. These two economic cycles overlap in the figure of the symbolically named Victor. The sexual contract provides only limited benefits to Slavica, the stand-in for the feminized nation.

In sum, *I Am from Titov Veles* situates the main characters in the postcommunist present, negotiating the haunting past and the unknowable future. It eschews traditional socialist filmmaking and Western European feminism, instead projecting a fantasy of femininity as a mode of survival that relies on circulating the only commodity that these women own, their bodies. Sisterhood, instead of being a symbol for solidarity or equality, marks an economy in which the women exchange sexual favors with men in order to take care of each other. Teona Strugar Mitevska articulates such a feminist-feminine vision through a cinematic language of sartorial, sensual, and affective filmmaking in which colorful costumes, mythic allegories, and spectacular fantasy scenes offer a contrapuntal composition to the industrial ruins and material decay of postsocialism. Its cinematic fantasies value female reproduction and assert female film production, but they also expose the promises of communism's industrial labor and capitalism's sexual contract as futile. The film depicts precarious life but frames such experience in a cinematic-political response that is fundamentally different from the Western leftist tradition, discussed previously in this chapter, and its feminist articulation, covered in the next sections. *I Am from Titov Veles* embraces a feminine-feminist aesthetics eschewing both social and socialist realist depictions of precarity.

Precarious Drifting through Neoliberal Berlin

Having discussed the political and realist cinematic language of Western European auteurs of the cinema of labor and a postcommunist aesthetic departure from the conventions of socialist realism, this section turns to feminist responses to neoliberal labor regimes by three female filmmakers whose work emerges out of collaborative production contexts. The following German and Austrian films focus on precarity but frame their response in fundamentally different ways. Independent filmmaker and feminist Tatjana Turanskyj's *Eine flexible Frau* (*The Drifters*; Germany, 2010) and *Top Girl oder La déformation professionnelle* (*Top Girl*; Germany, 2014) comprise the first two films of her trilogy *Frauen und Arbeit* (*Women and Work: Make Love, Not War*), while her most recent film, *Orientierungslosigkeit ist kein Verbrechen* (*Disorientation Is Not a Crime*; Germany, 2016), tells the story of a female journalist covering the refugee crisis in Greece. Turanskyj is cofounder of the German feminist organization Pro Quote Film, which advocates for quotas in film funding for women.

The Drifters depicts the downward spiral of unemployed architect Greta M., who drifts through a postboom Berlin at the end of the first decade of the twenty-first century. Greta desperately demands work in her profession as an architect. A telemarketing company briefly employs her to sell prefabricated houses. Greta has a tense relationship with her son and her ex-husband. She comments cynically on women who succeed in the neoliberal market economy and is openly envious of those who are pregnant and for whom heterosexual love offers access to a middle-class identity. Unable to function successfully in the post-Wall neoliberal economy, Greta neither embraces middle-class professionalism nor finds utopian possibilities in feminist solidarity. Greta's drifting through Berlin becomes symbolic of precarity's lack of direction; neither the narrative nor Greta moves toward a goal. A camera that lacks focus through the consistent depiction of random streets and unrecognizable sites communicates a general sense of being lost.

The film captures the effects of restructuring creative professionalism as freelancing, which turns workers into entrepreneurs. Greta becomes unemployed when her transnational architectural firm closes its offices in London and Berlin. She experiences pervasive but invisible under- and unemployment. At a party in her former architecture firm, her friends discuss urban development in Berlin. One female architect accuses other guests of being nostalgic for the past of alternative work collectives and demands that they get used to Berlin's gentrification. When another woman admonishes her, "Ten years ago, you still had a utopian vision," the speaker wonders whether she is the only one at the party who is gainfully employed. The scene indicates that those with employment are indistinguishable from those who are unemployed.

The Drifters puts to rest any utopian possibilities of collective work (see also Halle 2013). Greta wants what she will not receive: love from her teenage son, respect from her divorced husband, money from her past employers, a job opportunity from her successful friends, and the possibility to express her urban artistic vision. If Greta embodies what Berlant has called a "post-Fordist affect," responding to the neoliberal present that produces "new affective languages ... of anxiety, contingency, and precarity," she nevertheless does not articulate optimism, cruel or otherwise (2011, 19). In a departure from the utopian aspirations of second-wave feminism, Greta instead expresses what Sianne Ngai (2005) labels "ugly feelings," such as envy, irritation, anxiety, and paranoia. She performs neither femininity and good work habits nor political resistance.

Women compete against each other or relate in hierarchical relationships as their leadership roles behoove them. The second-wave feminist understanding of patriarchy, based on women as victims and men as perpetrators, does not offer an appropriate political analysis of twenty-first-century films when individual women have advanced. The film demonstrates that neither the Marxist model of class exploitation nor a simplistic feminist model of patriarchy can fully explain the precarious working conditions of female creative professionals. Greta embodies the postutopian solitude after collective experiments associated first with West Berlin's alternative culture and then with the creative possibilities opened up by the Berlin Republic have given way to financial crisis, outsourcing, and survival of the fittest. In sum, the film's feminism emphasizes the particularity of precarity for middle-aged professional women in the creative class. It refuses advocating femininity, neoliberal entrepreneurism, or what Berlant calls "cruel optimism." Instead, the film exposes neoliberalism's strategies of transforming workers into entrepreneurs, which for women implies not only advertising and selling labor power in the form of skills and knowledge but also reifying the female body and its attendant feminine characteristics.

A Comedy of Glass Ceilings and Outsourcing

If *The Drifters* charted the daily life of those middle-aged women in the metropolis cast aside by global outsourcing, then Maren Ade's *Toni Erdmann* (Germany, Austria, Switzerland, Romania, 2016) focuses on the adventures of a young female manager who specializes in downsizing for global companies located in the former Eastern Bloc. Ade also participates in alternative production context, as she belongs to the small production company Komplizen Film in Berlin, which financed the film, as well as other successful independent global art films by female filmmakers. As Germany nominated the film for the Oscars and it dominated the European film awards in 2016 and the German film awards in 2017, *Toni Erdmann* proved to be exceptionally successful. Its original screenplay tells the story of corporate manager Ines and her relationship to her father, Winfred Conradi, a recently retired music teacher. Winfred belongs to the liberal postwar generation, whereas Ines specializes in laying off workers for other companies. During a surprise visit in Bucharest, her father impersonates a range of characters, from business coach Toni Erdmann to the German ambassador. First, Ines considers her father a hindrance to her networking, but her professional persona cracks at an absurd naked birthday brunch, when her father arrives in a Bulgarian Kukeri costume made out of long-haired goat skin. Subsequently, father and daughter embrace in a public park, and the film concludes with Ines's visit to Germany for her grandmother's funeral, where she reveals that she now works for a company in Singapore.

The film contrasts Ines's desperation in her attempts to advance professionally and her boss Gerald's subtle sexism with her own ruthless calculations to reduce the number of employees in Romanian companies. Hester Baer suggests that Ines "knows only work and the constant quest for self-optimization"; she is, in other words, an "exemplary neoliberal subject" (2017, 1). The film carefully reveals subtle sexism when Herr Henneberg, whose company has outsourced the downsizing of his subcontractors to Ines's firm, invites her father to join his party but asks Ines to take his wife shopping. The first turning point occurs when father and daughter drive out to the countryside to assess the situation of a subcontractor whose workers Ines intends to let go. She turns the tables on her father by making him playact as another business manager from Germany. When they go out to the site, Ines's father jokingly points out that one of the workers on the oil field is not wearing gloves. His boss immediately fires the worker, and Ines's dad begins to comprehend that his humor does not have the intended effects. His general criticism of what he perceives as his daughter's professional lack of ethical treatment of others receives a strong rebuttal from her when she tells him that she can explain to him all the ways in which his actions in Germany economically affect the people in Romania, irrespective of his liberal attitudes.

The majority of the narrative restricts the setting to a hermetically sealed business world with meeting rooms, rooftops, and car interiors. The look onto "a real Romania" occurs from Ines's point of view out of her office window into a yard behind a fence below. Locals enter either as part of the service industry or in subservient roles in business transactions, even if they are internationally trained. At the same time, Ines remains permanently stressed and insecure about her performance, preparing meetings and reflecting on them with a coach via electronic media. A system of permanent coaching and self-assertion reinforces her insecurities, which propel the monetized psychological services previously associated with friendship. Work extends into the evenings at restaurants and bars, and weekends at malls in outings in which Ines strives to entertain and impress Henneberg. Her attempts at professionalism lead her to reinforce unwillingly the role of the housewife, entertaining her male colleagues and caring for their well-being.

Increasingly, Ines takes up her father's jokes, finding joy in the absurdity that he introduces into the profit-driven business world. The comedy, Baer suggests, does not follow traditional comedic conventions. In Baer's analysis, *Toni Erdmann* "disorganizes the conventions of comedy" to reflect "on a formal level the insecurity of the present" and "to evince feelings of insecurity and discomfort" (2017, 3). While the film includes moments in which Ines transcends her role as cold-hearted business woman, it ultimately foregrounds her participation in the global system of increasing efficiency that relies on outsourcing and downsizing with mobile capital. When Ines suggests a radical solution of

FIGURE 2.4. *Toni Erdmann* (Maren Ade, 2016)

cutting all jobs, assuming that would lead her client Henneberg to choose the more modest plan that she had developed and wants to implement, he instead selects the most cutthroat solution.

Despite Ines's moments of humanity, the film emphasizes Western European businesswomen's participation in the neoliberal restructuring of the former Eastern Bloc. It shows how ruthless global capitalism implicates those who actively advance its corporate form and those who imagine themselves outside of its exploitative structures. *Toni Erdmann* offers a detailed account of how neoliberal restructuring reorganizes places and how it deforms subjects, including their relationships to each other and their daily work practices.

Precarious Falling and Female Friendship

In contrast to the solitary heroines of *The Drifters* and *Toni Erdmann*, the characters of Austrian independent director Barbara Albert's *Fallen* (*Falling*; Germany, Austria, 2006) form a group of female friends that enables if not solidarity, then at least a dialogic reflexivity on the loss of utopia and the disappearance of the traditional industrial working class and the solid middle class. While less internationally successful than *Two Days, One Night* and *Toni Erdmann*, this film offers an explicitly feminist contribution to the discourse of women's work under the conditions of neoliberalism in Europe. The subtle restructuring of work constitutes the background, and the narrative concerns the ways in which women support each other. The women also masquerade as successful to hide what they perceive as personal failure: employment below their educational level and their past aspirations, retraining and part-time positions, jail time, and single motherhood. *Falling* contrasts with accounts of postfeminism outlined in the opening of this chapter and demonstrates independent feminist art cinema's vision after utopia.

Albert is a writer, actress, assistant editor, and producer. Born in 1970 in Vienna, she now lives in Berlin. Her first feature film, *Nordrand* (*Northern Skirts*; Austria, Germany, Switzerland, 2000), portrays the lives of young women, including migrants from former Yugoslavia in the mid-1990s who live in the outskirts of Vienna. Her second film, *Böse Zellen* (*Free Radicals*; Austria, Germany, Switzerland, 2003), shows the interconnectedness of different lives, and her film *Licht* (*Mademoiselle Paradis*; Austria, Germany, 2017) is a period film depicting a female blind piano player in eighteenth-century Vienna. She has collaborated with documentary filmmaker Michael Glawogger, whose oeuvre has focused on the global landscape of labor, for example, *Slumming* (Austria, Germany, Switzerland, 2005), *Workingman's Death* (Austria, Germany, 2005), and *Whores' Glory* (Germany, Austria, 2011).[6] Albert coproduced Andrea Štaka's *Das Fräulein* (*Fräulein*; Germany, Switzerland, Bosnia, 2006) and Jasmila Žbanić's *Grbavica* (*Esma's Secret—Grbavica*; Bosnia and Herzegovina, Croatia, Austria, Germany, 2005). She also cofounded the film production company COOP 99. As have most directors discussed in this chapter, including the male directors of the leftist tradition, Albert has resisted the pressure of the investment-heavy film industry and engaged in alternative production and labor practices.

Falling, which has received less critical attention than Albert's first feature, takes seriously the current political and economic conditions for women.[7] But in contrast to many films that explicitly address contemporary neoliberalism or capitalism, *Falling* does not focus on a precarious lower class struggling to survive, as, for example, the Dardenne brothers' *Le silence de Lorna* (*The Silence of Lorna*; Belgium, France, Italy, Germany, 2008) or Alejandro González Iñárritu's *Biutiful* (Mexico, Spain, 2010, discussed in chapter 1). It depicts a seemingly middle-class cross section of women in their midthirties—Nina, Carmen, Brigitte, Alex, and Nicole with her daughter, Daphne—who reunite in a small Austrian town at the funeral of their former high school teacher. During the day and night they spend together, the narrative reveals the lies they tell each other to keep up the facades of success, the increasing economic gap among them, the unreliability of the sexual and marriage contracts, and their loss of utopian political movements. The film thus connects the disillusion of the Left and feminist hopes to the present of increasing economic gaps among women. The film concludes with a sense of economic insecurity that has become the women's reality. Instead of a fundamental transformation, it portrays minor expressions of agency when they return to their everyday lives. These actions, the film implies, result not only from their mutual support in the present but also from their memory of their hopes for an alternative future that they had once nourished in the past.

The film mobilizes the affective bond of friendship as the women remember the house where they once wanted to live as a political collective. The women's precarious working conditions produce shame that each associates with her lack of success. Carmen left the small town early and moved to Germany. The others accuse her of having abandoned them, as she embodies the glamour and luminosity that McRobbie (2009) claims the media promises to young women. The film seems to accord Carmen that status with a golden BMW, which becomes the vehicle for the women's nightly tour. However, the conclusion reveals that she does not act in front of the camera, as the others assume, but works as a dubber. As the women meet at a funeral, their black outfits erase their class differences, even though Carmen appears more refined and sophisticated than her friends. The revelation of her lack of success at the film's ending also challenges spectators to rethink their readings of the character. It reverses the narrative convention of the makeover show, which celebrates the always-surprising success through a one-hour transformation in the reveal at the end. Instead, the film's conclusion uncovers that Carmen's repeated attempts to reach somebody on her cell phone, which appeared as a sign of her success and importance, signaled instead her desperate search for work.

The women explicitly reflect on the passing of the great ideologies and collective hopes. They work in the service industry that emerged around under- and unemployment, as one of them trains the long-term unemployed, while another dreams of becoming self-employed in the wellness industry. When they sit around the fire during the night, one of them calls Carmen a traitor, to which she retorts: "And who are you? The fighter for the working class?" When her friend responds that the working class does not exist anymore, all the women agree that the time of ideologies is over. Subsequently, when the police arrest one of them in the mall because she overextended her time-limited release from prison, they are unable to offer any effective resistance.

The film's conclusion depicts small gestures in the women's private lives that take the place of fighting for grand ideologies. Alex breaks up with her boyfriend, and Carmen spits on the grave of their former teacher. The film's ending combines everyday activities in the visual track with a political song on the audio track, thereby contrasting the past utopian ideals with the mundane everyday life to which the friends are accustomed. The film does not endorse a feminist or leftist utopian aspiration. Neither does it model individual success or collective power. Instead, it uses the female-friendship genre to outline the loss of the political utopia and to emphasize mutual support and small acts of resistance. The women's inability to fulfill the radical political demands or liberal middle-class aspirations of professional success for women fills them with shame. Instead of delineating what Guy Standing calls "the precariat"—"the new dangerous class," consisting of those employed in casual, temporary, and part-time and short-term labor, including migrants, interns, and those with low incomes (2011, 9, 15, 18)—Albert shows a group of women passing as middle class who are haunted by the shame of precarious conditions and engaged in constant retraining. The film's postfeminism captures the adjustment to the economic reality after feminism. Instead of promising choice through consumption, it instead exposes the fallacies that surround notions of freedom, be it sexual or economic, without negating the importance of agency in enacting existing choices.

Conclusion

This chapter reflects on the centrality of diverse neoliberalisms to the articulation of a feminist cinema in twenty-first-century Europe. It counters a homogenizing theoretical discourse about a monolithic and all-encompassing neoliberalism by demonstrating the diversity of filmmakers' vision of precarious work. The danger of a new universalism emerges from the lack of differentiation among neoliberalisms and the inscription of the precariat as a new class that substitutes for the past industrial working class in the cultural imaginary of labor. The chapter acknowledges the theoretical centrality of neoliberal economics and precarity for women's work in the twenty-first century while it emphasizes the specificity of the experience of precarity across classes, professions, and regions. More often than not, discrimination based on gender, race, and citizenship continues to be embedded in what appear to be new forms of neoliberal organization of work.

The chapter's assertion that a feminist cinema exists in twenty-first-century Europe results from attending to independent cinema, including lesser and more well-known films from across Europe. The precarious and harried solitary female worker as the emblem of neoliberalism has risen to prominence in the films by traditional political auteurs of Western Europe who are trained in the cinematic language of social realism. Films from the former Eastern Bloc are wary of industrial labor as a path to women's liberation but also formulate a strident critique of the capitalist promise to women. Capitalism provides the contemporary language of the victor, as in *I Am from Titov Veles*, and configures women symbolically in a heterosexual romance of a strong masculine West that saves a feminized East.

Even though this book as a whole does not focus only on explicit feminist representations of women's work, arguing instead that the topic proliferates across European films, this chapter demonstrates the existence of a political feminist vision of working women in the first decade of the twenty-first century. Whereas the screen heroines traverse landscapes that symbolize the moment after the loss of the great ideologies of the Left and of feminism, the filmmakers discussed in this chapter operate in alternative economic contexts. Their films thus embody the paradox of advancing a critique of neoliberal capitalism without offering a solution, while the conditions of their production reflect the agency they assert within the complex funding system of the European film industry. This independent art cinema traces the mundane effects of precarious employment and gestures of resistance to neoliberalism. In contrast, popular cinema in Western Europe narrates nostalgic visions about past industrial labor centering on female characters—the topic of the next chapter.

CHAPTER 3

Heritage Cinema of Industrial Labor

> The body under the skin is an over-heated factory.
> —Antonin Artaud, "Van Gogh, the Man Suicided by Society"

> The first camera in the history of cinema was pointed at a factory, but a century later, it can be said that film is seldom drawn to the factory and even repelled by it.
> —Harun Farocki, "Workers Leaving the Factory"

> Heritage, for all its seductive delights, is bogus history.
> —Robert Hewison, *The Heritage Industry*

This chapter's readings attest to the ongoing cultural significance of industrial and mechanical labor in our contemporary imagination of work. The films' temporality and ideology differ between the former West and East as the aftereffects of the Cold War haunt contemporary European cinema about women's work. A process of cultural reimagination of the factory and office work is under way in Western European countries. The new heritage cinema of industrial and mechanical labor, often in the form of biopics, from Great Britain, Germany, and France tell stories about women overcoming barriers to equality, freedom, and success. The female gendered representation of labor struggles revises cinema's historical imagination, centered on male workers, and expands the repertoire of heritage cinema. It also appropriates a feminist rhetoric for individualistic success stories. Female protagonists conjoin industrial and feminist pasts, claiming both for a definition of a white nation within Western Europe. When individual films offer counternarratives that poke fun at France's reclaiming the past of labor conflicts, they can rely on an audience familiar with such cultural appropriations. Similarly, Eastern European films do not engage in the nostalgic recuperation of the industrial past and instead situate factory labor in the present. Outdated machines do not offer the film's female protagonists paths to equality, liberation, or self-fulfillment, in contrast to the past socialist realist celebration of the worker hero. In sum, this chapter traces the revision of the depiction of factory labor projected into the past and organized around female characters. The films mobilize industrialization for national progress devoid of migrant and minority labor.

The term "heritage cinema" originates in early 1990s British film studies. The rise of heritage in Great Britain included educated leisure and tourism and the management of culturally significant monuments. Since its coinage, it has referred to Western European films that offer an immersive experience of historical moments and national literature. Heritage cinema emerged during the 1980s in Great Britain and since the 1990s in France and Germany. Its films represent Western European national art cinemas on the global market. The twentieth-century history of heritage in Great Britain results from an interest in the maintenance of the country house, on the one hand, and from economic and industrial decline, including the 1970s recession, on the other (Hewison 1987). Since the early 1990s, heritage discourse has transformed into an academic field and a global practice.

Film scholar Andrew Higson (1993, 109) observes that heritage cinema circulated images of Englishness internationally as nostalgic spectacles. Responding to Great Britain's decline as a world power, heritage cinema turns a fantasy about the upper class into national identity (110). Films such as *Another Country* (UK; Marek Kanievska, 1984), *A Passage to India* (UK, United States; David Lean, 1984), *A Room with a View* (UK; James Ivory, 1985), and *Maurice* (UK; James Ivory, 1987) contrast to multicultural films set in the present, for example, *My Beautiful Laundrette* (UK; Stephen Frears, 1985) (110). Heritage cinema, according to Higson, offers an ambivalent and humanist response to Margaret Thatcher's politics in the 1980s in the context of the National Heritage Acts (1980 and 1983), which transformed publicly accessible historical buildings and spaces into commodities (110–112). Films tend to focus on a country house set in a beautiful landscape, while literary adaptations fetishize period details and invent a "male-centered" past from the perspective of the present (112–114).

Moving "slowly and episodically," the films lack "close-ups and rapid cutting" (117). The irrecoverable past creates a sense of loss that accompanies the pleasure of re-creation, concludes Higson (47).

In response to Higson's ideological criticism of heritage cinema, film scholars recuperate its progressive identity politics. Richard Dyer (2001) points to the presence of gay characters, while Rosalind Galt (2011, 7–9) argues that the marginalization of "pretty" as trivial undergirds the negative view of heritage cinema. Dyer suggests that the films offer "a vision of integration even in homophobic societies of the past" (2001, 48). Galt emphasizes the "feminine space of memory-work" in films about working-class families that give voice to the "psychic urge to mourn that which we are glad to lose" (2006, 14). Dyer and Galt question Higson's premise that heritage is inherently conservative. Despite Dyer's emphasis on social marginality and Galt's reminder of nostalgia's ambivalence, Higson's critical gesture regarding heritage cinema's celebration of the past allows the reification of marginal identities in twenty-first-century heritage cinema to come into view, for example, in French and German films that emerged later.

Heritage cinema itself became more diverse as it rose to prominence in France and Germany, moving beyond the limited view of British aristocrats. As the "hegemonic French cinema of the 1990s," it memorialized the colonial past (Powrie 1998, 479). With a "didactic imperative" the French government sponsored the opening of *Germinal* (France, Belgium, Italy; Claude Berri, 1993) and sent video copies of the film to schools to celebrate France's working class and heavy industry (Austin 1996, 166–167). In Germany, heritage cinema supposedly performed memory work for viewers who had only mediated knowledge of historical events, portraying understanding between Jews and Germans during the Holocaust (Koepnick 2002). The films endow the Nazi period with "splendid decors" and "aural pleasures" (49). These film studies approaches differ from Alison Landsberg's coinage of the term "prosthetic memory," which implies a more positive attitude toward heritage cinema, claiming that it does not call for "a retreat from the social world but a new way of participating in it" (2004, 46).

While cinema studies assume that films trade in mediated memories, the field of heritage studies, in contrast, cherishes authenticity—and this inflects the perception of heritage cinema as well. International heritage scholarship did not acknowledge industrial sites before the twenty-first century either at UNESCO or in the *International Journal of Heritage Studies,* founded in 1994 (for two special volumes on labor and heritage, see Kallio and Mansfield 2013; Shackel, Smith, and Campbell 2011).[1] In a report entitled "Is Industrial Heritage

Under-Represented on the World Heritage List?," Michael Falser claims that industrial heritage sites are "important milestones in the history of humanity" and collated an extensive list of such heritage locations from all periods and regions across the globe (2001, 9, 16–147). By the late twentieth century, only 28 out of 529 cultural sites of the World Heritage List belonged to industrial heritage, and 22 out of these were located in Europe, with hardly any from the twentieth century (see Falser 2001, esp. 6–7, and the appendix, 151). Since the beginning of the twenty-first century the number of such locations has increased. In sum, industrial heritage is on the rise in the early twenty-first century, both in scholarship and in the memorialization of historic sites. While the latter are still few in number, their increased presence indicates a significant departure from the almost absolute exclusion from the previous understanding of heritage.

In his original 1987 treatise, *The Heritage Industry*, Robert Hewison claims that heritage responded to deindustrialization in England. More recent research in economic history emphasizes that deindustrialization in Western Europe becomes visible from the perspective of the nation-states (Plumpe and Steiner 2016). From a global perspective, "the loss of industrial labor in the developed countries is less than the increase of the developing world" (Steiner 2016, 18).[2] Werner Plumpe and André Steiner argue against the term "deindustrialization" because the consumption of industrial products increased, and their manufacturing sectors have been moved to countries that produce more cheaply (2016, 12). Steiner paints a differentiated picture, demonstrating how in West Germany, for example, some industry sectors expanded between 1970 and 1987 (automobile production and information technology), while others disappeared (textiles, mining, and iron and steel) (2016, 31–32). In West Germany, industry declined because World War II reconstruction was completed, emerging markets competed, and Fordist production reached its limits (26–28). Production shifted to service in Great Britain, West Germany, Italy, Belgium, Austria, and Switzerland (17).

The recent intervention by economic historians against a totalizing understanding of deindustrialization offers a more nuanced account from a global perspective. At the same time, it supports the perception of deindustrialization for certain sectors, particularly in Western European nations, which gives rise to casting industrial and mechanical labor as heritage. This heritage cinema of labor claims industry's pastness while highlighting its progressive, forward-moving quality. Heritage cinema provides the framework for such a matrix, even though the notion of linear progress that inheres in modern labor changes the films' pace from the slow rhythm associated with the leisure of the upper class to increasing speed and mechanical beats.

The three films that make up the first half of this chapter exemplify this nostalgic view of past industrial and mechanical labor and differ from Higson's original emphasis on slow pace, spectacular surface, and the long shot. Cinematic heritage imports filmic features associated with the industrial film (see also Hediger and Vonderau 2009a). This twenty-first-century heritage cinema centers on female characters, commodifies feminism and the labor movement, and disavows the historical presence of an ethnic and postcolonial minority workforce.

Heritage cinema of industrial and mechanical production not only returns to a particular historic moment in its diegesis but also cites earlier cinematic conventions through the use of archival footage, period music, and anachronistic techniques of transition such as the opening and closing iris or the wipe. The colorful and sensual evocation of the swinging fifties and sixties addresses spectatorial pleasure, while a mise-en-scène of heavy industry, metallic soundscape, and drab color scheme cites the early Soviet machine aesthetic. Rewriting actual historical labor conflicts with a mainstream understanding of feminism evacuates radicalism from both labor activism and the women's movement.

Several films are biopics, a genre that paradoxically fictionalizes the lives of historic personalities to make them "real to us" (Bingham 2010, 8). In the early twenty-first century, the genre invokes feminism but offers individual success stories. Bronwyn Polaschek isolates the "postfeminist biopic" as "an emergent subgenre in film" (2013, 1). She sees the genre's palimpsests as reflecting the "complexities of the historical context of the setting of the film and also of the actual context in which it was produced" (3). Her reading of four biopics of historical female artists suggests that the genre lends itself to playing out different feminist understandings of art and aesthetics, in other words, it allows for a negotiation of different instantiations of feminism. The simultaneous circulation of films that nostalgically depict industrial labor in iconographic strikes and those that situate dirty work in factories in the present reminds us again of Ernst Bloch's (1977) notion of the simultaneity of nonsynchronism.

Heritage Made in England

Made in Dagenham (UK; Nigel Cole, 2010) depicts the 1967 strike by the female sewing staff at the Ford plant in Dagenham, England. The strike was a response to a two-year agreement about pay between Ford management and the unions that introduced a new grading structure aimed at "higher productivity" with a "focus on 'efficiency' and 'modernization'" (Cohen 2012, 52). At the time, the popular press "seized with glee upon the 'petticoat' aspect of the strike" (62).

FIGURE 3.1. *Made in Dagenham* (Nigel Cole, 2010)

The film continues that notion by emphasizing femininity with brightly patterned dresses and warm colors. However, according to Sheila Cohen, the slogan "equal pay for equal work" did not refer to pay equality between men and women but emerged from "the perceived discrimination of downgraded skilled labor to unskilled labor" (52). The Ford sewing machinists saw themselves as "workers, not women," and male union leadership introduced the equal-pay demand (52). When the strike cut off the supply of seat covers and forced Ford to stop production, the company lost one million pounds of revenue each day, and management turned to Minister of Labor Barbara Castle and Prime Minister Harold Wilson of the new Labor government (55).

The historical background of the strike's success reveals the Labor government's attempts at appropriating gender to contain the labor movement. Castle suggested an equal-pay bill to break the strike but did not fulfill the women's demand of regrading. The women received a pay raise and had to strike again in 1985 for their work to be upgraded. Trim shop steward Rosie Boland claimed in an interview in *Socialist Worker* in 1968: "Let's face it, if the women had got C grade, which we are still fighting for, it would have broken Ford's wage structure" (Sagall 1968). When confronted with the women's refusal, Castle used a feminine ruse to disarm the striking women by "sharing a cup of tea and engaging in cozy feminine chat," a form of "personalized 'intimacy'" in line with Ford management (Cohen 2012, 55–56). Even though the striking women did not frame their demands as feminist, they understood that "the refusal to concede upgrading was discrimination against them as women" (53). In sum, the strike's historic success was not a self-evident feminist achievement but resulted from a complex interplay of wage demands by female factory workers and a government's placating strategy that used gender to displace the women's claims.

Made in Dagenham fictionalizes the historical event and claims authenticity by integrating archival footage. An opening collage includes Ford's period advertising with bikini-clad women eroticizing car sales and family picnics evoking postwar leisure, as well as historical footage of the female strikers having tea with Castle. The final credit sequence shows the women again, in the contemporary present, enjoying themselves while reminiscing about their victory. As Landsberg points out, such a "gesture" relies on the "real body of the survivor to guarantee or anchor the memory that the film has constructed" (2004, 126–127). Bookending the story—opening with Ford's promotional material and closing with the women in the contemporary moment—the archival footage suggests that women moved from sexist commodity to assertive countermemories and collective self-representation.

The film follows the convention of the biopic, which has proliferated in Europe in the early twenty-first century. *The Queen* (UK, France, United States, Italy; Stephen Frears, 2006), *La môme* (*La Vie en Rose*; France, UK, Czech Republic; Olivier Dahan, 2007), *Coco avant Chanel* (*Coco before Chanel*; France, Belgium; Anne Fontaine, 2009), and *The Iron Lady* (UK, France; Phyllida Lloyd, 2011) chart the path to success of women whose names are utterly familiar to the public. In 2016 alone, *Paula* (France, Germany; Christian Schwochow), *Marie Curie* (*Marie Curie: The Courage of Knowledge*; Poland, Germany, France; Marie Noelle), and *Lou Andreas-Salome* (*In Love with Lou*; Germany, Austria, Italy, Switzerland; Cordula Kablitz-Post) rely on the name recognition of their eponymous heroines. The latter three films depict a painter, a scientist, and a psychiatrist, respectively, who overcome gender discrimination to achieve fame in their fields. The genre offers consumable hagiographies of exceptional women who exceeded the restrictions of their gender.

Made in Dagenham creates social types to make its narrative of the working class's collective action palatable: the main character, Rita, is a young working woman with a husband and two children who becomes the film's hero when she calls for the first vote to strike. Her older friend, Connie, serves to link the 1960s to Great Britain's World War II heroism through her husband, who suffers from PTSD and commits suicide. Brenda embodies swinging London with her fashionable hairstyle and minidress, while Sandra is the young single working girl easily manipulated by Ford. But the film's investment in industrial labor and the collective working class nevertheless puts pressure on the genre conventions of the biopic and expands heritage cinema.

The film's revision of working-class solidarity hinges on the representation of mutual support across class boundaries by Castle and the character Lisa, the wife of British Ford manager Peter Hopkins. The film organizes these alliances in symbols of femininity associated with leisure and domesticity: sex, clothes, and children's education. Lisa—the educated and undervalued housewife à la

Betty Friedan's 1963 *The Feminine Mystique*—plays a key role for the rewriting of class solidarity as individual help across class lines. The film imagines Lisa and Rita's class-crossing bond via their maternal concerns regarding a teacher who bullies their sons. Their first encounter emphasizes class politics when Rita visits her son's teacher to complain about his corporal punishment. In response, he humiliates Rita by predicting that her son's class background has predetermined his academic failure. Later Lisa reveals that she has the same complaint and calls the teacher a bully. The narrative introduces class discrimination only to expose it as a ruse for masculine aggression. Maternal concern connects Rita and Lisa more than class identity divides them.

Later in the narrative Lisa ventriloquizes the perspective of a contemporary audience. She visits Rita to tell her that Lisa's history degree from Cambridge University enables her to recognize extraordinary people, and she asks Rita not to give up the fight. The exchange on the walkway to Rita's apartment encapsulates the dramatic irony of biopics, namely, that the contemporary audience recognizes the exceptional individual, while the diegetic characters underestimate her, as they are blinded by their historic limitations. The notion of the exceptional individual, however, flies in the face of the premises of feminist and labor organizing (see also Cobble 2004; Kessler-Harris 2007).

The film rewrites feminism in postfeminist terms of material consumption when the female characters exchange fashion brands across class boundaries (see the discussion about postfeminism in chapter 2). In preparation for the meeting with Castle, Rita visits Lisa and borrows a dress, which serves as the symbolic link between her as worker, Lisa as wife of a manager, and Castle as female politician. Castle appears as a down-to-earth, self-defined, "fiery red-head" who yells at her two male undersecretaries that "equal pay is common justice." After their historic negotiation, the minister and the women meet reporters, and Castle remarks on Rita's dress: "That's Biba. . . . I saw it in a magazine." Rita answers about Castle's dress: "That's C&A," to which the minister responds: "Why pay more?" The exchange associates Castle with the thriftiness of the working class and Rita with high fashion, reversing the economic underpinning of class difference.[3] The narrative relays that Rita has to borrow an appropriate dress to visit the minister in Parliament, but the scene's emotional impact emerges from the victorious community that the women present to the journalists and photographers in the film and to the film's audience and that seemingly supersedes class differences.

The film connects Castle and the strikers before they meet. The women demonstrate in front of Westminster Hall, attracting honking cars and catcalls from men, which brings Castle to the window of her office. As the women have not fully unrolled their banner, instead of "We want sex equality," it reads "We want sex," a joke that pivots on the supposed semantic proximity between women's equality and sexual desire, occurring in a long tradition of sexist jokes. It relies on the notion that the Freudian slip reveals the true desire: underneath the rational demand for equality lies an irrational desire for sex. The film casts this as the moment of recognition between Castle and the female demonstrators as she states under her breath: "I know the feeling." The minister's misreading of the political demand for gender equality as expression of sexual desire rewrites prefeminist labor activism as postfeminist sexual desire.

The film endows postfeminist body politics with the power to defeat adversaries. Sandra wants to become a model instead of working in the factory. In order to break the strike, management offers her a photo shoot for the company's catalog. Rita arrives in the nick of time to dissuade her, and Sandra returns to the photo shoot, having painted "Equal Pay" across her belly. Her gesture, the film implies, defeats the Ford management, as the photographer and the American Ford manager turn away from her body in defeat. Sandra's body-political statement evokes actions by the contemporary feminist group FEMEN.

The view that women express and mobilize agency through the sexualization of their bodies stands in sharp contrast to second-wave feminism. In her foundational feminist film-theory essay "Visual Pleasure and Narrative Cinema" ([1975] 1988), Laura Mulvey famously argues that classical Hollywood used male characters to advance narratives and female "to-be-looked-at-ness" to arrest the narrative in a visual spectacle. Sandra, with a political slogan written with lipstick on her bikini-clad body, demonstrates how Mulvey's analysis does not apply to contemporary postfeminist film, which advances its narrative with female characters staging their own "to-be-looked-at-ness." By harnessing the historical labor politics for feminist biopolitics, the film disavows the work that goes into a strike. The shot of Sandra's sexualized body in the advertisement for the DVD *Made in Dagenham* commodifies the nude female body part to sell the product.

The film invokes the patriotism associated with Great Britain's World War II for its construction of industrial labor as national heritage. Rita forges a link to the past in her speech at the Union Delegation meeting, the film's emotional turning point. She ties Connie's husband George's fight in the RAF and the legacy of World War II to the women's strike, while the camera frames her from behind centered in the shot, looking at an out-of-focus sea of men. When Rita addresses the all-male attendees, "We are the working classes: the men and the women. We're not separated by sex," her speech exceeds the diegetic historic moment.

A contemporary audience witnesses that gender organizes workplaces, union memberships, and wage differences. Rita interpellates the audience of the film into a vision of an egalitarian community of the working class. When Rita's husband, Eddie, arrives and they kiss, the heterosexual harmony cements the political vision.

The film's understanding of heritage relies on the whiteness of the mutually constitutive industry and nation, contrasting with the workers of color who appear in the documentary footage. The film integrates fictional reenactment and archival footage in the narrative.[4] In an interview spliced into the film twice, a group of men respond negatively to the question whether the women should receive equal pay. This archival footage shows a multicultural workforce, including black workers with a foreign accent, in contrast to the cast and extras of the fictionalized narrative. Such material supports the documentary truth claim but also produces a textual tension within the narrative.

The disavowal of the historic diversity of the working class in Great Britain mirrors the submersion of racial and ethnic difference into the soundtrack. The narrative opens and closes with shots of the workers riding bicycles in slow motion toward the factory gate accompanied by the reggae soundtrack of Desmond Dekker's "Israelites" and "You Can Get It If You Really Want," written by Jimmy Cliff and sung by Desmond Dekker.[5] As these two tracks open and close the film, they suggest a development from despair to success. The final song's second-person address, "You can get it if you really want," interpellates a global audience into the women's historic success and echoes the dynamic ride toward the camera. The film's final text across the image informs the audience: "Two years later in May 1970 the Equal Pay Act became law. Similar legislation quickly followed in most industrial countries across the world." Progress was "made in Dagenham" to be exported to other advanced nations. The cinematic apparatus defines the working class as white and constitutive of the nation, and it subordinates the postcolonial subjects into the soundtrack, where its aural pleasures evoke the fantasy of multiculturalism.

In sum, *Made in Dagenham*'s attention to historical women's labor organizing first introduces and then denounces class conflicts with body and sartorial politics that mask labor exploitation. The film thus elides the work that goes into labor activism and turns class solidarity into individual friendship relations, which is integral to the film's emotional appeal. In order to claim factory work as heritage, the film disavows the labor of union organizing, the emotional work of feminist solidarity across lines of class division, and finally, the historical reality of a postcolonial and minority labor force.

Projecting Feminism onto the East

German director Volker Schlöndorff's biopic *Strajk—die Heldin von Danzig* (*Strike— the Heroine of Gdansk*; Germany, Poland, 2006) depicts the struggle of the antigovernment union movement Solidarność—Solidarity—in Poland in the 1980s. Also about a forgotten woman, the film equally employs the genre conventions of the biopic, integrates archival footage, and restages key scenes familiar to an audience. Schlöndorff came to fame as part of New German Cinema, the West German film movement between 1962 and 1982. By turning to the former Soviet Bloc, he cites the socialist realist emphasis of labor, evoking industrial heritage as mediated history. The film tells the story of Agnieszka Wowalska, a barely veiled stand-in for Anna Walentynowicz. Her firing from the Lenin shipyard in Gdańsk, Poland, initiated the 1980 Solidarity strike. As her alter ego in the film, Anna Walentynowicz worked first as a welder and then as a crane operator. Like *Made in Dagenham*, the film subtly revises historical events in its portrayal of workers' solidarity that challenges the state. It departs from depicting proletarian culture and the strike as heroic masculinity. Yet whereas *Made in Dagenham*'s cinematography and colorful mise-en-scène feminize the factory, *Strike—the Heroine of Gdansk*, in contrast, depicts a world devoid of feminine qualities, invoking a presumably visual vocabulary of socialist realism.

In the workplace of the shipyard, steel dominates. The opening shot in particular plays with a surprise effect when the viewer realizes that the character dressed in gray and huddled close to the ground while welding reveals herself to be a young female worker. The gray monocolor expresses the grittiness in the tradition of Sergei Eisenstein's black-and-white film *Stachka* (*Strike*; Soviet Union, 1925). *Strike—the Heroine of Gdansk*'s documentary mode includes an even pacing, a consistent chronology, and the integration of archival footage. The aesthetic language mimics socialist realist cinema, the preferred mode for films about work in the former Eastern Bloc, including the factory as a privileged setting in

FIGURE 3.2. *Strike* (Volker Schlöndorff, 2006)

literature and film. The projection of female productive labor onto the European East contrasts to the past in postwar West Germany, where women came into view in the national economy primarily as consumers (see Carter 1997). Establishing shots of cranes and smokestacks, shots of shadows of characters against a high-contrast background, and crane tracking shots of the interior setting of the factory pay homage to Eisenstein's original classic and cite what by now has become an iconography of industrial film. The soundtrack consists of rhythmic hammering that evokes the pacing of mechanized production.

Strike—the Heroine of Gdansk integrates different cinematic modes of mediating history (fictionalization, archival footage, restaging) in its opening. "Gdansk, summer 1961" defines historical footage before the onset of the narrative. Throughout, the film crosscuts footage of historical events with reenactments such that the past seems to be continuing seamlessly into the present and documentation appears to flow into fictionalization. Iconographic shots jolt the memories of those who remember the television footage and photographs about Solidarity's strike in Gdańsk. Reenactments of televised moments, for example, Lech Wałęsa signing the agreement between the strikers and the government in 1980 with a giant pen, reinforce the film's overarching truth claim.[6]

In order to offer a narrative of individual triumph of a woman both exceptional and representative as it inheres in the biopic, the film has to depart significantly from its supposed source, Walentynowicz's autobiography. The film depicts the period from 1968 to the signing of the agreement between the strikers and the government at the end of August 1980, before the imposition of martial law in December 1981, in other words, only the period that led to the success of Solidarity. Emphasizing the strike at the shipyard that her firing initiated, the film departs from Walentynowicz's (2012) autobiography in important ways. She grew up in rural Poland, where her parents died when she was ten years old, and was left at the mercy of a family who treated her with violent disdain. After working as a maid, she succeeded by becoming a laborer at the shipyard in the city and decided to raise her son alone. She called the shipyard her second home but refused to join the party (35). Walentynowicz recounts her conflicts with the party about labor rights and with Wałęsa, which later marginalized her in the Solidarity movement. In her autobiography, the strike appears as one victorious moment followed by jail time and bitter fights for recognition and restitution for the remainder of her life. In contrast, the filmic account begins with her move to the city and ends with the heroic triumph of Solidarity, acknowledging Walentynowicz's bitterness only in the brief epilogue.

At the film's conclusion, the convention of the biopic—employing the real person to shore up truth claims—turns into an empty gesture as the coda takes up the genre convention in the credit sequence.[7] In *Strike—the Heroine of Gdansk*, a black screen announces "25 years later," and the aged Agnieszka walks along the sea with the shipyard in the background, embodying the victory over historical adversity and reflecting in a voice-over how the strike not only changed Europe but also signaled a loss of solidarity in the movement in Poland. In the final long shot, we see the actress Katharina Thalbach as Agnieszka. Most likely the absence of Walentynowicz resulted from a well-known disagreement between her and Schlöndorff. The fact that the coda only cites but does not act out the familiar convention reinforces the character's reflections of loss articulated in hindsight.

Strike—the Heroine of Gdansk and *Made in Dagenham* rewrite the gendered cinematic imagination of industrial labor of the strike narrative, which had centered on male proletarians. Both films restage iconographic scenes and incorporate original footage, but in order to advance their narratives of the victorious collective or individual, they carefully select from and revise the historical archive. *Made in Dagenham* subtly shifts from class to gender, and *Strike—the Heroine of Gdansk* sidesteps the conflicts between Walentynowicz and Wałęsa and the clampdown by the state. The films recuperate industrial labor projected into the past for a mainstream feminism through the biopic, the genre emblematic for individualizing history. Popular cinema espouses an interest in industrial labor at a time when its disappearance in Great Britain and Germany gave rise to post-Fordist flexible work. The figure of woman serves to mediate the imagination of industrial labor as Western heritage.

Work as Sport

"Nostalgia for typewriting is everywhere," suggests Darren Wershler-Henry in his fragmented history of the typewriter, the term that historically referred to both the machine and the female typist (2005, 6).[8] The French film *Populaire* (France, Belgium; Régis Roinsard, 2012) focuses on labor and love in the times of the typewriter and celebrates work as sport in a story about a secretary who wins speed-typing competitions and her boss's heart in midcentury France. The film mixes the sports film genre with the rom-com, which was experiencing a "spectacular rise . . . in France in the 1990s and 2000s" (Harrod 2015, 1). The interweaving of office work and romance has shaped "the public's imagination" of the white-collar environment (Berebitsky 2012, 12). The obsolescence of the typewriter enables the nostalgic recuperation of the fantasy of the 1950s heterosexual and patriarchal office romance, which the film projects as the foundation of the modern nation. Enabling visible speed—"the only new pleasure invented by modernity" (Duffy 2009, 4)—makes the machine the hero of this heritage film. Instead of resurrecting a real person in its final credit sequence, *Populaire* includes grainy, black-and-white, archival footage of the IBM Selectric typewriter.

Populaire tells an every-girl's-fantasy tale about Rose Pamphyle's move from the French village Saint-Fraimbault to the town of Lisieux in Normandy. She interviews for a position as secretary with insurance broker Louis Échard, who immediately recognizes her talent of speed-typing and hires her on the spot in order to coach her. While she shares his mansion to maximize their time for training, she falls in love with him. Rose wins first the regional and then the national competition in Paris, where they consummate their sexual relationship. Louis then leaves Rose, sacrificing his love for her chance to win the international speed-typing competition in New York City. The Japy Company hires Rose to advertise its brand of the pink typewriter Populaire to women.[9] When Rose competes in the world speed-typing competition, Louis arrives at the last minute with his American friend Bob and confesses his love for Rose, which coincides with her victory and Bob selling Louis's idea for the Selectric typewriter to American businessmen from the company "ICM." The film's happy ending establishes the couple and France's superiority in speed. Bob's phrase "America for business, France for love" inscribes a division of labor into their shared progress in the West.

Feminism and labor conjoin in *Populaire*'s ambivalent nostalgia, typical of heritage cinema. The film invokes familiar feminist tropes and narrative conventions, such as a young woman's liberating move from a small town to the city and independence through wage labor. In the 1950s in France "mobility was the categorical imperative of the economic order" (Ross 1995, 22). Projecting a desire for liberation into the 1950s neither questions nor disrupts patriarchal structures; instead, it brings the dynamics of heterosexuality into the service of the nation. The emphasis on the working girl associated with the big city creates a palimpsest of historical moments from the nineteenth century, the 1920s, and the late 1950s shot through with an awareness of the present.[10]

Populaire's narrative critiques feminine branding in suggesting that the pink typewriter does not allow its users to type fast. Yet the film's setting and mise-en-scène reify femininity. Rose enters the capitalist marketplace as one commodity to sell another when the Japy team hires her to represent its brand. When her pink Japy typewriter prevents her from reaching her full potential for speed at the international competition, she discards it in favor of her old machine from her dad's mom-and-pop store and wins. The nostalgic gesture advocates a return to the past as a time before typewriters were branded to

FIGURE 3.3. *Populaire* (Régis Roinsard, 2012)

target women. But while the narrative purports to expose the construction of pink femininity, the film's aesthetics is one of rose-colored excess. The period's fashion iconography of tight bodices, full skirts, and "bullet bras," as well as of cars, architecture, interior design, and music, reflects the attention to detail for a nostalgic viewing pleasure. Wipes and the use of an iris evoke old-fashioned film style. Through its self-referential title, *Populaire* confidently announces itself as a popular film from France that speaks in a global vernacular. Different from the French New Wave or *cinéma du look*, it proves wrong "historians [who] have portrayed France as receiving rather than producing mass culture" (Schwartz 2007, 4). The film's return to the 1950s echoes "the marketing of 'Frenchness'" in "a pas-de-deux" of "Hollywood and Paris" (6).

Populaire conjoins the vision of female self-realization through modernization with a fantasy of labor consisting of mechanical mastery with one single objective: speed. Typing makes work visible in a way that computing has obscured it (see Hediger 2009). The home computer has eroded the distinction between leisure and work by moving secretarial labor from the office first into the home and then into coffeehouses, trains, and planes. Performing as mobile secretaries, accessible and responsible at all times, and administrating lives in increasingly complex digital environments have become the norm for most. *Populaire* not only makes work physically visible but also turns it into a sport (see Zarnowski 2013). Labor turned sport consumes Rose, as she practices typing until she falls asleep at her machine at Louis's dining room table.

A richly layered musical soundtrack, rhythmic typing, and expressive dancing create aural and kinesthetic pleasures. The film's music mines the archives of cultural production at the intersection of work and leisure with songs celebrating secretaries and using the typewriter as instrument to create the beat to pop music.[11] Mambo, cha-cha, and French rock and roll combine with the rhythmic sounds of typewriters in a kinetic tour de force of speed-typing. The integration of popular dance music from the period illustrates Joel Dinerstein's claim that "rhythmic flow" was the "unifying aesthetic principle of Machine age modernism," when "big band swing, tap dance, and the lindy hop were public models of humanized machine aesthetics" (2003, 8, 12). The kinesthetic appeal of typing competitions that turn labor into a spectator sport results from the integration of the rom-com, which Claire Mortimer calls "a woman's film" (2010, 1), and the sports film, which captures "the drive towards overcoming obstacles" (Babington 2014, 11). The female athlete / male coach dyad, typical of the female sports film, keeps women under patriarchal control (66). The sports film's standard victory combines with the rom-com's union in the happy ending.

Typical of a sports film, *Populaire* includes competitions that punctuate and structure the narrative and that connect to the surrounding drama (Babington 2014, 49). The competitions invite an audience's immersion into the kinetic speed of typing. At the onset of the first event, the camera slowly moves backward to reveal the women in colorful dresses sitting at individual tables with their typewriters in front of them, as in a typing pool. Once the competition starts, the film's average shot length decreases dramatically, and the camera dynamically changes positions and angles, coinciding with the cuts. The scenes crosscut quickly among close-ups of a typewriter's keyboard, over-the-head shots of competitors, and Louis in the audience, who models spectatorship for the film's audience. Repeated close-ups of the timer remind us that the women race against each other and against time, turning the timekeeping of labor into a seemingly playful competition (see also Wershler-Henry 2005).

The pacing of the editing, the hitting of the carriage return levers, and the rhythm of the soundtrack reinforce each other. Les Chaussettes Noires' 1960 rock-and-roll song "Dactylo Rock" accompanies the typing and the rhythmic movements of changing paper, which make visible the physicality of mechanical labor turned sport. The song text conjures up flexible, young, attractive,

FIGURE 3.4. *Populaire* (Régis Roinsard, 2012)

and romantically available secretaries who are happily singing while working, expanding their work hours without complaints. The song cites and speeds up American Gene Vincent's "Be-Bop-A-Lula" (1956), part of rock and roll's transnational exchange as it developed from 1940s African American rhythm and blues. The soundtrack presents the secretary as an ambivalent figure outside the home charged with recreating the domestic sphere in the place of work. When Rose dines at a nightclub with Japy father and son, the cha-cha of the soundtrack turns into a diegetic performance, another carefully crafted instance of the film's soundscape. The big band performance of "Les secrétaires cha cha (Las Secretarias)" combines the tapping on the typewriter, the fun-loving figure of the secretary, and exotic rhythm.[12] Originally developed in Cuba as a result of the hybrid musical influences of Eastern Europe and Africa, the cha-cha traveled first to New York City and then across the ocean to France. The song reflects the global popularity of the secretary as a figure of modernity.

The three competitions punctuate the narrative and map Rose's process of maturation onto an expanding geography from regional to national to international space. Louis and Rose's sexual encounter coincides with their presence at the heart of the nation. They are driving under the Eiffel Tower—the national icon of modernity—accompanied by Ella Fitzgerald's 1956 "I Love Paris" on the soundtrack, a transnational text evoking a rich history of Paris as a haven for African Americans. When Rose runs from the car through Paris, the scene pays homage to the urbanite chanson singer Cleo in Agnès Varda's *Cléo de 5 à 7* (*Cleo from 5 to 7*; France, Italy, 1962). The national coding bathes their romantic sex scene in blue and red, two of the three colors of the French national flag. Rose's Parisian, modern, and tight red dress indicates her maturity, contrasting with the wide skirt and former ponytail, which signaled her shared innocence with the 1950s.

Rose's coming-of-age embodies France's postwar process of maturation as she ascends from petit bourgeois to middle class, which comes to represent the nation in the postwar period (Ross 1995, 149). The couple embodies the whiteness advertised to women via hygiene and consumption in the midfifties (84). The film allegorizes the couple's embodiment of the nation in relation with the United States through the role of Louis's American friend Bob, who is the husband of Louis's former lover Marie.[13] The image track maps the national couple onto a geography of binational relations with the United States, while the soundtrack remains the site of transnational exchanges and appropriations.

However, in the age of DVDs, the expanded film text includes extra material that maps the historicity of typewriter technology onto the expanded EU. The bonus material *Typists Rule* describes how the film's producers had to procure outdated machines and make them look new. More importantly, however, the French actresses did not know how to use a typewriter, and they were not aware that typing on these outdated machines differs from using the computer. Instead, they "went to the Czech Republic to find experts who used this specific technique on these machines," relates Nicolas Bedos, the actor who plays Japy junior and shares his view: "Girls do that [type on typewriters] in Eastern countries. I find it incredibly anachronistic." Thus, while the film claims a heritage of mechanical labor for the French nation, the expanded text of the DVD casts Eastern Europe as what Dipesh Chakrabarty calls "the sphere of the nonmodern" (2000, 39). The extra material demonstrates how asserting industrial and mechanical labor for Western European nations projects premodernity onto the East. Leaving heritage cinema behind, the subsequent discussion pertains to a film that deconstructs national industrial heritage cinema from within.

Queer Camp and Industrial Heritage

François Ozon's film *Potiche* (France, 2010) subverts the ways in which labor conflict functions in heritage cinema. Its vernacular of global popular film relies on a queer sensibility of melodrama and camp (on queer cinema, see Griffiths 2008; on Ozon, see Chilcoat 2008). Based on the play *The Trophy Wife* by Pierre Barillet and Jean-Pierre Grédy, the film queers the celebratory history of postwar conflict between labor and capital, as well as between gay and feminist liberation movements. *Potiche* employs camp's subversive—and not explicitly critical—mode to question what Landsberg (2004) calls the "prosthetic memory" of French social and political movements for a national imaginary. The film mobilizes and resignifies the rich semantic field surrounding two of France's most famous stars: Catherine Deneuve appears as the bourgeois factory owner, Suzanne Pujol, and Gérard Depardieu is the communist, Maurice Babin. Deneuve combines an association with perversion from her early roles and her later embodiment of the metonymic figure of the French nation, Marianne (Deneuve served as the model for a bust of Marianne in 1985). Depardieu evokes his roles as central characters in French heritage films of the early 1990s such as *Cyrano de Bergerac* (Jean-Paul Rappeneau, 1990) and *Germinal* (Claude Berri, 1993) (see also Powrie 1998).

Ozon exaggerates the gestures of nostalgia inherent in heritage cinema, including Maurice and Suzanne's shared memory of sex in the forest or their elaborately choreographed disco dancing. The film's camp style exaggerates the vocabularies of both social realism and nostalgic heritage cinema so that they become visible. The film appropriates the language of popular film to subvert the conventions of mass culture. It resists the contemporary reification and commodification of subcultural practices, including camp. In addition, it undermines the notion of the heterosexual couple as the foundation of the nation, as in *Populaire*, instead imagining alternative kinship organization. The narrative exposes conventional domesticity and traditional family structures, including heterosexual coupling and reproduction, as important functions for inheritance and the ownership of capital.

The French/Belgian coproduction appears as a lighthearted comedy that takes place in Sainte-Gudule, a fictional small French town. Set in 1977–78, the film tells the story of a labor conflict between the bourgeois Pujol family, which owns an umbrella factory, and the company's labor union. When union members kidnap Robert Pujol, he suffers a heart attack, and his wife, Suzanne, takes over the factory, resolving the strike, innovating production, and increasing profits. The narrative reveals that Robert had sexual affairs, as did Suzanne, including with former communist, now mayor, Maurice Babin. These past encounters call into question the family lineage. Suzanne loses her directorship of the factory, becomes a feminist, and runs for mayor. The film concludes with her victory celebration, during which she sings, surrounded by a crowd of supporters.

Two interrelated strands propel the narrative forward: one concerns crisscrossing sexual affairs that question the patriarchal family lineage and ownership of the factory. The other narrative strand tells of class warfare's most traditional weapon: the strike. The latter sets the events in motion, a reversal from the tradition of political film, where the portrayal of class exploitation builds up until the final escalation and confrontation, as in *Made in Dagenham* and *Strike—the Heroine of Gdansk*. Camp questions the memory of the beloved dead patriarch–cum–factory owner, as well as the reification of liberation movements. By portraying the mother as a sudden and unexpected feminist and her conservative daughter as aligned with the emasculated father, for example, the film undermines the narrative of generational progress that inheres in the accounts of feminist, sexual, and leftist liberation movements.

The excessive color and emphasis on decoration of the bourgeois household invoke classic Hollywood's melodrama and camp. In an early shot, Suzanne sits in front of the living room's picture window and writes a poem. The shot echoes a similar composition in Douglas Sirk's *All That Heaven Allows* (United States, 1955), a key melodramatic text about the transgression of class boundaries. Whereas other films, such as Rainer Werner Fassbinder's *Angst essen Seele auf* (*Ali: Fear Eats the Soul*; West Germany, 1974) and Todd Haynes's *Far from Heaven* (United States, France, 2002), excavate the repressed homosexual and interracial desires from *All That Heaven Allows*, Ozon instead exaggerates the original film's class conflict and implied sexual transgression.

Ozon also retrieves something else repressed in the melodrama of the 1950s, namely, actual sex that results from the eroticization of the tabooed class other. Early on, when Suzanne tries to intervene and calm the strike, she visits Maurice Babin. They gaze into the night from the window of his humble worker's apartment and share a memory of their sexual encounter when they were younger and she was already married. The memory of their sexual encounter exaggerates the contrast between Suzanne's feminine dress and jewelry and Maurice's working-class muscular body. *Potiche* questions the gendering of the working class as masculine with the attendant feminization of the bourgeoisie.

Camp's strategy exaggerates representational codes to expose their naturalizing function. When Suzanne jogs through the forest, she marvels at nature. By turning nature into kitsch through the use of a whistled song, sunbeams shining on the path, soft focus, and the different cute animals that Suzanne encounters, *Potiche*'s opening scene estranges nature, announcing camp as its main mode of address. Susan Sontag postulates in her pathbreaking essay "Notes on 'Camp'": "All camp objects, and persons, contain large elements of artifice" (2001, 279). In *Potiche* this applies to characters, mise-en-scène, and narrative.

Potiche depicts excessive femininity in Deneuve's Suzanne (as camp is often criticized of doing), but it also exposes the artifice in the social realist depiction of the factory laborers. A salient example of this occurs when Suzanne visits the factory to negotiate with the workers about their demands. She wears a multistrand pearl necklace, a little white fur jacket, and a flowing and flowery dress. When they meet at the negotiating table, two-shots of Suzanne and the secretary, Nadege, at the head of the table alternate with shots of several male workers. The men embody the reality effect associated with cinema verité. They are unkempt, with wild beards and long hair, and one appears cross-eyed. Their everydayness is incongruous with the rest of the film. The lack of stylistic continuity makes realism visible as a style. It thus loses its naturalizing effect, instead appearing constructed. Incongruity defines camp, which first depends on decontextualization. Sontag explains that "camp sees everything in quotation marks. It's not a lamp, but a 'lamp'" (2001, 280). In other words, an audience suddenly understands: these are not workers; they are "workers," and the visible realism constitutes them as such. Social realism appears as artifice in the context of the film's excessive acting, star presence, and mise-en-scène. In their contrast, both styles—social realism and star glamour—traditionally are reductive signifying systems for the depiction of labor and capital.

The sexual escapades confuse inheritance and confound class boundaries. When Robert hears that his son, Laurent, is involved with Floriane Marquiset, the daughter of a baker, he reveals his past affair with the baker's wife, as Floriane could be his son's half-sister. His wife averts the threat when she reveals that she herself had affairs at the time, implying that her son might not be her husband's offspring after all. The institution of the patriarchal family company unravels when Suzanne reveals she does not know the identity of her son's father. Suzanne's many past affairs make any kind of patrilineage—in terms of either family, economy, or ideology—impossible to trace for the male characters, both capitalist and socialist. The film's portrayal of sex undermining capitalist ownership echoes the feminist critique of the imbrication of sexual and class politics and of the mutually stabilizing function of patriarchy and capitalism. What appears on the surface as sexual farce reveals an understanding of the use value of female sexuality and its reproductive function for the working of capitalism.

Potiche does not depict family ownership and outsourcing as two mutually exclusive modes of organizing production, as a nostalgic account of capitalism prior to globalization would have it. Instead, the plan to outsource emerges from the family operation when Suzanne's son-in-law, Jean-François, suggests moving production to Tunisia. Suzanne's idealization of her father's capitalist paternalism, which structurally exploits labor but engages in the social contract, evokes the current mourning of the loss of the European model. The new economy signaled by the outsourcing of labor turns production and distribution into flexible units in which owning the means of production does not imply social responsibility either to the labor force or to the region or nation. *Potiche* does not endorse the neoliberal reorganization of labor and capital, but it questions a contemporary nostalgic articulation of loss that turns the conflict between capital and labor into a heroic national memory. *Potiche*'s camp of capital and labor asks whether the current critique of neoliberalism may sometimes slide into a melancholic attachment to class conflict as part of a national past.

A minor figure points to the existence of the global migrant worker, Pilar, the maid, who is from Portugal. In contrast to labor's rightful place at the negotiating table, Pilar is an isolated figure who does not have recourse to labor negotiation and who is replaceable, as Suzanne enjoys taking over her chores during her absence. Pilar signals that globalization's transnational labor migration is already in place in the domestic setting, the site of reproductive and invisible work.

Capitalist Dreams and Postcommunist Labor

Whereas *Potiche* subverts the emphasis on heritage surrounding labor conflicts through camp by mimicking nostalgia for the past, the Eastern European film

I Love Budapest (Hungary; Ágnes Incze, 2001) situates work in factories in the present. Ágnes Incze's first feature, *I Love Budapest* depicts the lives of two young women in the metropolis. They balance dirty and underpaid factory labor with trying to make it in the glamorous mirage of newly arrived capitalism. Its deceptively simple tale of the young heroine moving from the countryside to the city implies a scathing critique of the possibilities that both the dilapidated remnants of socialism and the promises of capitalism hold out for women. The drudgery of factory labor contrasts with the seductions of capitalism, but neither offers a reliable future promise for the film's two main characters. Incze made the film two years before the 2003 Hungarian referendum on joining the EU and three years before the country joined the EU in 2004.

Immediately after the collapse of the Eastern Bloc, euphoria in the Hungarian film industry turned into the realization that Hungarian films would have to compete with Hollywood (Cunningham 2004, 142). In the early 1990s, "cinemas closed, revenue from film admissions dropped, the number of people actually going to the cinema fell dramatically ... and Hungary was swamped with foreign films" until the mid-1990s, when "the downward trend reversed" (143, 150). Even though John Cunningham values the rise of independent cinema, his survey of Hungarian cinema between the collapse of communism and the early twenty-first century privileges the two auteurs Bela Tarr and István Szabó, who dominate national Hungarian cinema on the global circuit. *I Love Budapest* is a marginal film in national Hungarian cinema, but its lack of production value accompanies a particularly insightful representation of the transition to capitalism and its implications for the economic possibilities for women.

I Love Budapest counters what Elaine Weiner has called "market dreams" in "postsocialist spaces" (2007, 3). She argues that the "grand narrative" of "capitalism vanquishes communism" promises to free people and casts the neoliberal market as hero and the communist state as villain (4). However, this tale demands that those who were formerly in the grip of communism must give up their "'bad,' irrational behaviors (irresponsibility and dependence)" and take up "'good,' rational behaviors (self-reliance, personal responsibility, and independence)" (4). *I Love Budapest* exposes such a market dream.

Two political economists of the region, Dorothee Bohle and Béla Greskovits, offer a thorough account of "capitalist diversity" in East-Central Europe, situating Hungary among the Visegrád group (2012, 1). They argue that the countries of East-Central Europe in the 1990s and the first decade of the twenty-first century have integrated different kinds of capitalisms and that Hungary had already undertaken economic and political reforms during communism (141). Therefore, the impact of EU accession on the region was indirect, as the countries experienced enormous foreign direct investments that contributed to "reindustrialization, job creation, and enhanced competitiveness," led to "embedded liberal regimes," and created "intraregional rivalry" (167). Those countries then assumed a "leading role of export-oriented complex transnational industries," including of "cars, machinery, and equipment, electrical and electronics products, and chemicals including pharmaceuticals" (171). This account precedes the global financial crisis, when "the precariousness of the postsocialist order has once again come to the fore" and Hungary experienced "reform fatigue and disenchantment" (223).

I Love Budapest's critique of future-oriented capitalism and factory work haunted by its communist past emerges entirely from the perspective of young women. The representation of factory work responds to what Anikó Imre sums up about the Hungary's past: "Communist cultures emphasized production and demonized consumption" (2009, 65). In contrast to the heritage films about labor made in Western Europe, *I Love Budapest* is set in the present moment. It neither idealizes labor nor fetishizes the past. Instead, it rejects nostalgia, but it does not replace it with a celebration of capitalism's promise of a future good life.

In *I Love Budapest*, Anikó moves from the countryside to Budapest to be with her friend Móni, who is dating Krisztián. Anikó and Móni keep their work in a factory a secret, as it does not fit the cosmopolitan image that they want to project. Krisztián hides the fact that he is married so that he can play the role of a young and unattached urbanite. He makes money through illegal deals, while Móni teaches Anikó the rules of the free market of modern love. But Anikó likes conventional Miki, who gets shot working for Krisztián. When Anikó and Miki flee, chased by the police, their car lifts off and flies away. The film ends in a fantastic dream of their flight across the rural landscape.

I Love Budapest structures time through repeated shots in the factory, indicating the continued cultural force of labor. The depiction of industrial labor adheres to the traditional emphasis on machines and drudgery. Each of the factory scenes begins with a shot of a machine moving rhythmically and accompanied by loud noise, typical of industrial footage. The camera pans across heavy machines, showing their interconnectedness in an outdated, grimy, and dirty factory left over from the communist past. The interior appears in monochromatic cold and dark blue. It is the setting for intimate bonding among the female workers.

The women in the factory wear dirty work clothes with headscarves to protect their hair, or they are nude in the shower. Their short hair matches their pragmatic attitudes, and they embrace masculine qualities such as strength.

They form a collective social bond, and one of them takes a maternal interest in Anikó. This woman argues against the fetishization of beauty and instead advocates for health, for example, when Anikó does not want to wear a mask in the factory despite the dust. Close-up shots with a handheld camera do not center the image on Anikó and her coworkers. Light sources focus on objects or the background, in instances obscuring characters' faces. An early sequence ends with a long close-up of Anikó's toes in the shower, typical for the social realism associated with the cinematic depiction of labor: finding beauty in the details of the everyday.

Repeatedly, the handheld camera casts Anikó in a close-up with a low angle from above instead of a frontal shot. Characters criticize Anikó for her daydreaming, but the film does not advocate for her coworker's summary of the daily drudgery of her life as alternative. Anikó and Móni believe that their capital lies in their looks, sexuality, and bodies. In contrast to Móni's explicit sexuality, which enables Krisztián to exploit her, Anikó holds on to old-fashioned moral views. The new capitalism promises financial and romantic rewards for the young women's sexualization, but the film exposes this as an illusion. While the girlfriends spend their money on perfume and tight T-shirts, Móni's apartment consists of cardboard boxes that function as closets and tables. Their desire for glamour contrasts with their actual living conditions, revealing the capitalist dream as potential nightmare. The factory is therefore also the site of contrasting body politics. A factory scene shows Anikó with her coworker in the communal shower. The familiarity and intimacy through shared work contrast with the emphasis on beauty in the heterosexual contract, which creates competition among women.

Capitalism does not offer a viable alternative to industrial labor, as it interpellates women into the commodification of their sexuality. The depiction of factory work in the tradition of the filmic representation of industrial labor contrasts with dreams of consumption linked to femininity. The film's conclusion aligns us with Anikó when she becomes active and flees with Miki in the car. It magically takes off and flies across the city and the fields in a way that is reminiscent of Merzak Allouche's *Salut cousin!* (*Hi Cousin!*; France, Algeria, Belgium, Luxembourg, 1996) and Ridley Scott's *Thelma & Louise* (United States, France, 1991), films that create utopian hope for their struggling characters. The flying car literalizes the characters' dreams by superseding film's realism and transgressing the boundaries between city and country. Cinema exceeds the everyday by allowing audiences to imagine and kinesthetically experience the impossible.

Conclusion

In sum, whereas the Western European films discussed in this chapter project industrial labor into the past but endow it with a nostalgic idealization, the Eastern European film portrays factory work in the contemporary moment but in dilapidated environments. *Made in Dagenham* and *Strike—the Heroine of Gdansk* associate labor with the past as a precondition for its idealization. *Populaire* similarly claims anachronistic mechanical work for a faux feminism. *Potiche*'s camp of industrial labor and class conflict as national heritage queers not only the conventions of depicting work but also the social configurations of family, reproduction, and inheritance. *I Love Budapest* subverts the fantasy of progress that the contemporary heritage cinema ascribes to industrial and mechanical labor.

If Western European films nostalgically recuperate labor to claim white nations in ways that continue the historical postwar divide of East and West, depictions of labor migration into Europe occur in different East–West and North–South configurations resulting from past colonial relationships, organized labor migration, outsourcing to other countries, undocumented migration, and human trafficking. The next chapter emphasizes the ways in which films about labor migration of minority and postcolonial subjects situate their narratives radically in the present, in stark contrast to the films discussed in this chapter. However, chapter 4 continues the emphasis on sound's relation to migration and mobility. Whereas chapter 3 demonstrates how heritage films of industrial and mechanical labor submerge transnational cultural exchange and minority discourse into a soundtrack that provides an emotional backdrop to the dominant image, chapter 4 foregrounds the countermovement of filmmakers who mobilize voice to emphasize migration for the European discourse about work.

CHAPTER 4

Voice in the Cinema of Labor Migration

> The voice is elusive. Once you've eliminated everything that is not the voice itself—the body that houses it, the words it carries, the notes it sings, the traits by which it defines a speaking person, and the timbres that color it, what's left?
> —Michel Chion, *The Voice in the Cinema*

> What determines who moves with whom?
> —Jacqueline Bhabha, "The 'Mere Fortuity of Birth'?"

> What passport would the ill-fated child of Madame Butterfly and Captain Pinkerton carry?
> —Linda K. Kerber, "The Stateless as the Citizen's Other"

The previous chapter argues that the image track of industrial heritage cinema inscribes whiteness into Western Europe nations, while the subordinated soundtrack of popular music plays a supporting role that propels working bodies forward with increasing speed. The soundscapes appropriate ethnically coded music excised from the visible white nation. This suppression of transnational cultural transfer into multicultural soundscapes accompanies the films' implied trajectory of progress associated with industrial labor. The emergence of industrial heritage cinema in Western Europe responds to the outsourcing of factory work to the Global South and Eastern Europe. But women also migrate within and into Europe, the topic of this chapter. The films discussed here negotiate women's relationship to labor and migration through the cinematic mediation of the human voice. Foregrounding the female migratory subject, the chapter continues the attention to image and sound in the analysis of films' imagination of women, work, and migration in early twenty-first-century Europe. In order to assert subjectivity and agency for their main female characters, the films emphasize their voices, more often than not through voice-overs.

The analysis of the politics of voice relies on an intersectional feminist study of films about women who migrate for work within and into Europe. Film's reliance on separate image and soundtracks enables filmmakers to endow sound with an independent function to enhance, reflect on, or counter what is visible on the screen. Since the depiction of labor historically relied on synchronized image and sound in film's projection of realism, the argument asserts that migration ruptures the traditional European imagination of labor. This transformation manifests itself in the politics of voice depicting female migrants on-screen (for a survey of different theoretical contexts of voice, see Dolar 2006).

The films about women moving for work use voice to establish a space for the contemplation of the social condition of labor in the context of global migration. In other words, contemporary forms of labor develop into migration patterns, while technological advancements shape the way labor and migration intersect in increasing processes of globalization. Aware of the association of voice with authenticity and as a carrier of affect, filmmakers use voice to endow female characters with subjectivity, interiority, and agency.[1] Characters address spectators in voice-overs reminiscing about the past or reading diaries or letters, sometimes haunting the image from a different historical or biographical moment. Sound's transcendent quality captures migration processes across space and time.

Voice also functions in forms of immaterial labor, producing an affective dimension and emotional surplus. Presenting female migratory characters with their own voice constitutes a political gesture. The question what form such politics of voice takes in each film motivates this investigation. Cinematic strategies range from seizing the migrant's own speech in order to ventriloquize the receiver country's fantasies to subverting sound conventions in order to open up a space for critical reflection on the prosaic social reality on the screen. The centrality of the female voice in narratives and documentaries about labor migration connects films from 2006 to 2010. As the directors do not inhabit the subject position of their cinematic characters, the films collectively circle around Gayatri Spivak's foundational question "Can the Subaltern Speak?" (1988).[2] The films offer an affirmative response to her question, but in the process of doing so, they reveal the conditions of such speech in the cinematic, social, and imaginary space of Europe.

Mobility and Migration in Europe

Mobility and migration define and challenge the New Europe. The "free movement of goods, people, services, and capital" defined the European Economic Community in the 1957 Treaty of Rome, while "material and symbolic boundaries" separate Europeans from non-Europeans (Verstraete 2010, 4, 9). In her important study of mobility as European ideal and migration as its counterpoint, Ginette Verstraete, however, overlooks migratory movements within Europe. Labor migration occurs into and within Europe in ways that reflect histories of routes and economic inequality among its member states, as well as between Europe and elsewhere.

The term "labor migration" evokes movements of population groups from one nation to another to fill shortages in particular sectors, for example, when Turks moved to West Germany in the 1960s. Labor migration includes settling in Europe to take up work; state-sponsored long-term labor contracts, under which women leave families and children behind; or short-term revolving work residencies, when workers receive a limited visa and plan periodic returns. This chapter relies on a more expansive understanding of the relationship between labor and migration based on the diversity and complexity of migration movements, as well as their filmic depictions. In 2010 alone 3.1 million people migrated into an EU country, and 2.0 million left an EU country (Fainde 2010).

Migration within Europe as it emerged after the 2004 EU enlargement to include Eastern European countries affects sender and receiver countries, as well as Europe as a whole. In her discussion of East–West migration within the EU, Jane Hardy (2010) focuses on the migration of Poles to Great Britain before the global financial crisis, the refugee crisis, and Brexit. Circulatory post-2004 migration responds to high unemployment in sender countries and produces a form of "brain waste," as those migrating for work enter professions that require a lower skill level than the workers may have (Hardy 2010, 48). In particular, "high income lifestyles" in the receiver countries stimulate "demand for low wage service sector jobs in hotels, restaurants and gyms and sometimes as domestic labor" (49). A focus on bilateral migration, for example, Polish/German, masks the fact that such movements are links in chains, as workers from countries outside the EU, including, for example, North Korea, take up jobs where out-migration has created labor shortages (52). These characteristics equally apply to migration into Europe, even though the journeys are more challenging and treacherous.

Migrating for work into Europe is gendered. Female labor migrants upset deep-seated cultural imaginaries about ingrained gender hierarchies, including the public/private split and the "sexual division" between masculinity associated with mobility and transcendence and femininity aligned with immobility and immanence (Verstraete 2010, 8, 35). At the same time, the export of women's domestic labor and care from the Global South takes place in a gendered global economy (Parreñas 2008). The European market has a demand for migrant women for "cleaning, cooking and housekeeping inside private houses; caring for sick, disabled, elderly and young people . . . ; and providing sex in a wide variety of locales," situating women in disproportionately high numbers in informal economies (Agustín 2007, 53). In receiver countries, the high number of undocumented female migrants in low-paying domestic and sex work has racialized and ethnicized these sectors (Anderson 1999, 125; see also Cox 1999). Domestic work has moved from tasks of maintaining and reproducing human life to "a role which constructs and situates the worker within a certain set of social and economic relationships" (Anderson 1999, 120). In Great Britain, for example, recruitment creates ethnic stratification as agencies and employers invoke presumed national characteristics (Cox 1999). The employment of migrants in the domestic sphere makes visible the labor inherent in the tasks and detaches them from the heterosexual family and the sexual contract, enabling members from the EU to participate in the paid labor market, while undocumented workers from outside remain invisible to the public.

Women's surge in the labor force in conjunction with the deterioration of the welfare state has increased the need for domestic work, such as caring for children and the elderly (Anderson 1999, 117). In London, for example, paid domestic labor has grown simultaneously with the widening of the income gap during the 1980s (Cox 1999, 138). Bridget Anderson emphasizes "the important role played by non-citizens in sustaining the European family as a viable social, economic and reproductive unit" (1999, 117). Migrant women from Eastern and Southern Europe and the Global South carry out the household labor considered women's work, exposing the internal economic and cultural cleavages within the EU, as well as those between EU member states and non–member states (Gutiérrez-Rodríguez 2010, 2). Eastern European women assume "the immaterial, caring labor traditionally performed by a wife within the institution of marriage" (Parvulescu 2014, 2). This includes post-Fordist labor in the "globalized markets for adoption, egg donation, surrogacy, stem cell tissues, and clinical trials" (10). Taking care of children and the elderly is both "a source of exploitation" and "a vital foundation for the sustainability of our lives" (Gutiérrez-Rodríguez 2010, 8). Migrants reproduce European families in a division of labor.

Public discourse, including documentary and popular action films, articulates this gendered dynamic in the form of a phobic and moralistic focus on sexual trafficking. In contrast to such popular imaginary, Kamala Kempadoo compares the situation of trafficked women to that of "other migrant women who sought to make a livelihood for themselves and their families in a highly gendered and racialized world order" (2005, xi). She asserts that "the neoliberal economic interests of corporations, multilateral agencies, policy experts, and national governments" undermine "human rights and social justice" (xiv). Twenty-first-century feminist theory has to confront the global division of labor, the racialization and ethnicization of domestic work, the privileges of Western European women, and the changing configurations of the family. Domestic labor and care work have become detached from the (hetero)sexual contract.

European Cinema of Migration

The increase of migration in recent decades has led to a European migration cinema (see Ballesteros 2015; Berghahn and Sternberg 2010). Generally, scholars follow a chronological model of the history of migration cinema in Europe that proposes distinct phases associated with consecutive generations. Sarita Malik (1996) calls the problem films of the 1970s and 1980s in Great Britain "the cinema of duty" because they depict solitary male migrants who suffer and thus evoke pity and understanding from the implied audience of citizens of receiver countries. A decade later, minority cinema performed "pleasures of hybridity," which Deniz Göktürk (1999) also perceives in the context of West Germany and the Berlin Republic and which capture sexually diverse and multiethnic communities. This chronology, however, associated with a generational model, relies on the logic of progress (Heidenreich 2015, 19–20). Despite this postmigrant playful cinema, films still advance "cultural repertoires of images," Nanna Heidenreich points out and emphasizes the headscarf and "the limited space of the woman" as markers of the foreign (15, 17).[3]

Two interconnected characteristics come to the forefront in contemporary European cinema of women's migration: temporality and sound (see also Celik 2015). Exilic and diasporic filmmakers "deprioritize the ocular and explore the aural and the tactile so to instigate the memory of home and the experience of uprootedness in a wealth of affective registers," according to Ipek A. Celik (2015, 24). She connects the emphasis on aurality to a "temporality of crisis," as public and popular media tie migrants to "emergency situations," for example, as victims of human trafficking and suspects in terrorism, which puts European identity at risk (3).[4] While this chapter echoes Celik's analytic emphasis on temporality and sound, it departs from her argument in two ways. It argues that the emphasis on sound expands the perception of time instead of reflecting a sense of crisis. In addition, it proposes that films that foreground voice to capture agency portray female migrants as transcending victimization.

Sound and Voice in the Space of the Cinema

Sound's transcendent quality captures migration processes across space and time. Cinematic sound extends beyond the screen: this characteristic permits it to express the border-crossing movement of migration. In theatrical screenings, sound "*envelops* the spectator" (Camper 1985, 371, italics in the original) and fills the space, while the image "remains confined to the rectangle of the screen" (Doane 1985, 166). Sound's ability to surround spectators endows music and voice-over with affective impact. Sound expands beyond what is visible in the image, literally when it originates off-screen and metaphorically when it invokes transcendence (Camper 1985, 374).

Traditional synchronous sound unites body and voice on-screen (Doane 1985, 164). But the screen frame does not constitute the limit of the diegetic space, and characters speak from beyond it in a "voice-off" that assumes the presence of a body that could appear (165). Similarly, an interior monologue creates "a temporal dislocation" of the voice from the body (168). An unconscious hierarchy privileges the visible over the acoustical dimension of film.

Timbre, pitch, and volume create perceptions of gender, race, ethnicity, and nationality. Even though Mary Ann Doane (1985, 174) warns of exaggerating voice's feminist potential, she sees its intimate link to the body as the reason why it has garnered scholarly attention. Kaja Silverman (1988, viii) considers norms equally important in defining expectations for the female voice as for the female body. Voice, she argues "command[s] faith in cinema's veracity" (43). Feminist filmmakers have appropriated the voice-over because it gains authority by transcending the body and inverting the "sound/image hierarchy" (48). As this chapter emphasizes how voice comes to the fore in films about migration by women from the Global South or the abject East, it points to the limitations of Doane's and Silverman's attention to gender alone. Migration produces particular articulations of gender, for example, becoming ethnicized and/or feminized through the move to another country and into another labor sector associated with lower status.

The qualities of voice have led scholars to formulate theories about its central function for a cinema of migration. Hamid Naficy's (2001) early and influential term "accented cinema" defines the material, economic, aesthetic, and symbolic dimension of films about migration, diaspora, and exile. Those films rely on the frequent use of letters (5). The accent, in contrast to the dialect, appears when a subject speaks in a language different from the mother tongue. Multiple languages increase in what Yasemin Yildiz calls "the postmonolingual condition," which results from migration and mobility, for example, in the EU (2012, 3). In sum, the cultural overdetermination of voice as authentic expression of the self turns it into a privileged site for the negotiation of politics in films about female labor migration within and into Europe.

Made between 2006 and 2010, the films discussed in the remainder of this chapter reflect a moment before the global financial crisis, which led to internal remigration, for example, of Polish workers who returned to Poland from Great Britain, and before the refugee crisis of Afghani, Syrian, and North African migrants arriving in Europe. The latter occurred in the fully mediated environment of multiple sharing platforms that brought forth new forms of filmmaking, such as documentaries based on iPhone recordings, for example, *#MyEscape* (Germany, Elke Sasse, 2016). Films also responded to the refugee crisis with a return to the figure of the single, young, male character, a stand-in for the anonymous mass of refugees, for example, in Aki Kaurismäki's *Le Havre* (Finland, France, Germany, 2011) and *Toivon tuolla puolen* (*The Other Side of Hope*; Finland, Germany, 2017). This migration cinema translates the crisis into linear narratives of flight. The urgency and extent of the refugee crisis run the danger of eclipsing earlier forms of migration cinema in which, as this chapter attests, women's work played a crucial role.

The following analyses cover a range of films that mobilize voice for a metacommentary on women, work, and migration in Europe. Successful mainstream films, such as Sarah Gavron's *Brick Lane* (UK, India, 2007) and David Cronenberg's *Eastern Promises* (UK, Canada, United States, 2007), employ female voice-over readings from letters and diaries, literary history's minor and private genres associated with women. The voice-overs resurrect the temporal and geographic distance collapsed by contemporary electronic communication media. The next section turns to the mediation of voice in two documentaries from 2010, Alan Grossman and Áine O'Brian's *Promise and Unrest* (Philippines, Ireland) and Martina Priessner's *Wir sitzen im Süden* (*We Are Based Down South*; Germany). The former uses letters and diaries as a metaphor for long-distance intimacy, while the latter focuses on the affective labor at call centers. The chapter concludes with a discussion of the sound strategies in Anja Salomonowitz's political art film *Kurz davor ist es passiert* (*It Happened Just Before*; Austria, 2006), in which ethnically white Austrians ventriloquize the experience of women migrating to Austria.

Epistolary Voice-Over

Postcolonial migration becomes the precondition for wage labor as a path to liberation in Gavron's film adaptation of Monica Ali's 2003 book *Brick Lane*. The film's vernacular of the British heritage cinema contrasts to the experimental aesthetics of minority and queer British independent cinema of the late 1980s and early 1990s.[5] *Brick Lane* takes up and mainstreams now-anachronistic 1970s feminism to women who move from the Global South to the West. Its spectatorial pleasure relies on the nostalgic aestheticization of prefeminist sensual femininity, which the film depicts as a condition to be overcome. When Nazneen sews pants in her apartment, her wage labor emerges from her domestic tasks, reflecting presumptions about the innate abilities of subaltern women that offer a path to independence from the sexual contract. *Brick Lane*'s focus on a female migrant who is not a victim remains exceptional for a film with high production value that achieved international success, even though a story of a woman from the Global South finding liberation in the West encapsulates a familiar narrative trope.[6] Repeatedly, image and sound have a contrapuntal relationship, in which the former captures the destination country and thus privileges ocular-centric rationality, while the latter evokes the lost country of origin, enveloping spectators in acoustic emotionality. Belonging to both sound and image, the voice links the two and oscillates between them.

Brick Lane tells the story of Bangladeshi migrant Nazneen in London after her father arranged a marriage to the older Chanu, who lives in London. During her time in England, Nazneen exchanges letters with her sister Hasina, who remained in Bangladesh. Nazneen begins sewing at home for money to finance her trip to see her sister and falls in love with the much younger Karim. In response to the increasing Islamophobia after 9/11, Chanu decides to return to Bangladesh. Nazneen rejects both Karim's marriage proposal and her husband's proposition to remigrate in order to stay in England with her two daughters.

The opening establishes a binary contrast between the present in London and the past of the lost homeland, setting the stage for Nazneen's increasing self-assertion through labor. The prelude at the outset, before the credit sequence, creates the space of Bangladesh, devoid of geographic or temporal specificity, as the past of Nazneen's childhood. Southeast Asian–themed music accompanies the beautiful landscape, creating a soundscape that envelops spectators with Nazneen's melancholy voice-over, endowing the images with the instability of memory. Close-ups of butterflies, long takes of meadows, and the slow motion of Nazneen and her sister in the vast and richly colored field evoke the unstructured and expansive time of premodernity, from which the female migrant emerges (see Lim 2009; Chakrabarty 2000).

Bangladesh, with its mythical timelessness, is the site of women's suffering when Nazneen's mother commits suicide in the river. A shot of her floating in her red sari surrounded by water lilies aestheticizes the trope of the female corpse (see Bronfen 1992). The film uses fades to black as transitions between the children's play and the mother's suicide, enhancing the fluidity and unreliability of memory. The prelude ends with Nazneen traveling by boat to meet her future husband, collapsing the journey to England in the ellipsis of a cut. Instead of migration, marriage transports Nazneen into domestic labor and the metropolitan present. The sound bridge of Nazneen's voice recounts her mother's belief in women's fate, projecting a lack of female agency onto Southeast Asia to set up the possibility of choice in the West, including that of productive labor.

The language of the heritage cinema projects a preindustrial timelessness onto Nazneen's past and country of origin, setting the stage for the ennobling function of labor in the migration narrative. *Brick Lane* claims a place in the national imaginary for postcolonial migration via heritage cinema. The film offers visual splendor as an alternative to the dominant portrayal of Bangladesh as poverty stricken. The luscious colors of a green field, in which the young sisters are running in bright dresses, evoke the shots of beautiful English landscapes in such heritage films as Joe Wright's *Pride & Prejudice* (France, UK, United States, 2005) and Ang Lee's *Sense and Sensibility* (UK, United States, 1995). The girls on a path through a Bangladeshi village in a shot with striking colors, classical symmetrical compositions, and careful lighting call to mind the road through British country villages, as in James Ivory's *Howard's End* (UK, United States, 1992). Individual heritage films have portrayed passages and journeys in the

FIGURE 4.1. *Brick Lane* (Sarah Gavron, 2007)

context of past colonial empires, as in Regis Wargnier's French *Indochine* (1992) and David Lean's British *A Passage to India* (United States, 1984). Heritage films' cinematography displays the spectacle of the colonial or imperial past celebrating a social order that their narratives question with stories of transgression of "established boundaries of class, race, sex and gender" (Dave 2006, 28). In general, landscapes function as conduits to memories with an aural space that enhances their beauty (Harper and Rayner 2010).

For a subaltern migration story, claiming to be part of the heritage cinema makes a political statement, but one that contains its own limitations. The ambivalence regarding the status of beauty when projected onto a feminized postcolonial landscape finds expression in conflicting feminist approaches toward the cinematic spectacle. Feminist film theorists who follow the lead of Laura Mulvey (1988) are suspicious of women's "to-be-looked-at-ness" in conventional narrative film. In contrast, Rosalind Galt accuses feminist theory as having inherited "a suspicion of prettiness" based on neoclassical aesthetics and Marxism's "iconophobia" (2011, 237, 239). She argues that "making the pretty into a critical term is an unequivocally feminist move" (236). However, Mulvey rejects the spectacle for the same reason that Galt recuperates it: because it is devalued as feminine. The problematic of a film such as *Brick Lane* does not lie in the beauty of the mutually constitutive Bangladesh landscape and femininity. It concerns the way that the film offers them visually for aesthetic pleasure but narratively casts them as a state to be left behind.

Beautiful Bangladesh of the undefined past contrasts with the gritty, dirty, and gray streets of contemporary East End London through which Nazneen moves during the credit sequence. The opening juxtaposes the pleasure of spectacle of Bangladesh fractured through childhood memories to the domestic labor in London in the cinematic language of social realism. A musical sound bridge and a dissolve announce the shift from the past to the present, with matching cuts of close-ups of Nazneen's young to her mature face, implying a move from Bangladesh to London, play to work, and girl to woman. In both shots her sari covers her head and frames her face. The veil, of course, has a long history as an emblem of Orientalist understanding of femininity, on the one hand, and a symbol of women's oppression, on the other. It projects a semantic field of "oppressed woman, forced marriage, and honor killing" and implies the potential for unveiling (Heidenreich 2015, 178). Nazneen's close-ups invoke this range of connotations from sensuality and oppression to possible unveiling and liberation.

London appears temporally and geographically specific. The credit sequence's opening shots that show Nazneen returning home from shopping

FIGURE 4.2. *Brick Lane* (Sarah Gavron, 2007)

include the street sign Brick Lane as the geographic marker of East London. Intriguingly, London's East End historically was a "space that has never been clearly or adequately defined, delineated or drawn. It is not, and has never been, a village, town or borough" (Newland 2008, 17). Writers portray the "enigmatic imaginative space" as "palimpsest" in which the "'Otherness' of Brick Lane" continues (17, 156, 230).[7] Nazneen's energetic walk, the passing people, including a garbage man, and the quicker cuts associate modernity with professional and domestic work.

The collapse of narrative time in the cut from the playing child of the past to the mature working woman of the present captures the interpellation of Nazneen into a housewife through marriage. Early scenes in the narrative contrast her unpaid domestic work with her husband's attempts at a successful career thwarted by a glass ceiling for minority men. *Brick Lane* suggests that present-day England discriminates against men of color and that the Global South oppresses women but that the West opens a space for the latter to achieve self-actualization. A sex scene with a disaffected Nazneen remembering her youth evokes Silvia Federici's (2012a) argument about sexual reproduction as labor (see also chapter 1). Such depiction suggests that the oppressive family structure necessitates feminist liberation.

The aural dimension of music and voice transcends the social reality of London and links Nazneen to her past and her homeland. Theme music marks the onset of her memories of her and her sister playing in the past. The epistolary voice-over inscribes the geographic and temporal distance that underlies migration. Such a narrative construction differs from contemporary global experience of "time-space compression" (Harvey 1990), "distant love" (Beck and Beck-Gernsheim 2014), "place-polygamy" (Beck 2000), or digital copresence enabled by new media technologies (Köhn 2016). As the human voice reveals "the 'inner life' of the character," it accords spectators privileged access to Nazneen's subjectivity and intimacy (Doane 1985, 168). At the same time, the enveloping and transcending quality of sound also creates a sensorial experience of the lost homeland's nostalgic plenitude beyond the image of the destination country.

Nazneen's nostalgic memories and epistolary exchange offer female kinship as an alternative to the alienation of the industrial metropolis and the heterosexual contract, which demands domestic labor. The film emphasizes the difference between paid and unpaid labor while also revealing their porous boundary. Nazneen's sewing surfaces as an innate domestic skill that we never see her develop. The sequence that depicts the arrival of the sewing machine, which her neighbor Razia gives her as a gift, connects her daughters' play and laughter with the memories of Nazneen's past, linking her wage labor to the happiness of her childhood. Labor ennobles the migrating character in a discourse of uplift that validates individual self-actualization.

The film's editing turns Nazneen's beauty, which includes the accoutrements of traditional femininity (colors, fabrics, patterns, and the modesty of the veil), into a synecdoche for Bangladesh. In the context of a global gendered division of labor, the consumable prettiness coincides with her female labor in the informal sector that produces clothes for Western consumption for less than a sufficient wage. The film and book, for that matter, depict the abuse in the informal sector through the character of Mrs. Islam, who lends money and extorts excessive interest. While the film critiques the exploitation of migrant women by exposing the low wage for labor in the home, it simultaneously participates in the visual politics that idealize Bangladesh as raw material to be extracted.

The film's happy ending concludes with a liberated Nazneen in a final crane shot showing her enjoying leisurely play with her daughters while making snow angels. The laughter recuperates the aural and visual motives of the past into the present. Magical snow removes physical markers of the courtyard and deterritorializes the space, as in previous shots of her memories of the past. Nazneen's sari, cardigan, coat, and uncovered hair capture her hybrid identity and the main symbol of Western liberalization of Eastern women: the loss of the veil. The postcolonial narrative trajectory, in contrast to the feminist films set in present-day neoliberalism, gives rise to a story line about wage labor's ability to transport Nazneen into magical modernity.

The Haunting Voice of *Eastern Promises*

Canadian director Cronenberg's thriller *Eastern Promises* similarly separates voice-over from action and connects the former to the lost homeland of a dead trafficked prostitute who haunts contemporary London, again the city of destination. The film's action narrative centers on the traffic of women from Russia for enslavement in sex work in the metropolis. The film opens with a dramatic collapse of Tatiana, a pregnant young Russian woman, in a convenience store. After being rushed to the hospital, she gives birth to a daughter and dies, leaving behind a mysterious diary written in Russian. Anna, who works at the hospital as a midwife, subsequently searches for Tatiana's family members by having her uncle Stepan translate the diary. The translation reveals that the Russian mafia traffics Russian women into forced prostitution. Its patriarch, Semyon, raped Tatiana. Anna and undercover Scotland Yard agent Nikolai, who infiltrated the mafia, prove the crime with the baby's DNA, which leads to Semyon's arrest and the happy ending of Anna and Nikolai with the orphaned baby.

Scholars such as Isolina Ballesteros praise the film for reflecting "on the indignity and ethical implications of turning women migrants into commodities to be bought and sold in capitalist markets" (2015, 103). Ballesteros values that Tatiana's diary confines the details of the "enslaved women's sordid lives" to a disembodied voice-over that prevents exploitative and violent images (103). She presumes correctly that the voice-over claims female agency, subjectivity, and authenticity. The spoken text connects these notions to poetics through repetition and symbolically evocative language. However, similar to *Brick Lane*, the voice in *Eastern Promises*, enunciating the brief lines over the film's action, evokes a timeless past in the country of origin that floats in the present of the destination country.

After Tatiana's death, her voice reads repeatedly from her diary over the film's action: "My name is Tatiana. My father died in the mines in my village, so he was already buried when he died. We were all buried there. Buried under the soil of Russia. That's why I left, to find a better life." The poetic simplicity invokes a mythical origin that casts the homeland in nostalgic terms despite its horror. The metaphor of collective death captures past masculine labor in a patriarchal national history that created the global dispersal of a female labor force available for forced prostitution and thus vulnerable to the exploitation by criminal patriarchs abroad. The fact that two different actresses share Tatiana's role emphasizes the split between image and sound that inheres in film. Sarah-Jeanne Labrosse performs Tatiana's body, while Tatiana Maslany speaks the voice-over.[8] The former collapses actress, character, and the figure of the prostitute circulating globally in the visual medium, while the latter appears as the already-dead localized specter who haunts the transnational narrative. The ghostly voice and its melancholy articulation about loss envelops the space of the Western metropolis. Tatiana's contradictory lines project onto her premodern origin a collective timelessness and placelessness that echo the limited screen presence of her character as the film's enigma.

The temporality of traditional, generation-based migration organizes contemporary modern London. As a second-generation female Russian migrant, Anna represents an assimilated British citizen. Anna and Tatiana embody the two poles between which images of migrants oscillate. According to Heidenreich, they occur "between the power of genealogical sequence of generations (the family as a system of tradition with no escape) and the imagination of total detachment from genealogy: without social network, whether understood as family or other forms of attachment" (2015, 106). Anna's migrant family includes her Russian uncle Stepan, who, in distinction to Semyon, appears in the domestic sphere engaging in the feminine task of translation. The family contrasts to the narrative crisis that Tatiana and her daughter's total lack of attachment creates. As Anna self-confidently rides a motorcycle through the city and works in a multicultural hospital, the multigenerational migration process implies assimilation to Western society with liberated and self-confident women.

Nameless women forced into prostitution belong to a discourse on human trafficking overdetermined by the depiction of all-encompassing violence that excludes the question about labor. The argument's different threads merge in one particular sequence. The trafficked prostitutes appear on-screen only in a scene set in an isolated house when Nikolai and Semyon's son Kirill visit. Kirill taunts Nikolai to have sex with one of the women to prove his heterosexual masculinity. According to narrative logic, Nicolai has to comply to maintain his cover. However, Ballesteros proposes a "gay subtext of the film"—Kirill's "closeted desire for Nikolai"—and so the film's play with invisibility and visibility operates on multiple levels (2015, 104). Tatiana's voice-over reads the diary over Nicolai's violent sex act, in which the prostitute becomes the object of exchange between the two men, illustrating Eve Sedgwick's (2015) verdict that this cements their homosexual bond. The combination of the bodily presence of the unnamed trafficked women in the objectifying sex act accompanied by the voice-over of the dead woman reifies the prostitute's commodification and exchangeability. The audio track turns the naked, passive, and sexualized woman on the image track into the symbolic stand-in for all trafficked (and already dead) women. Through her pregnancy and writing, Tatiana leaves the collective invisibility of illegal and forced migration. Her death and reproductive capacity create the trace of rape in her daughter's DNA, reducing reproductive labor to biology.

In conclusion, *Brick Lane* and *Eastern Promises* rely on the divergence between image and soundtrack. They associate the image with the destiny of migration and sound with its origin. Whereas the image claims objectivity based on visible materiality, sound evokes subjectivity reflecting free-floating ephemerality. The films reproduce a hierarchy that privileges image over sound, in which the voice-overs suggest that the past haunts the presence and imply that migration creates a temporal disjuncture. Letters and diaries are handwritten in the original language, enhancing the anachronism of the private media and genres historically associated with female authorship. They symbolize the distance to the homeland and the characters' reflection on attachment and displacement. In *Brick Lane*, this cinematic strategy associates the destination country with labor as a means for self-expression and female liberation from the sexual contract. *Eastern Promises* empties prostitution of sexual labor by framing it as human trafficking and reduces reproductive labor to biology. The film's central narrative trope of rape metaphorically stands in for the larger crime against women, but in that process it also erases their agency, for which it substitutes the melancholic memory of a mythical past and homeland. The next two readings examine documentary films that employ voice to expand the space that contemporary communication technologies collapse.

Epistolary Voice-Over and Long-Distance Intimacy

Promise and Unrest is a politically committed documentary about the everyday life of a Filipina nurse in Ireland and her long-distance care of her own children in the Philippines during the period that ends with the global financial crisis. As women migrate into gendered occupational roles (Kofman et al., 2000), they often leave their children with relatives or migrants from more rural areas or poorer countries in what Arlie Russell Hochschild has termed "global care chains" (2000) and engage in "distant love" (Beck and Beck-Gernsheim 2011). In *Promise and Unrest*, the filmmakers mobilize the separation of voice from image to capture the dynamics of the split life of labor migrants who move back and forth between two countries, here the Philippines and Ireland, and who are emotionally engaged via social media with their homeland while working abroad. In other words, instead of advancing a linear narrative about movement from sender to destination country, the film relies on cinematic strategies of editing and sound to capture the women's mediated presence in two different locales.

The film documents the lives of mother and daughter Noemi and Gracelle Barredo, crosscutting between Ireland and the Philippines. Noemi shares her apartment in Dublin with Elvie, also a Filipina caregiver. Noemi's sister Neriza looks after Noemi's two children, Noy Noy and Gracelle, in the Philippines. During the period covered by the documentary, Noemi's family builds a new house, Gracelle finishes high school and moves to Dublin, Noemi's father dies, and finally Noemi loses her job because of the global financial crisis. In the accompanying voice-over, Noemi reads from letters to her daughter, Gracelle, her son, Noy Noy, her mother, Nanay, her father, Tatay, and her younger sister Neriza. Sometimes Gracelle also reads from letters to her mother or reflects on her life and her relation to her mother in diary form.

In conventional documentaries, the disembodied voice-over—located outside of diegetic space—speaks with authority directly to the spectator (Doane 1985, 168). Feminist documentarians respond to this tradition by inscribing autobiography with historiographical agency (Waldman and Walker 1999, 22). Following the conventions of feminist documentaries, Noemi provides the voice-over. After a process of politicization, she begins to articulate her concerns in the language of labor rights in the context of transnational immigration. She transforms the free-floating affect that, according to Encarnación Gutiérrez-Rodríguez (2010), characterizes domestic labor and care work into political demands to decouple labor rights from immigration restrictions.

Care work is poorly compensated on the global market. The Philippines has a vested interest in keeping the price for women's labor low in order to maintain its export and receive remittances. The work of women "outside the nation" changes the understanding of the role of women in the family (Parreñas 2008, 27). Rhacel Salazar Parreñas shows that the participation of Filipina women in the international labor market "enhances their status in the family, increases their consumption power, and provides them with autonomy to make decisions independent of men" (2008, 9). Labor migration enables women to gain economic power, rupturing "the gender ideological split that defines men—the *haligi ng tahanan* (pillar of the home)—as breadwinners and women—the *ilaw ng tahanan* (light of the home)—as homemakers" (6). Yet the work as nurses and nannies maintains the cultural perception of women's domesticity. Agencies support and the Philippines profits from the notion that Filipino women are particularly well suited to be caretakers based on the presumption of innate characteristics such as patience, passivity, efficiency, and empathy (31). Global labor migration has led to neither higher wages or better employment opportunities for women in the Philippines nor pressured men to care for the children or elderly relatives left behind in the country. The association of Filipinas with low-paying work, Parreñas demonstrates, mirrors their gendering as feminine in a global imaginary. The "ideology of women's domesticity engenders the low wages of Filipino women," and, in turn, globalization is a "gendered process": the "masculinization of the transnational professional class in the metropole relies on the feminization of the periphery," explains Parreñas (37).

Global mobility has changed the traditional organization of the family. Instead of the sexual contract, the two sisters, Noemi and Neriza, engage in a delicately balanced division of labor that decouples biological reproduction from maternal care. Noemi differentiates between her love for her daughter and her care work, repeatedly emphasizing that she left her daughter, Gracelle, behind "because of love." She expresses her affection for Gracelle by buying her things and asking her to understand her mother's long-distance love. Gracelle responds to the conflicting demands of the absent mother by wanting to become a flight attendant. Her voice-over describes her mother's one-month-long visit to the Philippines with sentimental phrases about family life: when "Mom" is "home for the holidays," she "buys me special things." Aware of the family economy, Gracelle explains that her mother sends money to her sister, who gives it to their mother to budget and distribute to different family members. Gracelle's comment that in the early years of her mother's return she did not recognize her illustrates her view of the limits of receiving material objects as a substitute for their bond.

The film maps the geography of the contemporary female labor migrant not only onto the international distance but also onto the domestic spaces in both locations. Migrating for work, leaving children, and sending remittances for the construction of a family home create multilocational domesticity, which assumes different forms in the two places. Gracelle can tell who has relatives abroad by the size and the appearance of houses in the Philippines. Noemi's work allows the extended family to represent a higher status in the Philippines, in contrast to her existence in Ireland, where she belongs to a barely visible service sector. *Promise and Unrest* rarely shows exterior scenes in Ireland; Noemi and Elvie remain in their apartment. The scarcity of images of Noemi in public space reflects what Parreñas calls "placelessness," which refers "to the absence of a fixed geographic space that migrant Filipina domestic workers can call their own" (2008, 98). Working in homes where they do not have access to a private sphere forces them to congregate in public settings, for example, at bus stops, and express "spatial deference" to the native users of public space (103). The film not only depicts but also enacts this placelessness by documenting the limitation of space in Noemi's apartment and never showing her in the new house built with her remittances.

The voice-over transcending continents contrasts to the limited space visible on-screen, especially in the shared small and cluttered apartment. The inability of the camera to be mobile in its tight space affords the audience only partial views of the apartment. The film's long takes reproduce the lack of space. The women repeatedly sit in the same places at the table, or, once Gracelle has

FIGURE 4.3. *Promise and Unrest* (Alan Grossman and Áine O'Brien, 2010)

arrived, they lie on their beds, talking, while the daughter sits at the computer. The apartment in Dublin includes practical things to cook but no decoration. Long takes give audience members time to survey the table and chest of drawers, where jars of lotion sit on top of each other. A calendar from a Chinese restaurant hangs on the wall in a mise-en-scène of the diaspora. Noemi and Elvie's cramped living arrangements do not offer intimate space in their shared effort to maximize their remittances. Decorations that create domesticity adorn the house in the Philippines. Stills evoke the tradition of home movies and photographs, in which family members stage themselves in a performance of domesticity.

The long-term documentary cuts between Ireland and the Philippines without showing time spent on airplanes. Even when Noemi's grandfather dies and she undertakes an emergency trip back to the Philippines, a cut substitutes for the journey, expressing the mobility of subjects in the global economy in what David Harvey calls "time-space compression" (1990, 260–323). Electronic communication media develops from VCR to computer with the interactive abilities that enable live conversation in real time. Noemi keeps her cell phone in hand. On the apartment's television Noemi and Elvie primarily watch a video about the construction of Noemi's house in the Philippines.

The letters that the voice-overs read, with their epistolary style and self-reflexivity, invoke a lost temporality through an outdated medium. They suggest an actual geographic distance that electronic communication media collapses. Their dialogue creates a metanarrative in the soundtrack that reflects on the intimate relationship between mother and daughter. Disembodied voices comment on the challenges of long-distance relationships, while the image track, with synchronized sound, depicts local and immediate interaction. The gap between the performance on the screen and the subjectivity expressed in the letters expresses the conflicting demands of the everyday life of global labor migrants. On-screen, Noemi and Elvie joke about the similarity of their paid work and their unpaid domestic and maternal labor. For example, when Noemi wants her daughter to move to Dublin, she jokes how Elvie would then be a "child minder." Such jokes capture the survival strategy of humor, while the letters work through the emotional depth that the situation demands. As the letters lay bare the extent of the hardship that inheres in the separation and deferral of a return, they expose the light-hearted affect as coping mechanism.

Promise and Unrest shares with *Brick Lane* and *Eastern Promises* the detachment of sound from image and voice from body. The voice-over also recounts letters and diaries, anachronistic media in an age of communication technologies such as cell phones and computers. Synchronized sound depicts Noemi and Gracelle engaging with those technologies. The voice-overs offer intergenerational insights into the conditions and effects of migration, including the hardship it produces for migrating women, their children, and their extended family. As in the other two films, the voice-overs mobilize the assumption that authenticity, agency, and subjectivity inhere in voice. However, in contrast to *Brick Lane* and *Eastern Promises*, *Promise and Unrest* does not cast migration as a linear process from premodernity to modernity in which the voice-over serves as a reminder of the collective mythical past left behind. Instead, the documentary employs editing to reproduce the effect of space-time compression and synchronized sound to demonstrate the women's use of communication technology. The immediacy of electronic communication and the epistolary metadiscourse capture yet again Ernst Bloch's concept of the "simultaneity of the nonsimultaneous."

The temporal and spatial distance of letter and diary writing allows the family members to reflect on their split lives. The film exposes the coping strategies in the everyday, the performativity of caring femininity, and the women's awareness of the conflicting perceptions of class in two locations. They defer their domesticity into a future in the Philippines, which they access concurrently via mediated images. Voice is also at the center of the next section, which analyzes a documentary about the economic extrapolation of affective surplus produced in call centers in Istanbul, Turkey.

Affective Accents in Call Centers

Priessner's *We Are Based Down South* documents the lives of Turks who work in call centers in Istanbul that operate for German companies. The film's subjects grew up in Germany but do not have German citizenship and thus are bound to live in Turkey. Call centers have become emblematic for the outsourced labor enabled by communication technology. Voice and accent negotiate deterritorialized ethnicity and nationality, invoking trust and producing affect. In her discussion of affective economies in call centers, Kalinda Vora describes the commodification of "attention, concern, and human communication," defining "affective labor" as the work that "produces value through the capacity of human vital energy as a creative force to be invested directly into other human beings, thereby supporting their lives" (2010, 34, 35). The economic surplus of affective labor in call centers benefits the nation of the customers and not that of the workers, "resulting in a net flow of affective resources to consuming nations at the expense of producing nations" (34). The labor of the agents at the call center thus produces value for a different country.

The film's documentary account of the off-shore call center follows four Turkish Germans who live and work in Istanbul for German companies. Three of them—Bülent Kubulu, Murat Demirel, and Fatoş Yıldız—grew up in Germany but have only Turkish citizenship. Bülent was deported from Germany to Turkey because of criminal activity, while Murat and Fatoş were taken to Turkey by their parents when they were teenagers and were stripped of their German passports and citizenship. The fifth character, Çiğdem Özdemir, has dual citizenship and travels freely between the two countries and among different professions, embodying the mobility associated with a cosmopolitan lifestyle. Bülent, Murat, and Fatoş idealize Germany. Repeatedly they refer to it as their *Heimat* (German for "homeland") and recreate a German space in Istanbul. The low-paying jobs that allow them to speak German seemingly enhance their lives. Following genre conventions, the documentary cuts between the different characters who address the camera directly in close-ups or engage in everyday activities.

Innovations in telecommunications that allow "affordable real-time interaction with service workers abroad" enable call centers and the outsourcing of service labor (Vora 2010, 33). Call centers rely on the cheap labor force of the service industry "through outsourcing contracts and other forms of labor extraction" (34). Management controls workers through "computer-regulated communication technologies, such as dialing software and fully automated call volume, and through statistical and other more direct forms of performance monitoring" (35). Workers adopt a "machinic subjectivity" and project a persona with a new name and cultural knowledge about the country they call (35–36). The agents must show "culturally authentic emotions on the phone" to customers (36).

The constellation in Priessner's film results from the binational history of Turkish labor migration, which created a ready labor force of remigrants, in this case without German citizenship. As the characters have grown up in Germany, they are familiar with the cultural context of their customers. Their accent and language use create trust and perform the required affect, but they have to take on a German name to perform Germanness. The companies save cost, since they can rely on language knowledge, particularly of accented German. In this version of post-Fordist affective labor, the voice communicates authenticity through regional German accents. The main characters have a deep attachment to their work as a link to Germany. Even though they experience boredom and long journeys to the workplace, they value the sociability at work. They have friends and live through important events with members of their team. For example, Fatoş shares the moment that she is receiving her visa for Germany with her female colleague.

Their affective investment in work derives from their use of German language. With her strong regional German accent, Fatoş passionately engages in a phone conversation with a customer whom she called, coincidentally, on his birthday. At the same time, the work's repetitive nature, low skill level, and limited need for attention allow the workers to multitask and fill their time with other, often mediated, communicative activities. Fatoş instant-messages with her boyfriend in Germany while she talks on the telephone with a customer.

The main characters assume German names when they answer the phone for three national brands, Neckermann, Quelle, and Lufthansa, to create the illusion of a German workforce. On the telephone Bülent calls himself Ralf Becker. The work in the call center provides customers not only with information but also with affective care, including a sense of familiarity based on the shared language. This remediation emphasizes the affective and imaginary function of the nation in the global economy. The German companies can, through the aftereffects of Turkish labor migration to Germany, rely on a cheap labor force whose linguistic skills do not match their citizenships. Colloquialisms authenticate the workers as German for their customers.

We Are Based Down South deconstructs the assumptions about the embodiment of national belonging. Istanbul's location just outside the border of Europe turns Germany into a fetishized and legally inaccessible homeland. The characters are lonely, even though Murat and Fatoş are extroverts and Bülent and Fatoş have partners. Vora describes the loneliness that comes with "the alienated activity" in which workers invest their "vital energy," which "leaves the immediate world of the person who produces it" (2010, 42). Murat and Fatoş in particular appear as exuberant and generous, such that the film also lives off their affective energy.

The narrative acknowledges the ruptures and unevenness in the experience of the aftereffects of Turkish labor migration. The characters remember and recount their different stories of how they migrated to West Germany and returned to Turkey. The film does not tell narratives of collective linear migration and remigration but instead presents diverse accounts of multidirectional travel that nevertheless differ from free movement. For example, Fatoş's parents left her behind in Turkey with her grandparents until they brought her to Germany, where she was raised by German foster parents during the work week and her biological parents during the weekend. When her father found out she was dating a German, he took her to Turkey and asked the border police to invalidate her passport.

The film expands the scope of the account of Turkish labor migration to West Germany, which traditionally ended when the "guest worker program" in the 1970s concluded. The shift from material production to immaterial labor accompanies the development from migrating workers to mobile capital. When Fatoş visits her parents in their living room in Turkey, she proudly comments on the sofa that her father upholstered in the Black Forest furniture factory where he and many Turkish workers were employed. The reference to the skilled labor of her father in the factory, now reduced in its number of employers, in contrast to Fatoş's work at the call center illustrates that while the labor force of the postwar generation moved to the site of production, now capital locates to the place of cheap labor.

In conclusion, *We Are Based Down South* foregrounds the circulation of affect produced by voice in a global unequal economy. Vora explains the global division of labor: "If customer service work is located more and more heavily in the global South, then it becomes the work of people in 'places like India' to restore to humanity those who live in the West" (2010, 47). As the film shows, voice and accent are key to the affective labor in call centers, in this particular situation enabled by the involuntary return of those who feel German but are legally Turkish. Their employment relies on the notion of authenticity not only of voice but even more so of accent as markers of regionalism that endows a sense of national belonging. In contrast to the other films discussed so far, *We Are Based Down South* does not rely on formal aesthetic terms to engage with migration and labor in Europe. While the documentary does not deviate from fully synchronized sound, eschewing traditional and experimental forms of the voice-over, it records and thus points to the call center's isolation of the voice from its workers' fully embodied experience and in that process engages in a restorative practice.

Ventriloquized Clandestine Voices

Austrian filmmaker Salomonowitz's *It Happened Just Before* captures the continuum of documented to undocumented migration by women that ranges from human trafficking, sex work, and domestic labor to marriage. More than any other film in this chapter, *It Happened Just Before* unsettles the conventions of the relationship of sound and image without, however, breaking the indelible link between voice and body. Here, stories emerge from the wrong body. The film's political-aesthetic strategy in part serves to protect migrating women from the exploitative gaze and the potential of legal repercussions should their identities be discovered. More importantly, however, it makes a political statement about the simultaneous hypervisibility and invisibility of migrating women and their labor in Europe.

Five ordinary Austrians in their own private or work settings ventriloquize stories about individual migrating women. The narratives are composites from interviews that Salomonowitz conducted with migrating and trafficked women in order to retain their anonymity and highlight structural similarities. The five Austrians include a young male border guard, a midfifties female neighbor in a village, a bartender in a brothel, a female consul, and a male cab driver. Each tells a first-person story about a woman who has migrated to Austria in the private or work setting, engaging in mundane activities. By aligning Austrians with the image and migrating women with the story told by a displaced voice, the film's sound points to the women's invisibility within shared national and domestic private spaces.

The section "In a Brothel" also serves to demystify the space of prostitution and instead present it as a site of labor. The sequence begins with the bartender preparing his workplace before he opens for customers.[9] He counts money, arranges bottles, cleans tables, and distributes towels and condoms in the rooms. In his story, a young woman comes to Austria to be a dancer in a bar. She takes dancing and German lessons only to realize that she needs neither in the establishment where she works. Instead of a melodramatic scene of sexual exploitation, the narrative reveals the continuum of dancing and prostitution and the forms of subtle coercion, as the stories do not reveal outright force or violence but demarcate the women's limited agency. *It Happened Just Before* addresses the structural violence that creates the need for women to migrate, makes them vulnerable to different forms of economic and personal exploitation, and pervades the physically violent cases of human trafficking.

The bartender's attention to the detail with which he sets the scene for his future customers also exposes the banality of the economic transactions around sexuality. Such emphasis on the prosaic labor surrounding the sexual economy contrasts to many other films that create suspense around viewers' expectations of the sudden glimpse into the hidden space of violated and sexualized women, reinforcing the desire to see and uncover the forbidden. The subjects of the five episodes—who are not professional actors—speak directly to the camera, addressing spectators in static long takes. Such a filmic strategy identifies *It Happened Just Before* as an art film that relies on a theatricalization of the narratives of the everyday, refusing the conventions of social realism. In three out of the five scenes, the staging includes a cross-gender performance, challenging spectators to confront not only the nationalization and ethnicization of migration into Europe but also the gendering that traditional narrative cinema naturalizes.

Feature films create suspense by posing an enigma—trafficked women—with a deferred resolution—saving the women and punishing the perpetrators. Salomonowitz undermines this cinematic standard narrative. The film does not rely on suspense or the progression of time. The five segments relate to each other on structural and political levels but do not add up to an overarching narrative that unfolds over time. Salomonowitz creates spatial and temporal continuity within each segment but not among them. A viewer has to understand first that the characters on-screen do not tell their own story and then that the film itself relies on a paratactic structure. This organization situates the film at the intersection of art and politics, as each chapter becomes a visual exploration of a particular space and an auditory narrative by a woman who migrated to Austria. The affectless delivery and paratactic structure keep the spectator at a distance and allow for reflection based on the lack of immersion.

By refusing both exposition and resolution, Salomonowitz rejects the interdependent notions of the individualized problem and solution. Through its method, the film invites viewers to reflect on the connection between the resident Austrians and the migrating women. In some instances, the relationship results from sharing space, for example, an elderly woman who tells the story of a woman who appears as the neighbor within her story. In the other segments, however, the point of contact is work, as four segments show a border guard, a woman diplomat, a cab driver, and a bartender in a bordello. These professionals are not violent criminals, in contrast to mainstream feature films' binary of male perpetrators and female victims.

Salomonowitz's cinematic strategy produces a strong distantiation effect that serves to expose institutional and legal structures that make trafficking in women profitable. The stories are haunting, even if they do not invite identification or pity. The refusal to embody migrating and trafficked women through either sexualized spectacles of their bodies or melodramatic close-ups of their suffering faces avoids the inscription of pity. At the same time, the film does not vilify or celebrate the Austrians on-screen. Instead, it highlights institutional contexts from border laws and visa restrictions to sexual contracts and outlines coercion from seduction and physical violence to economic pressures and lack of choices. Work spans the range from sexual labor to domestic work.

Salomonowitz's film suggests that concrete structures create and organize trafficking. Her method captures societal blind spots instead of clandestine lives and emphasizes witnessing to give weight to women's stories. The particular employment of voice represents a simultaneous presence and absence of migrating women: their narratives appear in the everyday environments of Austria, but their bodies remain invisible. The strategy circumvents the pragmatic problems of filmmakers working with undocumented migrants and offers an allegorical representation of their existence in the countries of destination.

Conclusion

The politics of voice differs among the films on women's migration discussed in this chapter. *Brick Lane*, *Eastern Promises*, and *Promise and Unrest* associate the voice-over with older media such as the diary and the letter. They symbolize time for reflection and geographical distance, which contrast with the collapse of space and time in contemporary communication technology. *Brick Lane* projects the liberating function of labor onto the migrant from the Global South. In order to establish her character as in need of a modern identity, the film offers her melancholic voice-over as a memory of the underdeveloped past in the Global South. *Eastern Promises* similarly links the sound to the past in the place of origin and the image track to the present in the destination of labor migration. While the voice-over relies on a floating quality that envelops the spectator, it haunts the narrative from an undetermined past and undefined place. In *Eastern Promises* this strategy lends itself to commodify the visual representation of the trafficked and sexually exploited women and denies their agency.

We Are Based Down South documents the affective labor that occurs in call centers and undoes the reduction of workers to the function of their voices. The synchronization collapses the image and soundtrack in the realist documentation, but voice still encapsulates desire for an inaccessible homeland. The reverse and involuntary migration of the film's subjects complicates linear narratives of labor migration. Salomonowitz's strategy of paratactic episodes of ventriloquized stories asks spectators to search for the relationship between Austrian citizens and invisible migrating women. The filmmaker rejects the emphasis on the spectacle and physicality of the conventional cinematic staging of trafficked women as abject, passive victims. The next chapter continues the critical engagement with the cinematic representation of women migrating for domestic and care work with films that emphasize gesture as a carrier of affect.

CHAPTER 5

Care Work and the Suspicious Gesture

> Awkward, inefficient, or ill-directed movements of men . . .
> leave nothing visible or tangible behind them.
> —Frederick Winslow Taylor, *The Principles of Scientific Management*

> Gesture hovers on the brink of meaning.
> —Laura Mulvey, "Cinematic Gesture"

> Gestures solicit gestures.
> —Lesley Stern, "Ghosting"

On a small video screen and in a bare mise-en-scène, a solitary woman wearing an apron moves beautifully to the score of Georges Bizet's *Carmen*. Her intimately familiar yet also estranged gestures evoke ironing, cooking, caring, and serving. Japanese mime Mamako Yoneyama renders daily activities into stripped-down gestures in video artist Mako Idemitsu's *At Any Place 4: From the Tango of a Housewife* (1978) (see also Butler and Mark 2007, 249). The video isolates quotidian movements of otherwise invisible domestic chores from their contexts and aestheticizes them in a choreography of gestures. Her use of tango eroticizes these evocations of daily drudgery, and the classical opera score elevates the performance into the realm of art. The gestural composition blends physical and emotional expressions that define domestic and care work. The feminist performance art includes both aspects of gesture that are central to this chapter: on the one hand, the signification of rote and repetitive tasks and, on the other hand, the potential for agency.[1] This 1978 feminist art video from Japan goes to the heart of this chapter's concern: gesture—"normally understood in the most general sense, as bodily movement or pose"—conjoins and signifies the physical and affective dimensions of domestic and care work (Stern 2008, 199).

The ability of a singular gesture to encompass meaning differs from the economy of the sequencing movements of industrial and mechanical labor. The focus on gesture thus demands a theoretical foundation distinct from the history of serial photography of moving bodies by Étienne-Jules Marey and Eadweard Muybridge and the time-saving campaigns of Frank and Lillian Gilbreth and Frederick Winslow Taylor, who shared an interest in segmenting movement. Even though Taylor called for all-encompassing efficiency across sectors, he focused on industry and privileged masculine labor, such as handling pig iron in the Bethlehem Steel Company. Similarly, Frank Gilbreth based his "*enforced standardization*" on bricklaying (Taylor [1911] 2014, 41, italics in the original). They saw individual movements as building blocks of physical activity aimed at efficiency. In Gilbreth's film documentation on how to stuff envelopes, for example, movement either wastes or saves energy but carries no independent meaning.[2] Women come into Taylor's view as industrial laborers, such as the "girls" engaged in the "very simple though unusual work of inspecting bicycle balls in a factory" (43).

Even though these efficiency advocates intended to standardize domestic labor as well, immaterial care work has the potential to resist managed productivity. Taylor called for scientific management in "our homes" ([1911] 2014, iv), while Lillian Gilbreth advanced efficiency in the domestic sphere by organizing the layout of kitchens. The application of industrial management to the domestic sphere implies the primacy of the former over the latter. The potential to escape functionality inheres in intimate care work in the home, which evokes utopian notions of unalienated labor, authentic experience, and emotional attachment. A single gesture can encompass all of this, for example, in the tender touch of a sick child's forehead.

Continuing the focus on films about migration, this chapter shifts its attention from sound to gesture, honing in on the kinesthetic dimension associated with reproductive work in the home primarily in two genres: the romantic comedy and the psychological thriller. Chapter 3 has shown that in films depicting industrial and mechanical labor, bodies move in intensifying speed in an accelerating pace of editing and with a musical score that transforms factory rhythms into danceable soundscapes. In contrast to the mechanization of the industrial body, the individual gesture captures domestic and care work in the intimacy of the home and the hotel room, the space of secrets and belongings.

At Any Place 4: From the Tango of a Housewife also serves as a reminder of this book's arc from second-wave feminist theory—the emphasis on unpaid domestic labor as part of the sexual contract in the patriarchal nuclear family—to its current transformation. The theoretical approaches that emerged from the second women's movement rely on an understanding of family organized around the heterosexual division of labor and a "breadwinner wage," which, according to Nancy Fraser (2013a), undergirded the post–World War II Western European welfare state. In the twenty-first century, the presumed prototypical family structure that defined feminist theory's model of unpaid feminized domestic labor has given way to the predominance of dual-income families.[3] Gay, lesbian, and blended families, as well as single parents, also diversify the traditional norm. Even though the heterosexual division of labor has not disappeared, it is gradually waning, in part as a result of the demands of the feminist movement.[4] While women still provide on average more unpaid domestic and care work than men, the latter also participate more than in previous decades in European households. Women have entered the paid labor force in significant numbers in many European countries. In response to neoliberal demands of flexibility, they often take up more than one low-paying job in the service industry. Scholars have labeled this development "feminization," implying that it reflects traditional feminine work patterns. Female labor migrants who perform paid domestic work enable middle-class women to enter the paid labor market. When they take over the care work of the elderly and children or domestic labor, their presence reshapes family formations as well (Parvulescu 2014).

Feminist scholars in sociology, anthropology, and labor studies have responded to the increase in service work with accounts of intimate labor (Boris and Parreñas 2010) and emotional labor (Hochschild 2012)—and both concepts are central to this chapter's argument. Eileen Boris and Rhacel Salazar Parreñas define intimate labor as "tending to the intimate needs of individuals inside and outside the home," including "bodily upkeep, care for loved ones, creating and sustaining social and emotional ties, and health and hygiene maintenance" (2010, 5). Arlie Russell Hochschild explains the increase in emotional labor as a result of the rise of the service sector, which correlates to the decline of manufacturing. She sees female kindergarten teachers, nurses, and social welfare officers engaging in "emotional labor," which can be difficult to identify (2012, ix). The commodification of emotion in the professional smile, for example, by flight attendants, "convinces customers that on-the-job behavior is calculated," as "the emotional style of offering the service is part of the service itself" (5). For occupations in the service industry, as in her example of flight attendants, "to show that the enjoyment takes effort is to do the job poorly" (8). Hochschild describes how their training includes "deep acting," which "involves deceiving oneself as much as deceiving others" (33). Because acting is necessary for the performance of emotional labor, it can evoke suspicion and, potentially, retribution by employers and customers. If the job consists of performing care, the fact that it is paid undermines the perception of authentic empathy.

In film we find an additional layer of acting when an actor portrays a character who performs intimate or emotional labor. The actor can collapse or heighten the gap between the character's emotion and her performative reification in affective labor. Films also employ technical and formal strategies to cast doubt on or endorse the actor's gestures of care work. The individual gesture comprises the focal point where actors, the cinematic apparatus, and spectators negotiate these tensions between the actor's realist invocation of authentic feeling and the performance of commodified emotions.

Migrant women increasingly provide intimate and emotional work for pay in European households. Their status of labor migrants and their location within the private sphere accord them a role that is both sustaining and threatening to the family and home as constitutive of the nation. With the erosion of the welfare state, care work of children and the elderly moves into the private sphere, where it falls on either unpaid female family members or paid caretakers who, increasingly, are migrant women. Companies respond to suspicion vis-à-vis emotional labor in intimate spaces with technologies of surveillance, including, for example, nanny-cams (see Hayes 2016). In addition to suspicion surrounding their work, female migrants endure intersecting economic and sexual discrimination. Transnational migrants make up a vulnerable, feminized labor force "in the lowest wage sectors of the world's wealthiest economies" (Montoya 2016, 159). Tracking into a limited range of jobs racializes them, while culture sexualizes them (159). Private domestic services, especially childcare and the care of the elderly, have increased in Europe to the degree that noncitizens play an important role in sustaining European families (Anderson 1999, 117).

The three films in this chapter rely on gestures' ambivalence to frame female migrants in the private sphere: romantic comedies contain otherness through marriage, whereas the psychological thriller mobilizes phobic anxieties surrounding care work by noncitizens in the intimate spaces of the home and the hotel room. The presence of these narratives indicates a general awareness about the concerns surrounding emotional and intimate labor by female migrants. The films produce ambivalent texts that oscillate between the denunciation of the women's labor and an acknowledgment of their subjectivity. This fluctuation mirrors the status of the gesture in the paid emotional and intimate labor of care work.

In general, gestures encapsulate two different relationships of subjects to their work. First, they signify the ways workers embody labor regimes—in other words, not only how characters internalize a particular professional script but also how its gestural language shapes their body and affects. Second, gestures also allow agency to come to the fore, as they include the potential to exceed what is necessary, inherited, and acceptable to perform tasks. As ambivalence defines gesture, its performance can pose a challenge to the spectator's cognition, which allows thrillers to organize the uncertainty of perception around the migrant worker in the intimate space of the private home. The thriller rehearses the question whether the spectator witnesses care work or a ruse disguising an attempt to access the family as the heart of the nation to usurp its valued possessions: the most precious of all, the love of a child, or the most pernicious of all, the desire of a husband.

In other words, the reproductive labor of the servant, maid, or nanny includes love and tenderness of those in her care, either things or people. As affection can call forth reciprocity, domestic and care workers also pose a potential threat, paradoxically, especially when they do their work well, in other words, when they experience and express the appropriate feelings of empathy, care, joy, despair, and worry, for example (see Gutiérrez-Rodríguez 2010). The nanny or domestic in the intimate sphere must negotiate that she constitutes either a threat when her work relies on authentic feelings or a fraud when it does not. Consequently, the romance rewards the maid with love, while the thriller oscillates between genuine and performed emotions onto which the narrative projects ulterior and thus potentially sinister motives.

Surveillance meshes with erotic voyeurism in the private home in two intersecting regimes. On the one hand, the loss of a "nanny's love and loyalty occasions much anxiety" (Qayum and Ray 2010, 110). On the other hand, the phobic logic surrounding workers in the private sphere conjures up the figure of the uncanny female migrant worker getting away with theft, in part because her work enables her to enter the emotional economies, the private lives, the secret fantasies, and the intimate spaces of those for whom she cares. Such work, the thrillers imply, needs to be viewed with suspicion. The films turn the decoding of care and theft into a challenge for the implied spectators' cognitive abilities.

Gesture's propensity toward agency derives from the perception of its intrinsic authenticity and thus exists in a fundamental tension with the performativity that inheres in emotional labor. Nineteenth-century performer and teacher

François Delsarte viewed gesture as the "agent of the heart," in other words, as capturing immediate and authentic feeling (quoted in Cowie 2015, 82). Other scholars see gestures more generally as conjuring up an "imagery . . . *that is an integral part of the process of speaking*" (McNeill 2015, 17, italics in the original). Yet chapter 4 demonstrated that films mobilize notions of authenticity, in that case, the human voice, to different political ends. Consequently, the understanding of physical realness does not mean that films necessarily employ gestures to communicate authentic emotions. Instead, they also mine the association with true expression to its opposite end in order to question the legitimacy of the migrant and her labor.

The "'gestural turn' in criticism" (Schoonover 2014, 101) stems—at least in part—from Giorgio Agamben's essay "Notes on Gesture" (2000). Agamben's oeuvre locates gesture in philosophy and political theory, on the one hand, and cinema, on the other. While this chapter juxtaposes bodies engaged in industrial labor—consisting of sequential and efficient combinations of movements—to the individual expression of care that transmits affect via meaningful individual gestures, Agamben implies a historical relationship between the two. He suggests that Marey's, Muybridge's, and Taylor's "scientific-technological analysis" of movement produced a loss of gestures (see Levitt 2008, 198). Deborah Levitt (2008) explains that Agamben proposes that gestures existed in the private sphere but migrated to the public sphere in part through the invention of cinema—think Charlie Chaplin.

The theorization of gestures' racial and ethnic dimension has its own genealogy from the mid-twentieth century. David Efron's turn to cultural and communal influence on gesture in 1941 and Charlotte Wolff's psychological approach in 1945 countered Nazi claims of the biological and racial roots of gestural language. Efron found a significant difference in gestural habits depending on the level of assimilation when he created a catalog of gestures and their meaning by studying the gestures of Italian immigrants and Jews in the United States, on the one hand, and those of their offspring, on the other ([1941] 1972). Charlotte Wolff integrated biological with cultural explanation in her study of gestures. She interpreted gestures performed by mental patients in clinical studies as behavior that reflects "the core of personality" ([1945] 2016, xiii). According to her, gestures constitute a personality based on, for example, the "way in which a woman opens and shuts the door, how she walks, gives you her hand, takes a chair, remains seated, gets up, the way she lights a cigarette, tears up a letter, turns the pages of a book, arranges flowers" (5). Wolff highlights the "transmission of gesture by imitation" as the unconscious knowledge of others (11).

Based on these theoretical foundations, film studies scholars have recently turned to gestures in film. Lesley Stern lists three gestural regimes in the cinema: (1) "the profilmic performance of the film actors"; (2) "the cinematic performance—how filmic codes are deployed not merely to produce meanings but to generate affects"; and (3) "the spectatorial performance (mimetic enactment)" (2008, 186). Scholars consider gestures as part of the mise-en-scène that creates the film's mood (Chare and Watkins 2015, 1). Gestures can also manifest memories that "emerge unbidden, indexing the agency of the unconscious in bodily communication" (1). Laura Mulvey traces the "unfolding of a gesture," which the cinematic apparatus "harnesses" when it subordinates the animate body to its apparatus (2015, 7, 9).

Gestures encapsulate the possibility of agency. They are "learned techniques of the body" based on "cultural conditioning" and therefore constitute "a resource of resistance to homogenization" (Noland 2008, 2, x). In other words, they can subvert the routines imposed by standardization. Carrie Noland points out that because gestures evoke affects without precise signification, they create ambivalence. She has developed a theory of embodied agency, even though she acknowledges that the process of installing culture relies on disciplining the body through norms, including the repetition of gestures (2009, 3). Subjects acquire gestures in an intersubjective setting often through transmitting a habitus between generations (82). But gestures' kinetic dimension—when subjects experience their movement—can also lead them to resist gestural models and develop alternatives (3).

Feminist film scholars have turned to a "boundless corporeal lexicon of figures, gestures, and affects" in contemporary art cinema where that lexicon appears as a consequence of the delay and arrest that occur in the neoliberal economy (Gorfinkel 2012b, 311, 312). Attending to "gestural economies of exhaustion," Elena Gorfinkel suggests, enables a feminist perspective on the "small, minor, uneventful movements" that characterize female laboring bodies onscreen (314, 325). Fatigue results from post-Fordist affective and cognitive labor, which demands flexibility and permeates nonwork time (325).

This chapter emphasizes a different form of cinematic display of gestures, paying less attention to the particularity of the neoliberal economy, its labor regimes, and its cinematic instantiation and instead highlighting the continuity of lower-class labor, including minority and migratory women's paid labor in the domestic sphere. The notion of fatigue does not capture all the ways in which contemporary film makes use of the gestural language of labor. Gorfinkel argues that exhaustion results from a lack of access to meaningful and sustainable work, and she thus makes sense of the films about women on the economic margins that are the subject of her study. But as this book demonstrates, labor and sometimes meaningful work still occur under neoliberalism, on and off the screen, and call for readings. The performative open-endedness of gestures allows diverse instantiations in the filmic depiction of bodies in the moments of work and nonwork. Through gestures, films contain, discredit, but also resurrect work, as well as the subjectivity of those who carry it out.

The French romantic comedy *Les femmes du 6e étage* (*The Women on the Sixth Floor*; Philippe Le Guay, 2010) conjoins domestic labor with migration. Gestures define a group of Spanish maids in different instances in terms of class or ethnicity or occupation. The main character, María, is distinct among her peers through her gestural habitus. The subsequent reading of two Italian thrillers, *La doppia ora* (*The Double Hour*; Giuseppe Capotondi, 2009) and *La sconosciuta* (*The Unknown Woman*; Giuseppe Tonatore, 2006), establishes how they cast migrant domestic workers as (potential) thieves in the private spaces of the nation. Whereas the romance contains women's agency, the two thrillers endow gestures with suspicion. Such cinematic strategies respond to the collapse of the space of intimacy with the workplace, where conflicting demands for privacy and labor collide. Narrative conventions of the romance project desire onto the maid and contain it in the heterosexual couple, while the thriller challenges the spectator's cognition by mobilizing the ambivalence inherent in gestures of domestic and care work.

Economy of Gestures

The Women on the Sixth Floor takes place in Paris in 1962 when Spanish women worked as maids in French households. Patriarchal structures undergird this romantic comedy. The film's gestural language charts the film's trajectory from the feminine community to the heterosexual contract in the happy ending. Projecting labor into the past allows for nostalgic idealization similar to the recuperative narratives about industrial labor discussed in chapter 3. In *The Women on the Sixth Floor* an upper-class Parisian family hires a young Spanish maid named María, who lives above their apartment on the sixth floor. Bourgeois father and husband Jean-Louis Joubert, who is a stockbroker, falls in love with María and helps the other maids who live in the attic. In exchange, they take him into their fold. When Jean-Louis separates from his wife, he moves in with the maids on the sixth floor, flouting bourgeois conventions. María's aunt, who also works as a maid in the apartment building, realizes that María and Jean-Louis are in love. In order to protect her niece from potential heartache, she tells María how to find her young son in Spain, and María leaves in the night to be with her son.

The film concludes three years later, when Jean-Louis is looking for María in Spain, with a happy ending of their love.

The film announces the significance of gesture in its title sequence. Before the onset of the narrative, we hear female whispering in Spanish accompanying a black screen. Then, in a short vignette, four Spanish maids introduce themselves one after the other directly to the camera by providing their names and cities of origin and commenting on their work. In each case, a medium close-up follows an establishing shot of each of their faces so that their hands become visible on the screen. One of them moves her hands to signify ironing, sharing how much she enjoys the activity. These opening gestures accompany speech and encapsulate labor; they are "expressive" and "deictic" (Cowie 2015, 82). The former marks the women as working-class Spanish. The latter encapsulates the ambivalence of the women classifying their tasks. On the one hand, through these gestures, they retain agency. On the other hand, the work defines them and thus reduces them to its function.

The gestures of domestic labor act as synecdoche for the complex physical and emotional work that the women perform in the everyday. They code housework as familiar and anachronistically material. The audience recognizes specific tasks easily. The opening functions like an epigraph, announcing the significance of domestic labor for the women's identity and encapsulating their kinetic relationship to it. Their working-class accoutrements of heavy coats and headscarves and the breaking of the fourth wall recall documentary realism. The direct address also invokes contemporary reality-TV aesthetics, in which real-life characters introduce themselves directly to the camera to connect to spectators. The ensuing narrative of the six Spanish maids curiously does not include the women of the opening vignette. The latter remain outside the narrative as the trace of a shared history. The opening invokes collective self-representation, which the film increasingly abandons as the love story moves to the foreground.

The characters' gestural repertoire signals belonging to class, nationality, and gender. The kinetic embodiment takes place in a hierarchically organized architectural composition that aligns distinct gestural vocabularies with different spaces. The film critiques an architectural organization that makes service invisible but, according to the story, also enables community. Despite the fact that the title refers to the women on the sixth floor, only Jean-Louis develops as a character through the discovery of the hidden world of the maids, which projects a magical quality onto them—in many ways the source of the film's pleasure. The spatial organization of upstairs/downstairs has reflected and inverted a conventional trope of class organization since Fritz Lang's *Metropolis*

(Germany, 1927). *The Women on the Sixth Floor* justifies such vertical and hypervisible class configuration through its projection into the past. As domestic labor takes place in the shared space of the employer, the upstairs/downstairs metaphor does not easily apply to contemporary paid domestic labor in Europe. The long-running British TV series *Upstairs, Downstairs* (1971–1975, 2010–2012), set in 1903–1930 and 1936–1939, and *Downton Abbey* (2010–2015), which takes place between 1912 and 1926, rely heavily on the vertical differentiation of class performed as heritage. *The Women on the Sixth Floor*'s nostalgia mobilizes these kinds of intertexts to represent class distinctions, which enables the film to avoid confronting the affective charge of a shared intimate space.

The maids' lively and shared gestural language defines their community in their leisure time. They meet in different public spaces, such as the park and the church. Places for domestic laborers to congregate tend to be limited to public spaces, often transitional sites (Parreñas 2008). The women's gestures in private, including their touching, mark them as caring, sensual, and spontaneous. But they are also aware of the public gaze. When they meet in a friend's apartment, their gestural expression becomes exuberant as they sing, dance, eat, drink, and laugh in private.

The ambivalent nature of gestures enables the film's revisionist depiction of domestic labor, as in an early set-piece that rewrites the chores of cleaning as joyful choreography tied together by a pop song. Suzanne Joubert hires María for a test period of one day. After Suzanne leaves, María calls her friends to help her so that she will get the job. One of them turns on the radio, which plays Dalida's 1960 "Itsy bitsy petit bikini." The song narrativizes the transformation of women in the 1960s with the story of a beachgoer who dresses in a tiny bikini and self-consciously remains first in the changing cabin and then in the water until she is blue. The song's bikini-clad woman contrasts to the modestly dressed maids at work and turns their labor into play as they accomplish their

FIGURE 5.1. *The Women on the Sixth Floor* (Philippe Le Guay, 2010)

tasks with dance movements that follow the musical rhythm. They make grand gestures of vacuuming, drying dishes, or making a bed while swinging their hips to the song's melody, mimicking the idea of sexiness and expressing uninhibited sensuality. The editing emphasizes their parallel movements through matching cuts on gestures. Edits at the end of each stanza reinforce the musical rhythm by aligning the visual pacing with that of the song. They do not need to care about efficiency, since they are gaining time by working together. The scene encapsulates a shared communal moment. The illusion that the women complete all the housework during one song about leisure creates a fantasy of domestic labor emptied of its drudgery and exhaustion.

María's gestures distinguish her from the other maids and mark her—via her work—as serious, mindful, restrained, and determined. Instead of her work gestures limiting themselves to the completion of domestic tasks, her characteristic determined hand movements promise spectators knowledge about her person. María differs from the others through her restraint, expressed in her professional black maid's costume and extending to her movement. Her self-possession manifests itself in her upright posture and reserved but kind facial expression. When Suzanne shows her the apartment, María nervously but in a subdued fashion wrings her hands together, evoking the audience's empathy for a young woman in a foreign country learning the rules in a strange new environment. But when she works, precise gestures characterize her, for example, opening the curtains decisively and looking at her watch with a distinct wrist movement. In other words, the acting that brings forth María's gestures of labor functions in excess of what the tasks demand in order to define her character. Her physical restraint indicates an internal middle-class respectability. As her gestures promise the audience knowledge of her personality, the acting aligns spectators with her and prepares the ground for the love story.

The other women's gestural language serves as comic relief, particularly pronounced in scenes that reveal and make light of the structuration of intimate relations in the close quarters of service. One concerns their clogged-up toilet, a situation charged with the privacy of hygiene. Humor disavows the political problems that affect domestic servants. Decrying the despicable conditions of the attic where the maids live, early scenes depict the inadequacy of a clogged toilet and the lack of hot running water on the sixth floor. But when the anachronistic caricature of a French plumber arrives, the women respond with witty comebacks and laughter. The next day they exaggerate their appreciation into comedic excess that characterizes them as childlike. As in other, albeit American, twenty-first-century films that narrativize women's labor and purportedly shed light on racist discrimination, the depiction of the clogged toilet approximates scatological humor. Films such as *The Help* (United States, India, United Arab Emirates; Tate Taylor, 2011) and *Hidden Figures* (United States; Theodore Melfi, 2016), about African American female workers under segregation, equally create comic relief involving toilets, which were central to racial discrimination. In these American films, scatological humor strategically offers release for the audience in an otherwise emphatically melodramatic account of racist labor practices.[5] Similarly, *The Women on the Sixth Floor* acknowledges and then disavows the discriminatory practices surrounding access to appropriate spaces of hygiene for women.

Restrained gestural language, differentiated according to gender, defines the upper class of the family that has hired María. Jean-Louis's characteristic hands in his pockets combines a relaxed self-confidence based on inherited privilege with the absence of pretension that signals his ability to cross the class boundary. Upper-class Suzanne and her friends' gestural language serves to distance them from the maids, underscoring frivolous activity, such as smoking. Suzanne repeatedly claims exhaustion, which the narrative contrasts with her lack of physical activity. Individual shots juxtapose her complaints to María's distinct and tangible activities. The film portrays Suzanne as particularly inauthentic and sexually repressed—the enduring stereotype of the upper-class woman. Such a narrative conceit allows for the justification of the patriarch's sexual, emotional, and romantic encounter with the unattached, sexually available, live-in domestic worker. Late in the film, Suzanne's upper-class affect reveals itself to be a performance, as she originates from the countryside. Her calculated marriage to Jean-Louis enables her status in Parisian society.

The triangulation of wife, husband, and maid in the home complicates Carole Pateman's notion of the sexual contract (discussed in chapter 1). The characters act out the triangle when Jean-Louis sees nude María in the shower and then proceeds to have sex with his wife. According to Pateman (1988), the sexual contract accords the husband the labor power of his wife. But when his class affiliation implies that the wife should not work, he purchases the domestic labor power of another woman. Pateman does not discuss the interplay of sexual access and ownership of labor power. In order to justify Jean-Louis's choice to leave his wife and two children for the younger and exotic María, his wife appears less sympathetic and as a class impostor. In the recent surge of international films about maids—*The Help*, *La nana* (*The Maid*; Chile, Mexico; Sebastián Silva, 2009), and *Que hocas ela volta?* (*The Second Mother*; Brazil; Anna Muylaert, 2015), from the United States, Chile, and Brazil, respectively—the alternately sexually repressed or emotionally aloof upper-class housewife is a stock figure who narratively prepares her husband's desire for the maid or her daughter. Locating the man's supposed need to turn for sexual satisfaction to the maid in the wife's lack of availability individualizes systemic exploitative economic structures, even if sexual transgression is part of the power imbalance of heterosexually structured economies.

The traditional heterosexual couple closes the film and resolves the class conflict. Three years later, Jean-Louis travels to Spain, where he finds María in a village, leaving a house with a basket of laundry. Wearing a flowery summer dress that blows in the wind, she moves with a relaxed and animated stride through the expansive space, bathed in a warm, bright light. Such setting, costume, and composure contrast with her containment in the dark and stuffy interior of the bourgeois apartment in Paris. The gestural language of her work differs as she leisurely carries her laundry basket on her hip, evoking the exotic Mediterranean woman. But when she hangs the laundry, she uses the familiar precise hand movements. Her performance marks the subtle difference between "natural" work that appears as an extension of femininity and her past paid domestic labor, marked by formal restraint and precision. When she sees Jean-Louis, she stops her gesture of reaching for laundry midway. The subsequent crosscuts between close-ups of their two faces suggest their mutual intimate recognition in the absence of the hierarchical employment relationship. His visible class status, indicated by his red convertible, and her domestic abilities naturalize a highly conventional gendering of a future relationship. While the film had opened with close-ups of female domestic workers who defined themselves in relation to their housework, it closes with the return to the sexual contract as resolution.

The Uncanny Migrant Worker

Instead of containing the ambivalence, as the rom-com does, the genre of the thriller harnesses the ambivalence inherent in gestures to evoke suspicion regarding the female migrant's labor in the private sphere. It estranges gestures of domestic labor, such as cleaning, through camera angles, suspenseful sounds, and disorienting time lines, including intrusive flashbacks. Such narrative and technological strategies challenge viewers' cognitive abilities to detect the labor migrants' motivations. While in the thrillers *The Double Hour* and *The Unknown Woman* gestures of work function as a ruse to hide theft and violence, they also offer spectators access to possible alternative futures. Thus, the films train native audiences to distinguish false from true gestures, projecting onto the migrant characters a sinister agency with which they insinuate themselves into the private lives of the citizens of the nation. While a gestural habit shapes a laboring body, it can also provide access to a physical expression of resistance to labor's demands.

In *The Double Hour*, Sonia, a Slovenian chambermaid from Ljubljana, meets a former cop named Guido, who takes her on a romantic getaway to the villa where he works as a security guard. A criminal gang, however, attacks them and empties the house in a well-organized robbery. It appears that Guido is killed during the heist, and Sonia returns to work, increasingly surrounded by strange events. The narrative later reveals that Sonia was in a coma for three days after the attack, and everything that occurred after the robbery was a dream. When she wakes up, Guido is alive and in love with her. The film concludes with the revelation that Sonia had insinuated herself into Guido's life in order to gain access to the villa and that she is romantically involved with the boss of the criminal gang, who orchestrated the robbery and with whom she flees to Argentina at the film's conclusion.

The Double Hour also begins with a scene that establishes motifs but does not advance the plot. The opening scene presents the disjunctive relationship between mundane gestures and traumatic action. Before the title, a sequence of close-ups captures the traces of life in a hotel. Dirty glasses and napkins, leftover food, and shoes and magazines on the floor wait for staff to remove them and clean the room. The film then cuts to a cooking show on television, followed by a close-up of a hand massaging a sock-clad foot, presumably in a hotel room. We see the close-up profile of a young woman sitting on a hotel bed, absentmindedly rubbing her foot, inattentively watching television. She then lowers her foot and rubs her shoe. Sonia arrives and begins cleaning the bathroom, and the guest compliments her on her hair. When Sonia hears a noise, she slowly moves through the room to look out the window. From her point of view, the camera reveals that the hotel guest has jumped out of the window to her death. In a shocking cut, the next shot shows the face of yet another stranger in an extreme close-up: Guido at a speed-dating event talking to Sonia.

The spatially fragmented close-ups and the seemingly random encounter between the guest and Sonia, without establishing spatiotemporal context or introducing characters, challenge the spectator's cognition. *The Double Hour* never reveals more about the young woman, and her suicide remains an enigma, although it becomes a leitmotif throughout the film. The film's opening scene asks the audience to make sense of the action by interpreting the relationship between prosaic gestures and dramatic events.

The gestures of Sonia's work change through the course of the narrative. Until the film reveals that the many strange events occur in Sonia's mind during her coma, they create suspense about whether they occur in Sonia's imagination or whether the spectator is cognitively unable to grasp the film's action. At work after the heist, Sonia's gestures assume a new quality as she obsessively scrubs while simultaneously being unfocused; for example, she drops a guest's expensive bottle of perfume. In the hotel's hallway, she looks tired and slouches down next to her cart.

Sonia uses a set of distinct gestures when she meets Guido at the speed-dating event. She repeatedly touches her hair, moving it behind her ear and playing with it while she looks around the room, appearing nervous and insecure to Guido and to the spectator. Toward the end, the narrative reveals that she was acting, performing the shyness and innocence of an ideal femininity to elicit Guido's desire to protect her. Retroactively, it comes to light that humility, loneliness, and shyness, expressed in the repeated small gesture, constitute the scheme of seduction with which she specifically targeted Guido, who worked as a security guard at a villa filled with valuables, including art. Her performance as a lost innocent female migrant also dupes the audience, as her character garners sympathy. The film implies a warning against being deceived by a migrant's act of vulnerable femininity.

Sonia's gestures communicate shyness until she secretly meets her criminal lover, whom she slaps in the face and then passionately kisses. At this point the audience recognizes that she had planned Guido's seduction and the heist. When she meets her partner in crime, her fervent love-making in a truck and her brazen sexual appetite expose her modesty as a ruse to cover her passionate and criminal personality.

When Sonia awakens from her coma in the hospital, the narrative reveals that the action that took place in half an hour of screen time and three days of narrative time was a dream. Sonia undergoes a personality change that manifests itself in her gestures. She tenderly strokes Guido's face when she tells him that he has saved her. At home, Sonia calls her father while a tear runs down her face, expressing longing and regret. At the end of the telephone conversation, she violently holds her fist to her mouth to prevent herself from expressing her emotional despair.

A final sex scene between Guido and Sonia implies that Guido knows about her charade, because the organizer of the speed-dating event has inadvertently revealed to him that Sonia had targeted him. The choreography of their sex act communicates his resentment that she betrayed him and her love, which she will not act upon. The scene takes place in the hallway of her apartment, a spatial context that captures the transitional nature of their relationship. Close-ups focus on her repeatedly touching him. He in turn holds on to the doorframe, whereas she guides his hand onto her body. In contrast, he penetrates her but does not engage in tender caresses. She strokes his face, while the focus of the camera remains on her hands. An extreme close-up of her face with a tear suggests that she is aware of his knowledge and that she will leave. When they are sleeping, she strokes him again, signaling her genuine attachment to him. Their different gestural language reflects the narrative development but also relies on gendered notions of intimacy. The close-ups of Sonia's hands on Guido's face express tenderness and a craving for attachment. According to Eve Kosofsky Sedgwick, "the sense of touch" undermines the "dualistic understanding of agency and passivity," suggesting that Sonia attempts to overcome her victimization of Guido (2003, 14). In a final dialogue they reveal in coded language to each other that they both know the truth that Sonia used and betrayed him and that she will abandon him.

When Sonia arrives at the airport to meet her lover, he pets her face and gives her a tender kiss. She hugs him but does not touch him. Guido watches and records them from his car but lets them depart without calling the police. The film concludes with shots of Guido working in a new position as a security guard, the precarious job in neoliberalism par excellence, and drinking alone in a bar. The final shot shows a happy Sonia and her lover in Argentina having a photograph taken. In her coma-induced fantasy, Detective Dante had given her the same photograph, this time picturing her and Guido, and had claimed that he had found it among Guido's possessions. When she had shown it to her colleague Margherita during her dream, saying that she had never been to Argentina, Margherita suggested that it was Photoshopped. In the final shot of the picture, now being taken in Argentina, Sonia holds on to a necklace that Guido had given her in a gesture that connects her to him. A digital photograph does not claim truth, but touch expresses an authentic affective relationship to the past and the absent love.

In sum, Sonia's work as hotel maid was a strategic deception in order to engage in criminal activity, but her tender touch of Guido suggests genuine love, which she, however, does not act upon. Such projection contrasts to the fact that housekeepers in hotels are "at risk for sexual exploitation" to the degree that some hotels "hire security guards with the explicit responsibility of watching over the housekeeping staff" (Montoya 2016, 159). Whereas the narrative challenges spectators to differentiate between fantasy and reality within the profilmic world, for the majority of its time line the film makes cognitive comprehension impossible. *The Double Hour* mobilizes anxiety about the unknown laborer in the shared intimacy of the hotel room and among anonymous dating rituals. Its emphasis on surveillance perpetuates a paranoid fantasy about the domestic worker's access to guests' privacy. In the space of the hotel, inequity structures the encounter between the tourist and the migrant, and the latter's domestic and emotional labor seems to provide access to the privacy of the former. Sonia performs both intimate labor and femininity as artifice to infiltrate and deceive those around her. The hotel and the villa signal interweaving spaces for the plotlines of working as a chamber maid and seducing a security guard. Those two narrative threads disentangle the subservience and titillation that delineate the figure of the chambermaid, updating her character to a member of the twenty-first-century Eastern European labor force migrating within Europe.

Suspicious Gestures

Like *The Women on the Sixth Floor*, the Italian thriller *The Unknown Woman* weaves its tale around a female migrant who works in a private home, in this case, as a nanny. As in *The Double Hour*, the action unfolds in the present tense, and the main character, Irena, is a solitary migrant. She is played by Russian actress Ksenia Rappoport, who also portrayed Sonia in *The Double Hour*.[6] Instead of a romantic heterosexual union, the ending offers the encounter of the two women Irena and Thea, who the film misleads us to believe are mother and daughter. Similar to *The Double Hour*, *The Unknown Woman* casts aspersions on the main character and her gestures of labor, mobilizing suspicion of migrant domestic workers. As part of the genre convention of the thriller, the film withholds information and creates suspense, shrouding Irena's identity and her motivations in a mystery haunted by a violent sexual past that intrudes via flashbacks into her present life. The interweaving of incongruous sexual violence and mundane domestic tasks challenges the spectator's cognitive ability. The narrative instability produces ambivalence in the spectator, which the film links to Irena's unknown origins and mysterious motives. Flashbacks imply that her violent and sexual past motivates her mysterious acts in the present.

Ukrainian migrant Irena (who in the opening vignette is introduced as Georgia) is hired by the Italian Adacher family to work as nanny for their young daughter, Thea.[7] Disorienting flashbacks evoke the past of Irena's human trafficking, sexual exploitation, and forced prostitution by a hyperviolent pimp named Mold, who killed Irena's Italian lover, Nello. When Irena became pregnant, Mold sold her newborn infants to Italian families. Irena believes that Thea, the daughter of the Adacher family, is her and Nello's daughter. A flashback reveals that Irena attempted to murder Mold and stole his money. Mold survived, wants his money back, and in the course of events kills Thea's mother, Valeria Adacher. Irena murders Mold and buries him at the Adacher family weekend home, for which she is sentenced to prison. Even though Thea is not her daughter, years later, when Irena leaves jail, a grown-up Thea waits for her.

Similar to the other two films discussed in this chapter, *The Unknown Woman* begins with an enigmatic scene that exceeds the plot and establishes the film's tone. The film opens in a setting of a bare, undefined space reminiscent of a dilapidated palazzo. In the center stand three long-legged, slender women, dressed only in lingerie and wearing white masks. They depart, and three other women, dressed similarly, occupy their places. A disembodied eye peers at them through a peephole in a wall. The scene stages the women for visual consumption: they stand still, as if in a sexualized selection process. Their internalization of bondage eroticizes the stylized and choreographed scene. The absence of gestures implies the suppression of agency and their reduction to their bodies. The invocation of a sadistic gaze invokes expectations of soft porn. A male voice demands that "Georgia" stay, take off her clothes, and turn around to display her body. The absolute power of the disembodied male voice over the mute female body carries a sexual charge shot through with the potential of violence. The film intercuts the action with extremely brief and disorienting close-ups of a dark-haired woman riding a train, which challenges the viewer cognitively to connect the two different images and contrast an extremely stylized sexual fantasy with a mundane activity. The blonde woman, "Georgia," steps off the stage. Once she removes her mask, a close-up captures her looking directly at the camera. She is the same woman as on the train, but she appears in one shot as a sexualized blonde and in the other with a hardened face framed by curly black hair. This mystery person inhabits multiple identities.

The narrative never fully illuminates the brief opening scene. One possible way to read it would suggest that its titillation mainstreams the catalog of sexual fantasies into a narrative of forced migration and sexual exploitation and that the flashbacks in the style of B movies echo the scene's soft-porn aesthetic. The

FIGURE 5.2. *The Unknown Woman* (Giuseppe Tornatore, 2006)

erotic thriller bleeds "into and out of adjacent forms such as classic noir, neo-noir, porn, the woman's film, serial killer and horror films, and the auteur-led art-film" (L. R. Williams 2005, 26). A startling montage of incongruous shots sutures the spectator into the suspense of the thriller, which in part seduces with its cognitive challenge to integrate the fragments into a narrative whole.

Anca Parvulescu reads the opening as the casting call for the film itself. She suggests that the watching eye does not express lust and that the "naked woman in spiked high heels is not an erotic object" (2014, 70). According to Parvulescu, the "film has just cast her as the titular 'unknown woman,'" who will remain unknown because the European public does not acknowledge her invisible reproductive labor (71). Instead of a feminist approach grounded in a critique of fetishistic scopophilia, Parvulescu proposes an approach that detaches female nudity from erotic fantasy and offers insight into the centrality of "reproductive calculation" (71). She argues that the scene constitutes what Agamben calls "bare life," which commercializes the commodity of reproduction (2014, 71). The "sex-trafficking camp," according to Parvulescu, constitutes the site where women's valuable resource is exploited: their "reproductive potential" (2014, 72). She posits sex trafficking correctly on the continuum of women's work in the European market in response to the demand for reproduction (73–85).

Parvulescu brilliantly asserts the centrality of traffic in women for the discussion of contemporary biopolitics with a sophisticated reading of the film. Yet, in contrast to her analysis of the opening sequence as deeroticized and desexualized, it evokes the history of sadomasochism. The high heels, the perfect bodies, the erasure of faces, voices, and gestures create sexual tension that echoes the suspense of the film's generic structure of the thriller. The scene integrates masochism and sadism in a sexual economy that includes the former's staging of a fantasy, its deferral of the sex act, and the lack of touch with the latter's totalizing voyeurism. While the opening vignette sexualizes power in an enigmatic scene, the subsequent narrative implies that sexualization is part of the complicated matrix of reproductive labor.

Parvulescu's otherwise sophisticated rethinking of reproductive labor in terms of biopolitics marginalizes the actual work that occurs in the profilmic world. Her theoretical model shares this with other innovative approaches to women's labor under neoliberalism, including Lauren Berlant's notion of "cruel optimism" and Gorfinkel's emphasis on fatigue. Under neoliberalism, women still complete work that is not accorded any value and that thus remains invisible. To focus solely on bare life, cruel optimism, and fatigue runs the danger of engaging in another structural form of erasure that marginalizes the actual work that laboring subjects undertake. *The Unknown Woman*'s temporality results from past sexual violence in the form of bare life, which repeatedly intrudes on the character's attempt to remake her life through paid domestic labor. Focusing only on the character's past as sexually exploited at the exclusion of her reinvention as nanny illustrates the danger of reiterating the reduction of the figure of female migrant worker to bare life devoid of agency. In contrast, Irena accesses agency in creating nonbiological kinship through her care work in general and her transmitting a gestural language of resistance in particular. After all, Irena's sexual trafficking and her reproductive exploitation belong to her past, intruding violently into her current life of mundane domestic labor in flashbacks that challenge the spectator's cognitive ability to comprehend the action on the screen.

The film mobilizes ambivalence for suspense. Parvulescu suggests that Irena's only agency expresses itself in her killing of Mold (2014, 89). Taking into account Irena's care work with the child Thea throughout the course of the film, the happy ending of their intimate bond—when an aged Irena and a grown Thea meet—also implies the possibility of her reproductive labor as enabling agency. Irena creates fictive kinship and attachment to Thea through her gestural training of the little girl. The film misleads audiences by emphasizing their similar look—Irena and Thea both have dark curly hair. The repeated cross-cutting between Irena and Thea or including them together in two-shots and contrasting Irena's and Thea's dark looks to Valeria Adacher's blonde straight hair suggests that biology explains their attachment to each other. The film reveals this reading to be based on misleading visual representation when the ending reveals the two women's attachment to be a result of their affective gestural relationship throughout the narrative.

An early key scene casts doubt about Irena's gestures of labor. Because Irena believes Thea to be her daughter, she insinuates herself into the Adacher family. She first befriends the family's nanny only to injure her so that the family hires Irena. She also pays the building's janitor to allow her to clean the building's staircase. As the narrative does not reveal the reasons for her action, it casts suspicion onto Irena (see also Parvulescu 2014, 78). A high-pitched, suspenseful violin score and a low camera angle frame Irena cleaning the grand spiral staircase in the large apartment building. The scene begins with the round pattern on the floor doubled by the grand circular staircase framing the shot. We then see Irena working on the top floor. The grid of the banister obscures a clear view of her, and the pattern on a window in the background repeats the obstruction, challenging the spectator's visual grasp of the shot. The camera's rotation reinforces the motif of the spiral staircase, a familiar trope of suspense in films noir such as *The Spiral Staircase* (United States; Robert Siodmak, 1946)

FIGURE 5.3. *The Unknown Woman* (Giuseppe Tornatore, 2006)

and *Vertigo* (United States; Alfred Hitchcock, 1958). From a low angle, the camera points upward to Irena cleaning on the top floor and looking down into the hall, reversing the surveillance of the worker.

Irena's point-of-view shot and the eerie soundtrack estrange her mundane gestures of cleaning. A man arrives at the house, ascends the stairs, and enters an apartment. We only see his shadow, also evocative of film noir. Once he has disappeared, Irena hesitatingly and thus suspiciously moves down the stairs. A close-up reveals her hands wiping the brass sign labeled "Adacher" next to the doorbell. Her unfocused gestures take too long to complete the task at hand, turning the everyday activity of cleaning into a ruse through "the enigmatic quality of gesture" (Cowie 2015, 84). The film's use of camera movement and angle, as well as the soundtrack, frames her action in a suspicious gaze that echoes a culture of trepidation vis-à-vis domestic labor conducted by strangers in private homes.

Theft assumes a key function in the film's different psychological and material economies. Irena steals Mold's money and, more importantly, the Adachers' daughter's affection, symbolized in Thea's paintings that Irena takes to her apartment across the street from the building where the Adacher family lives. The notion of theft from the intimate sphere externalizes an anxiety that responds to underpaid labor in the informal and domestic sphere. The theft appears as a symbolic act, a projection onto the laborer accused of extracting value in the absence of visibly productive labor.

Early in the narrative, Irena breaks into the Adachers' apartment, and once she works for them, she finds and opens their safe. Irena first searches for the safe in the laundry room by touching the shelf and all the items it contains. She knocks on the wood, appearing to know about illegal activity. When she finds the safe, a close-up of her hands shows her caressing it. When she finally opens the safe, the low camera angle invites suspicion as she holds each of its contents individually, including jewelry, boxes, and official papers, which she presses against her heart, suggesting that the enigma concerns matters other than a simple theft or seduction. Rain on the window in the background heightens the noirish effect.

The film proposes parallel intrusive action vis-à-vis breaking into the safe and into the couple's intimate sphere. When she stays overnight, Irena searches the bedroom, moving increasingly into the inner sanctums of privacy. She explores the couple's intimate sphere. She undresses, puts on Valeria's clothes, and lies on the couple's bed after laying out Mr. Adacher's suit next to her. She then holds his imaginary hand. Irena appears to be usurping the role of the Italian wife, which, the film later suggests, she did because she was lonely and wanted to stage her desire for intimacy and normalcy. While Irena is lying on the bed, a flashback in bright colors shows her having sex in explicit scenes that shock in their interruption of the serene present moment. Instead of completing domestic tasks, her gestures invade the private sphere of the family, touching fabrics and invoking anxiety about intrusion.

In this film of proliferating enigmas, one particularly unusual narrative thread concerns Thea's affliction by a strange disease. She has no defenses when she falls; in other words, she is unable to use her own gestures to assert or defend herself, lacking the ability to respond physically to "kinetic sensations," the somatic effects of movement (Sklar 2008, 90). Irena focuses on Thea's affliction beyond the usual expectations or requirements of childcare. Irena transmits gestures to Thea in what Sally Ann Ness calls "gestural circuits of energy exchange" (2008, 266). In order to teach Thea, Irena first disables Thea from moving by tying her up. In the first scene, she creates a soft setting of bedding and wraps Thea in ropes so that she is unable to move her arms at all and only has limited ability to move her legs. Irena then pushes Thea down and challenges her to get up by herself without the use of her limbs. The moment Thea

FIGURE 5.4. *The Unknown Woman* (Giuseppe Tornatore, 2006)

gets up, Irena pushes her down again. The scene is violent, as Irena yells at a bound and defenseless child left alone at home with her guardian. Repeated quick edits crosscut Irena's pushing and yelling in close-ups, withholding motivation, making Irena appear monstrous, stopping only when Thea calls her a whore.

In the second sequence, Irena increases the challenge. The exercise takes place on the apartment's hardwood floor. A shot from above emphasizes the defenseless child, who is desperately crying and angry. In the emotionally difficult scenes, Irena continues to push Thea to the ground any time the child manages to stand. The film intercuts these practices with a flashback of Mold violently pushing Irena, also tied up, onto a bed. Shots of Thea's and Irena's close-ups of bleeding and crying faces in analogous compositions connected by matching cuts suggest similarity between past and present and between Irena and Thea. While Irena appears to be reproducing the sexual violence done to her with her actions vis-à-vis the child, the projection of Irena's past onto Thea's present carries overtones of sadomasochistic abuse. Spectators understand from the narrative that Irena is doing this to help Thea build her defenses. But brief shots of Irena in sexualized and violated poses intercut with her treatment of Thea and of Thea in similar positions as Irena sexualize Irena and Thea. Irena's past violent trauma turns into sexual titillation that overshadows the interaction in the present. The excessively sexual images of the past that haunt Irena invade the domestic, otherwise desexualized space of the family home.

Only much later, when Irena secretly watches Thea at her schoolyard, does the film expose what Irena has achieved. A little boy pushes Thea to the ground, and the other children laugh at her. But in contrast to earlier incidents, Thea gets up and beats the boy while Irena happily and proudly observes. Earlier, the film misled the audience to infer that Irena is reenacting the violence that she experienced at the hands of Mold with the little girl as victim, transferring her abuse onto the child. But later the film reveals that she trained Thea not to be a victim but to defend herself.

The ending radically contrasts to the genre aesthetics of the thriller and the narrative of traumatic sexual violence. Instead, it echoes Agamben's concept of "'coming community,'" which "will unfurl from a gestural politics that does not find its origin or destiny in a vocation or an identity" (Levitt 2008, 206). *The Unknown Woman* bares its critical potential only in the final shots, which validate Irena's desire for emotional attachment despite the extremely violent exploitation of her reproductive labor. The revelation that Mold forced Irena to work as a prostitute and took away her newborn suggests a connection between sex and reproduction that the stereotypical binary of the mother/whore traditionally denies. *The Unknown Woman*'s happy ending, when an adult Thea picks up an aged Irena after she has served time in prison, validates their intimate connection as a result of Irena's taking care of Thea, which focused on gestural transmission.

The film's ending privileges intimate care over biological genealogy. In the final scene, the recognition between the grown child and her former nanny contrasts with the misleading emphasis on Irena's and Thea's physical likeness. Many shots show them in profile looking at each other and emphasizing their equally curly black hair, which suggests that they might be mother and daughter. Their relationship instead results from Irena's care, particularly teaching Thea the gestures to defend herself against male violence. Thus, a focus on gestural language reveals that the agency of female migrants lies with the subtle teaching of resistant gestures to other girls and women beyond the biological inscription of reproduction. Gestures function in circuits of energy among women and thus serve to create alternative kinship relations based on attachments created by reproductive, emotional, and intimate labor.

Conclusion

The films discussed in this chapter, *The Women on the Sixth Floor*, *The Double Hour*, and *The Unknown Woman*, respond to the social changes regarding women, work, and migration in Europe. Cinema has pervasively sexualized care professions, including nurses and maids, for example, in the figure of the "sexy French maid." The three films differ in their negotiation of the history of sexualization. *The Women on the Sixth Floor* counters erotic fantasies surrounding the figure of the maid through the characterization of María as a particularly serious and hidden maternal character and Jean-Louis as an older caring man. Instead of sex, the film depicts idealized paternalism as the foundation of their love. *The Double Hour* relies on perceptions of sexualized chamber maids when it reveals Sonia's innocence as a performance to seduce Guido to facilitate the heist. In *The Unknown Woman* Irena's sexualization misleads the spectator, suggesting that what motivates the plot is Mold's forced prostitution of Irena, only to reveal that it is instead his exploitation of her reproductive labor that sets the action in motion.

The Double Hour and *The Unknown Woman* articulate a phobic fantasy according to which female migrant workers use domestic and care work as a cover for a theft that goes to the heart of the family and nation: its culture and children. They capture the gestural economies of intimate work in the domestic sphere. Whereas romance privileges the somber heroine with a precise gestural vocabulary that makes her an ideal candidate for domesticity, the thriller depicts work in the house as a possible ruse for criminal intentions. While *The Double Hour* and *The Unknown Woman* share disorienting temporalities and withhold information, challenging the audience's cognition vis-à-vis strangers in intimate spaces, their endings differ significantly: Sonia completes the theft and leaves the nation; Irena has entered a fictive kinship relationship with Thea. Thus, the latter film ultimately validates care work as instantiating affective bonds in transnational contexts and outside of biology. In the genre of the thriller, the maid and the nanny emerge as uncanny figures whose care masks their theft and whose gestures of work are not readable. Yet both films endow certain gestures with an authenticity that opens up the possibility of genuine attachment across boundaries of national belonging and beyond the confines of job descriptions. The next chapter continues the discussion of reproductive labor in the context of biotechnology and the biomarket in three dystopian films that place their action among migrants, refugees, and clones.

CHAPTER 6

Reproductive Labor in the Age of Biotechnology

> Travel counsellors can provide specialist advice and help on travelling to Spain for fertility treatment.
> —"Fertility Clinics Abroad"

> A surrogate mother is a lady who can help a childless couple by carrying their child in her uterus.
> —Giftlife Egg Bank

> One parent must go in person to pickup baby when born and go to USA Consulate to get passport issued in Africa, and bring back baby to USA. No other restrictions.
> —Indian Egg Donors

Biotechnology has significantly altered the understanding of life and thus of reproductive labor. Second-wave feminists responded to the invisibility of domestic and care work by criticizing the social construction of femininity as a ruse for extracting women's work without pay. In order to advance that critique, they collapsed biological reproduction of life with the social reproduction of the labor force. This understanding projected a paradigmatic image of the nuclear family consisting of a patriarchal breadwinner who received a family wage and a housewife who was responsible for the domestic sphere. Since the 1970s biotechnological innovation has altered the notion of what constitutes life and created the possibility to separate its production and reproduction among scientists, on the one hand, and tissue and egg donors, as well as surrogate mothers, on the other. Agencies disperse such labor across the globe but also among countries in Europe in a stratified division of labor. Women in the Global South donate or sell kidneys, blood, tissue, and eggs and serve as surrogates in an "integrated bioeconomy" (Cooper 2008, 149).[1]

While body parts, cells, and tissue have become commodities, donors and sellers do not generally profit from the investment in tissue, which can have enormous potential biovalue as genetic material that can be patented (Dickenson 2008). It is the patent line that carries the value, when "human biomaterials extracted from the body enter into research and commerce as objects" (Dickenson 2007, 5). The global "'body shopping' industry" includes private umbilical cord blood banks and fertility clinics that offer in vitro fertilization (IVF) (Dickenson 2008, viii). For example, high numbers of in vitro clinics in Spain regularly recruit and pay young, fertile women as donors from Eastern Europe, including Poland, Lithuania, Latvia, and Estonia. The women travel to Southern European IVF clinics to have their eggs harvested, which are then sold to women from Germany, Italy, and the United States in a global market of "baby-making" (1). Egg markets in Eastern Europe continue the uneven transnational economies of domestic, sexual, and maternal labor (see Cooper 2008, 149). Genetic material that promises desirable traits, such as beauty and talent, increases value and price. Market dynamics more than eugenicist nation-states influence genetic manipulation.

In the first decade of the twenty-first century, several films articulated dystopian visions of reproductive labor in the context of biotechnology. Its advances made organ harvesting and cloning possible. *Dirty Pretty Things* (UK; Stephen Frears, 2002), *Children of Men* (United States, UK, Japan; Alfonso Cuarón, 2006), and *Never Let Me Go* (UK, United States; Mark Romanek, 2010), all set in Great Britain, tell harrowing tales of harvested organs, global infertility, and bioengineered clones. The films reflect an awareness about biopolitics, defined as "the administration and regulation of life processes on the level of populations," which includes the legislation of biomedical advances and processes (Lemke 2011, 4). They move beyond such abstractions by showing how biotechnological practices rely on and reproduce economic disparities based on intersecting discrimination in contexts of class, gender, race, ethnicity, and national belonging. Their narratives, set among migrants and refugees, include female main characters and feminize their male counterparts. Racism in the context of biopolitics, according to Thomas Lemke, organizes "a dynamic relation between the life of one person and the death of another," such that one person's health directly affects another's decline (42). The three films address the spectator's sensory response to the violation of corporeal integrity, the loss of reproductive capability, and slow death as a consequence of organ harvesting.

At the same time, the films differ in their implicit economic, political, or humanist approach toward biotechnology. Their diverse positions result from the various ways in which they imagine the status of women's reproductive labor. In other words, films either idealize women's purported natural ability of childbirth to discredit technological alternatives or situate the current forms of women's reproductive labor, such as donation, surrogacy, and giving birth, in the long history of women's care work, including its outsourcing to women of color, female migrants, and those in the Global South. The films' differences, this chapter suggests, determine not only whether a film articulates a feminist position or not but also whether a response to biotechnology can have any critical force at all, since technological advances have already fundamentally reconfigured the relationship between nature and culture, biology and technology. Thus, a humanist attitude that relies on the notion of indivisible life denies the consequences of biotechnological advances. An approach that mobilizes an allegory of natural womanhood relies on an anachronistic understanding of life in general and gender in particular.

Despite the fact that feminist theory is poised to parse out the intersecting forms of discrimination that manifest themselves in the exploitation in biomarkets, feminism in general, including filmmaking, has not fundamentally revised its paradigms about reproductive labor in response to biotechnology—with the exception of the specialized scholars on whose work this chapter relies. Biotechnology operates along the gendered, ethnicized, and racialized economies of privilege and exploitation among Eastern and Western Europeans and between the latter and the Global South. However, the influence of biotechnology has also transformed the genre of science fiction. Instead of narratives cast in the future, the films in this chapter blur past, present, and future in dystopian visions of a future that has already arrived.

With a range of depictions, from crude operations extracting organs from living subjects in hotel rooms to advanced technologies of human cloning, these films reflect Ernst Bloch's notion of the "simultaneity of the nonsimultaneous." Individually and collectively, they depict the contemporaneity of extreme poverty, which reduces subjects to their bodies as their only economic resource, and the high-tech possibilities of cloning and organ transplanting. The technical and economic disparities turn subjects in the Global South and those financially marginalized within Europe, particularly women from Eastern Europe, into raw material for tissue, eggs, and babies. In order to foreground this dynamic, however, all three films collapse the global economy into the national setting of Great Britain, where they stage encounters between the different actors on the biomarket: those who donate and sell organs, those who receive and purchase them, and those who invest in and profit from the transactions.

Two strands of pertinent scholarship frame the topic. The first understanding of biopolitics concentrates on the nation-state's governing of populations. Michel Foucault initiated this approach with his foundational lectures originally delivered in 1978–79 (2008); Giorgio Agamben transformed it into his notion of "bare life" (1998); Melinda Cooper integrated it into an account of a biopolitical capitalism (2008); and finally, Thomas Lemke situated it in a broader history of philosophy, politics, theory, and science (2011). In these theoretical accounts, women's reproductive labor is curiously absent. Therefore, the second area consists of the substantive and far-ranging interdisciplinary feminist scholarship on biotechnology's effects on biology, reproduction, and kinship in the national and global contexts of race and gender. This research pays particular attention to the effects of biotechnological practices on gendered and racialized labor in the setting of economic inequality. Philosophers such as Donna Dickenson (2007, 2008) probe the ethical dimensions of biotechnology; medical anthropologists such as Sarah Franklin (2003) analyze how biotechnology transforms culture, including labor, kinship, and temporality; physicians such as Sayantani DasGupta (2010) focus on the impact on reproductive health, especially on women in the Global South; and legal scholars such as Michele Goodwin (2006) scrutinize the structural racism that organizes organ donations in the United States.

Foucault (2008) situates the emergence of biopolitics in liberal and neoliberal forms of government, which cast individual subjects, for example, migrants, as entrepreneurs. He notes that the transformation of sovereign power into biopower creates a racist discourse based on biology, for which disciplines such as statistics, demography, and epidemiology provide the tools to abstract life from its physical bearers. As the modern form of exercising power, biopolitics privileges the market, which interpellates the subject as *Homo economicus*, "an entrepreneur of himself" (226). This theoretical language sheds light on women in the Global South who sell their kidneys on the biomarket, even though Foucault ignores gender and women's labor in the reproduction of life.

Lemke's much longer historical perspective situates the 1970s as a moment when biopolitics emerged as a new form of governmentality and when its meaning changed as a result of the decade's "spectacular biotechnological innovations" (2011, 61). Those innovations included "the diagnosis of fetuses" as "part of prenatal care, and new reproductive technologies such as in-vitro fertilization" (26). In contrast to Foucault's and Agamben's attention to biopolitical power as a form of state control, Lemke is more concerned with nation-states granting decision making regarding life and its value to scientific and commercial interests (61).

The possibility of detaching the reproduction of life from a biologically female body would seem to transcend the need for a sexual division of labor and allow for a postgender utopia, as some second-wave feminists had hoped. In that regard, the works of Shulamith Firestone and Gena Corea represent the two opposing strands in feminist theory. In her book *The Dialectic of Sex: The Case for Feminist Revolution* ([1970] 2003), Firestone envisions the potential of reproductive technologies to liberate women from the burden of reproduction. In contrast, Corea's *The Mother Machine: Reproductive Technologies from Artificial Insemination to Artificial Wombs* (1985) views biomedical science as continuing patriarchal medicine's control over women's bodies.

Twenty-first-century feminist scholars highlight the continuity of reproductive labor from domestic and care work to those activities labeled "donation" (of eggs, tissue, and organs) in their research on organ harvesting, surrogacy, and assisted reproductive technology. They also emphasize the persistence and increase of racialization and ethnicization of reproductive labor as women of the Global South, Latino and African American women in the United States, and Eastern European women become raw material for eggs, tissue, and organs, as well as wombs for surrogate pregnancies. Thus, instead of releasing all women from reproductive labor, as Firestone had hoped, biotechnology carries the promise of liberating those women who have the economic means to purchase eggs, tissue, and organs or outsource pregnancy as a service. Biotechnologies turn the bodies of those who are desperate to sell body parts and biological services into raw materials.

The biomarket obscures its economic relations through a gift discourse. This occurs on a continuum, from blood and kidney donations to an international black market of organs, eggs, and surrogacy. The fact that subjects do not legally own their bodies, including extracted tissue, increases the pressure to donate. The pervasive evocation of altruism and help allows the biotechnological industry to "camouflage" its exploitation of so-called donors and ignore their health risks (Dickenson 2008, 42).[2] Richard Titmuss ([1970] 1997) conducted a sociological study of the gift relationship, arguing that the blood donation system in Great Britain was superior to that in the United States because it was not tied to monetary transactions. His validation of altruism shaped the discourse of blood and organ donation globally.[3] International regulations have lagged behind the global market of bioproducts, resulting in criminal organ trafficking and "transplant tourism," as laws differ significantly within Europe (Dickenson 2008, 9).[4] Dickenson's claim that "*any* form of tissue sale is in a sense exploitative, *whatever price is offered for it*," defines a humanist position that emphasizes the biological integrity of the human body tout court (11, italics in the original).

Whereas Foucault frames abstract racialized biopolitics in the context of the nation-state and Dickenson argues against tissue sale in absolute terms in the name of humanist ethics, Goodwin makes the case for a hybrid biomarket that would include donation and commodification. She suggests that the pressure on gifting creates the black market and that donations cannot fulfill the need for organs. She criticizes Titmuss's validation of the gift economy and the practice of organ donation and transplants for their implicit racist assumptions, an aspect of his work that bioethicists had previously ignored. Goodwin demonstrates that African Americans are more likely to donate and whites more likely to receive organs, while African Americans wait longer for organs, such as kidneys, and have the highest death rates during the waiting period (2006, 5). While Goodwin acknowledges the inherent ethical value in "altruistic procurement," she considers it inadequate because it does not fulfill the growing need, and thus black markets become an open secret (6). In contrast to other scholars' embrace of Titmuss's positive assessment of the gift relationship, she reveals that he opposed a market system for blood donation because it would attract "skid row" donors, who were often "negro," because commercial banks were located in "Negro and Ghetto areas," as she quotes from his book (7). Goodwin argues that Titmuss was concerned about the danger of infecting the blood supply for whites based on the assumption that "blood would flow *only* from Blacks to Whites" (8, italics in the original). While Goodwin acknowledges the dangers of an unregulated market, she emphasizes that altruism alone cannot fulfill the demand for organs. Thus, she advocates for a hybrid system that would include a partial commercial market regulated by government agencies or health care institutions (8).

The gift discourse in biotechnology continues the traditional expectation of altruism not only for African Americans but also particularly for women, especially regarding the donation of eggs for those affected by infertility and of umbilical cord blood for the future of their babies. The underlying ideology of care enables profits for private companies. The view of childbirth as nature instead of labor turns surrogate mothers into—in the words of Dickenson—a "biological *lumpenproletariat*" (2007, 54, italics in the original). Even though ovarian stimulation and egg extraction are not natural processes, the biotechnological market portrays providing egg and tissue as simple biology to drive down the price (56).

Dickenson links biotechnology's treatment of bodies as "open-access" to Carole Pateman's understanding of women's role in the marriage contract (2008, 164; see also chapter 1). She points out that the commodification of human body parts becomes visible when the biotechnological industry's projection of selflessness views the bodies of men as objects in order to turn them into donors of organs as well (165). Consequently, the films feminize reproductive labor but detach it from the female body except when concerned with giving birth. In other words, in both *Dirty Pretty Things* and *Never Let Me Go* organ harvesting, donation, and cloning concern female and male characters who are refugees, undocumented migrants, and clones. All three films demonstrate how bodies collapse raw material, labor power, and capital, expanding Dickenson's contention that biotechnology turns the body into capital (151).

The speculation that inheres in investments and developments of genetic material, for example, in patent lines, emphasizes futurity and therefore potentially transforms the perception of temporality. Scientists can develop stem cells taken from umbilical cord blood into other forms of tissue (Dickenson 2008, 44). Depositors of cord blood in private accounts can retain control of it for the future to remake a part of the body, which allows them to live "in a double biological time" (Waldby and Mitchell 2006, 125). As the different moments in the reproductive process become interchangeable, the technical innovations "collapse the chronicity of genealogical time" (Cooper 2008, 133). This speculative reinvention of the future, according to Cooper, coincides with the end of industrial production (11). She argues that such "speculation at the very core of production" effaces "the boundaries between the spheres of production and reproduction, labor and life, the market and living tissues" (10, 9). Film, as a spatiotemporal medium, has the ability to capture such a transformation of temporality through pacing created by editing and the soundtrack.

Dystopia as the preferred mode for narrating reproductive labor in the age of biotechnology captures speculative futurity. This differs from science fiction that depicts future technologies relying on a linear time line.[5] The three dystopian narratives do not simply take place in the future. Instead, they mark a transformation of temporality through mise-en-scène, on the one hand, and pacing and camera work, on the other. The cinematic vision of time differs from the understanding of the past as distinct from the present, which can be recuperated as memory and history, for example, in the heritage cinema of industrial labor (discussed in chapter 3). The ambiguity of time—through the meshing of past, present, and future—in the three films also derives from the dystopian impetus. The narratives comment on and exaggerate contemporary societal issues and imply a critical stance. By estranging their references from the representation of a recognizable and coherent present-day reality, however, their criticism becomes ambiguous and invites conflicting interpretations.[6]

Camera work comes to the fore, as reproductive labor appears to be invisible. The three films lack the increasing speed of the industrial heritage cinema or the attention to gestures of the films about care work and domestic labor. Instead, cinematic strategies include the use of a handheld camera with disorienting close-ups in *Dirty Pretty Things*, a technique that oscillates between focusing on foreground and background in *Children of Men*, and the use of extreme long takes in *Never Let Me Go*.

When films advance a humanist critique against the supposed threats of biotechnology and insist on the integrity of the human subject, they run the danger of importing an essentialist understanding of nature, including of gender and biological reproduction. To different degrees, the films reflect the struggle to depict the processes of bioeconomies and biotechnologies in their global mapping. *Children of Men* casts natural childbirth as the only and lost way of reproducing life, and *Never Let Me Go* emphasizes humans as indivisible wholes. They imagine an invisible state that harnesses women into their roles as bearers of the nation through a eugenicist discourse. In other words, dystopia as mode of critique implies the lost ideal of a humanity made up by indivisible subjects, a notion that relies on a biological understanding of gender and race. While all three films question instrumentalization, fragmentation, and monetarization of the individual body and its parts as unethical, they differ in the way they cast women's reproductive labor. The films either foreground the continuing economy of classed, gendered, and racialized reproductive labor or advance a humanist critique that imports traditional values in the form of naturalized heroic masculinity, female care, and a white nation.

The Underground Economy of Organ Harvesting

When Stephen Frears made *Dirty Pretty Things* in 2002, he had already established a career based on important gay and multicultural films from the mid-1980s onward, such as *My Beautiful Laundrette* (UK, 1985), *Prick Up Your Ears* (UK, 1987), and *Sammy and Rosie Get Laid* (UK, 1987). Throughout the twenty-first century he continued with globally successful British films, including *The Queen* (UK, United States, France, Italy, 2006), *Philomena* (UK, United States, France, 2013), and *Florence Foster Jenkins* (UK, 2016). In these latter films, established actresses Helen Mirren, Judi Dench, and Meryl Streep perform older, strong, main female characters. *Dirty Pretty Things* sits in between Frears's earlier explicitly political and his later, more mainstream films.

Dirty Pretty Things tells the story of a group of migrants, refugees, and people of color employed at the Baltic Hotel in London and circulating in the overlapping economies of service work and illegal organ trade. The hotel's night porter, Okwe, originally a physician from Nigeria, works as a minicab driver during the day and as a night porter at the hotel. He also rents a couch from Senay, who works at the hotel as part of the cleaning crew. Since Senay is a refugee from Turkey, it is illegal for her to sublet, and when immigration officers find out, she loses her job at the hotel. She begins working at a sweatshop, where her boss sexually harasses her. One night Okwe discovers a human heart clogging up a toilet in a guest room, part of the black market of human body parts that the hotel manager, Señor Juan, is running. When Senay intends to sell her kidney in exchange for a counterfeit passport, Señor Juan forces her to have sex with him and then blackmails Okwe to operate on Senay. After Señor Juan gives Okwe two counterfeit passports, Okwe drugs him and removes his kidney instead of Senay's. Subsequently, Okwe, Senay, and the prostitute Juliette meet a businessman in the hotel's parking garage to receive cash for the kidney. In the final scene, Senay leaves for New York City, and Okwe returns to his daughter in Nigeria.

The dark film melodramatically depicts the intersecting lives of its characters in the margins of society, with the hotel as a cover for the underground economy. The illicit trades include the employment of undocumented migrants, prostitution, and organ harvesting in exchange for counterfeit passports. The hotel captures the decaying postcolonial empire with the deteriorating old splendor of velour carpets, a grand central staircase, and porters in red uniforms. *Dirty Pretty Things*' "geopolitical space" is the multicultural "European global cityscape" (Rodriguez Ortega 2011, 21), populated by those whose political and social abandonment reduces them to their biological corporeality (Wills 2007, 118). While Okwe and Senay's Pakistani boss at the sweatshop hail from the former British colonies, the cast of characters also includes those from the New Europe, such as Señor Juan as the corrupt and drunk Spanish hotel manager, and adjacent countries, with Senay as Turkish refugee.

As the first feature-length narrative film with widespread distribution that explores the topic of organ harvesting, *Dirty Pretty Things* departs from traditional migration films that present treacherous journeys. The surprise ending, when Okwe, Juliette, and Senay turn the tables on Señor Juan, subverts expectations for minority cinema, which tends to integrate melodrama with social realism. Up to the moment when Senay jumps off the improvised operation table in the hotel room, we are to believe that the film will continue its melodramatic downward spiral. By slowly uncovering the horror of organ harvesting and the diminishing possibilities for dignified labor for Senay, *Dirty Pretty Things* reveals how the limited access to work increasingly reduces refugees and women of color to their bodies in cleaning, prostitution, and organ donating.

The film's success relies on the integration of generic conventions of melodrama, thriller, horror, and mystery to offer a critique of the combination of Europe's internal mobility and external closed borders that force migrants from outside of Europe into the underground (see also Rodriguez Ortega 2011, 23). Selling their organs constitutes the means through which the undocumented migrants access cosmopolitan European identities. The Spanish émigré, as organizer of the illegal body-trafficking business, represents the mobility of Europeans within the EU.

Dirty Pretty Things condenses the space of the global bioeconomy and focalizes the economic differences in London instead of mapping the transnational circulation of cells, organs, and surrogate pregnancies. Biocapitalism allows companies to take advantage of global mobility, for example, in research hospitals in India, where private firms conduct studies for Western pharmaceuticals by benefiting from the low labor cost and the country's genetic diversity. The film heightens the dramatic conflict by collapsing the distance and staging confrontations between those who normally do not encounter each other. The latter is the case when an Eastern European donor leaves her eggs in Spain for a German couple or when an American company arranges for a surrogate in India to carry a baby for an Israeli gay couple.

At the film's denouement, in its penultimate scene, when Okwe, Juliette, and Senay deliver Señor Juan's kidney to a nondescript white businessman in the parking garage of the hotel, Okwe's speech instructs the buyer as much as the audience. When the man asks Okwe who they are, he answers, "Because we are the people that you do not see. We are the ones who drive your cabs. We clean your rooms. And suck your cocks." He captures the continuity from service labor to organ harvesting. The "invisibility" results from the lack of recognition by those who avail themselves of service labor without registering those who perform it.

The film aligns spectators with Okwe's perspective by endowing him simultaneously with the body of the undocumented migrant and the superior gaze of the medical doctor. The audience shares his shock and outrage about the black market's horrific hygiene conditions and its "scandalous economics," to use Aida Hozić and Jacqui True's (2016) term. The film captures the sleep-deprived daze of the low-wage earner who holds several jobs. Okwe's constant exhaustion reinforces his position in the margins of society in an underground economy. He solves crises among those without access to doctors and hospitals because of their undocumented status. Okwe is constantly working, including in the domestic sphere. The film grants no release to the spectator, as neither the biological rhythm of day and night nor that of work and leisure structures the film. His overextension positions him in the blurry reality of the illegal zone where undocumented migration, underground labor, organ trafficking, and prostitution are located. As a physician, Okwe embraces an ethical imperative. The film criticizes the economic dynamics of the black market and the restriction on asylum and migration but offers the promise of medical professionalism.

The biomarket redefines the "extra-national subject" as a collection of organs (Lai 2010, 69). Scholars view the characters in *Dirty Pretty Things* as "dispensable to the state and 'unworthy' of its protection," reflecting Agamben's notion of "the figure of bare life" (Sparling 2014, 162). Larissa Lai, for example, explains that Okwe "belongs not to what Agamben calls *bios*, the life of the citizen, but to *zoe*, bare life" (2010, 71, italics in the original). She argues that the state exerts its biopower through regulatory controls, including birth certificates, death certificates, and passports (69). Yet such readings overlook the particularity of women, based on their historic association with reproduction, the role of their embodiment, and the legacy of sexual exploitation of those in vulnerable economic positions.

Frears's film, however, emphasizes the significance of gender by narrativizing the continuities of gendered labor and violence against women. When Senay works in a sweatshop, her boss uses her lack of access to legal protection and her economic dependence to abuse her sexually. The second time he does so, she runs away. When she returns to the hotel to sell her kidney, Señor Juan forces her to have sex with him in order to acquire the counterfeit passport. The film depicts the limitations of choices for undocumented migrant female workers, from domestic and sexual labor to selling body parts.

Senay's gendered corporeality has led some scholars to focus particularly on the visual representation of her body. Jenny Wills poses a variation of the central question in feminist film studies, that of women's "to-be-looked-at-ness" (Mulvey 1988, 62), namely, whether the "cinematography perpetuates the fragmentation and corporeality of the illegal alien body" (Wills 2007, 116). Wills discusses the film's excessive focus on Senay's eyes at the expense of her hands and concludes that the representation of Senay reproduces the emphasis on her body. Wills accuses the film of perpetuating Western ideologies that render female migrants silent but foreground their image on-screen (119). She points out that Senay's "employment patterns" are "mundane, uncreative, and silent," and her hands "remain unseen," even though her jobs rely on repetitive movements (119–120). Yet Frears's refusal to show Senay in the act of working underscores his political point: her organs have greater value on the biomarket in enabling her future than inheres in her labor power in illegal, low-wage jobs.

Therefore, Senay's decision to sell her kidney emerges as a rational choice, despite the fact that the film creates some ambivalence around her with scenes of her dancing and drinking in her apartment, stealing a fur coat from the sweatshop, and not being willing to sleep at a mortuary. In short, while the film endows her with some attributes of immaturity, hysteria, and irrationality, the narrative presents the selling of her kidney as her only and economically sound decision. Senay does not articulate it in those terms; instead, she expresses the reduction to her body by reclaiming it when she dances in the kitchen. The film stages the limits of the political critique against outsourcing pregnancies or selling organs, which comes up against the rational choice of an individual woman on the biomarket for whom leasing out her womb or selling her kidney can be an investment in, for example, the future of her other children. In contrast to reports that cast a horrified or moralizing gaze on donors and recipients, *Dirty Pretty Things* exposes the economic imperatives that fuel the black market while neither condemning the organ donors nor portraying them as absolute victims.

The film also feminizes Okwe, reflecting Dickenson's claim that "we all have female bodies now" because all bodies may be harvested (2008, 163). We watch him performing domestic labor repeatedly as he shops, cooks, and irons. But in contrast to Dickenson's rhetorical claim, Frears's film foregrounds that labor, biotechnology, and social context might feminize male migrants—and not all men—but that the sexualization of women of color occurs on a historical range of physical exploitation (163). As sexual assault remains the primary danger for Senay, the film emphasizes the history of violating bodies of women of color. By moving from her boss's coerced fellatio to Señor Juan's rape as "exchange" for a passport in addition to her kidney, the film implies a continuum from sexual attack to organ harvesting as forms of violating the female body.[7]

In sum, *Dirty Pretty Things* depicts the way that biotechnology has transformed the understanding of reproductive labor and the body, but also how sexualization of women persists in a biomarket that continues traditions of gendered and racialized exploitation. Compressing time and space, the workers of the Global South populate the postcolonial metropolis of the former empire. The continuum of female labor from cleaning, working in sweatshops, and prostitution to organ donating intersects with the gamut of sexual violence, rape, and harvesting of body parts.

Dystopian Motherhood

Children of Men shares *Dirty Pretty Things*' emphasis on biopolitics at the intersection of reproductive labor, migration flows, and population controls by positing a crisis of biological reproduction. It also takes place in London, in the year 2027, after all children have mysteriously died and a pandemic has rendered women infertile. The film's main character, Theo Faron, a disillusioned drunk, navigates the rundown city, littered with trash, populated by militarized police, and bombarded by public-service announcements against terrorists and refugees. Theo's former wife, Julian, works for an activist group called the Fishes. She enlists him to help get Kee, a pregnant "fugee" woman of African descent, to safety. Resistance fighter Luke orders Julian to be killed to try to foment an uprising around the soon-to-be-born only child in the world. Theo flees with Kee and a midwife named Miriam to reach the mysterious ship, *The Tomorrow*, which belongs to an organization called the Human Project. Kee gives birth to a girl in the Bexhill refugee camp and names her Dylan after Theo and Julian's deceased child. During an ongoing fight between soldiers and Luke's armed resistance group, Theo gets Kee and Dylan to safety. He dies in a boat on the open sea while the ship of the Human Project appears in the mist.

From the outset, the film has garnered much scholarly attention. The inclusion of a short discussion by Slavoj Žižek as extra material on the DVD frames the film in a theoretical context. The strands of scholarship that attend to the intertwined topics of biopolitics, race, gender, capitalism, and reproduction have arrived at different political conclusions about the film. They view it either as a progressive critique of the neoliberal embedding of biopolitics in a stratified society or as reiterating gendered and racialized stereotypes. The divergence of the political assessment of the film mirrors the split between the gender-blind discourse on biopolitics, on the one hand, and the substantive feminist scholarship on biotechnology's continuity of exploiting women of color's reproductive labor, on the other.

Scholars agree that in his adaptation of P. D. James's novel, director Alfonso Cuarón increased the references to contemporary global politics and situated the narrative explicitly among a multicultural cast. He thus brought to the fore the racial dimension of biopolitics and did so through his signature use of the camera. Several scholars follow Žižek's discussion of the camera work, which recasts the relationship between individual characters and mise-en-scène as a way to connect late capitalism to biopolitics. Feminist discussions of the film depart from this positive assessment. Integrating a critique of reproductive technology, they emphasize the shift from James's original literary depiction of Julian as the pregnant woman to the introduction of Kee's character. These two readings, however, are not mutually exclusive.

In his brief discussion, Žižek applies the term "anamorphosis" to the film's camera work to suggest that it provides the film's "critique of late capitalism." The term refers to a distorted image, often in painting, that requires the spectator to occupy a specific vantage point or use a special device for the intended picture to come into view. In the most famous example, Hans Holbein the Younger's *The Ambassadors* (1533), a skull appears only when the picture is viewed from a particular angle. Historically, anamorphosis's inherent possibility of two different perceptions allowed it to disguise caricatures and erotic images. *Children of Men*'s "anamorphosis" enables the mutually exclusive readings of the film either as successful critique of racist biopolitics or as failure due to racial and gendered stereotypes.

The "restless" camera asserts autonomy and decouples itself from Theo's gaze, turning him into the object and showing us what he refuses to see, namely, "the dead, the poor" (Ogrodnik 2014, n.p.). Long takes and a mobile, seemingly handheld camera emphasize the mise-en-scène and create a tension between foreground and background (n.p.). In the film's first half, important objects appear in the background of the frame, and in the second half they move increasingly to the foreground (Chaudhary 2009, 80–81). Those iconic images include references to Abu Ghraib, foot-and-mouth disease, the Holocaust, Pink Floyd, Michelangelo's *David*, and Picasso's *Guernica*.

In this line of reasoning, mass infertility becomes the dystopian allegory for neoliberal capitalism. Consequently, Kirk Boyle (2009), for example, who understands *Children of Men* through the lens of Naomi Klein's notion of "disaster capitalism," claims that the capitalist world economy that defines the dystopian society causes the infertility. The visual critique of capitalism expands the understanding of biopolitics as the refugees personify Giorgio Agamben's notion of "bare life" (Celik 2015, 44). By juxtaposing images from Abu Ghraib, animal cruelty, Michelangelo, and his *Pietà*, the film asks spectators to consider the "relationship between valorizing the human body and subjecting it to torture" (Chaudhary 2009, 100). Posing these larger ethical questions, Zahid R. Chaudhary claims that the film proposes the end of the fiction of universality. He suggests that by moving from the original nuclear family of Theo, Julian, and their child, Dylan, a "triad of white man–white woman–white child," to the nonbiological kinship of "white man–black woman–black child," the film endows "the new African Eve" with "hope for humanity" (74, 75). He therefore proposes that Theo's death signifies the end of the "universal subject of history in the West" (75). Kee's female baby thus implies the end of "paternal futurity" and a future determined by women to determine the future (75).

Not all scholars, however, believe that the effect of the camera work is as politically progressive. Some accuse *Children of Men* of perpetuating the "worst reactionary tabloid nightmares" with an "ideological topology, which relies on the eugenicist belief that an excess of hybridity would lead to sterility" (Bacon and Dickman 2009, 147, 150). The film's "*megarealism*," through the use of the immersive "*ThereCam*," fetishizes its seeming presence in the diegesis, best illustrated by the "blood-splattered lens" (154, italics in the original). In postdigital Hollywood, such cinematic code intends to transport spectators into the diegesis. For example, Cuarón's close-ups of and proximity with a large and ferocious crowd of demonstrators, vaguely and incorrectly identified as Muslims, intensify their perceived threat instead of reflecting on the mediated stereotypes that circulate in the public sphere (155).

Feminist readings criticize the film for stereotypically fetishizing Kee as the sole fertile character who is otherwise marred by silence. Within the parameters of the narrative, as a refugee of color, Kee does not adhere to the national ideal for reproduction (Sparling 2014, 161). Her pregnancy gives her temporary leverage, but ultimately she is vulnerable to statelessness (163). Feminists accuse Cuarón of blaming the female body for the crisis of infertility, turning its barrenness into the sign of failure and prioritizing the future child at the expense of the mother (165–168).

The film echoes the feminist paradigm of the private as political through the use of the camera work, which suggests a relationship between the characters and the mise-en-scène beyond the latter functioning solely as backdrop. The cinematic strategy connects the politics of the nation-state to the somatic, reproductive, and intimate functions of bodies. It suggests that the infertility does not result from women's biology but from societal context, including the violent treatment of migrants, the deterioration of public space, the privatization of art, the lack of communication, the rampant advertising for consumerism, and the prevalence of violence, destruction, and aggression.

Nevertheless, the film falls short of its own progressive intentions by ignoring women's reproductive labor. In an iconographic scene, Kee reveals her pregnancy to Theo in a barn at the safe house. In a secret meeting, she stands surrounded by calves. After she comments on cows getting their "titties cut off" to fit the milking machine, she exposes herself and shows her pregnant belly. The film fetishizes "Kee's fertile body" and endows it with "a mytho-scientific significance" as the bearer of the future of the human race (Chaudhary 2009, 96, 97). Lighting, composition, and music frame her as transcendent, echoing the

FIGURE 6.1. *Children of Men* (Alfonso Cuarón, 2006)

notion of a virginal birth as the long take invokes the icon of the Virgin Mary. When Kee begins to unbutton her loose top, Theo panics because he assumes that she is offering herself to him sexually, and he moves toward her, asking her not to do so. The film sets up the expectation of sexuality but then offers pregnancy to the audience. The camera shoots Kee from behind so that we see Theo's reaction, which coincides with the musical onset of the soundtrack, John Tavener's "Fragments of a Prayer." As the religious music elevates the scene, a reverse shot frames Kee beginning from the ground, moving upward through the calves, visually repeating the sense of awe that the music has introduced. Kee covers her breasts in a moment of stillness that reinforces the quality of a religious icon, perfectly framed in a medium long shot. The film reiterates the sense of religious wonder when Theo mutters "Jesus Christ" and Luke murmurs "miracle."

The religious references to virginal conception displace reproductive labor, which is absent in the scene of Kee giving birth when Theo and Kee are staying in a dirty room with a dingy mattress in the Bexhill refugee camp (see also Celik 2015, 43). The sequence shares the aural composition with the "revelation" in the barn. It begins without musical soundtrack, and Tavener's "Fragments of a Prayer" comes to mark the moment of transcendence when the infant is born. The narrative emphasizes Theo's conversion: whereas he used to drink liquor, he now uses it to disinfect his hands. The uncomplicated birth after years without knowledge about the process implies that it is a natural occurrence with no work involved. The absence of Kee's labor (including also her sex work, as scholars unanimously call her a prostitute) shapes the narrative and its politics. It mirrors the lack of attention to reproductive labor in the theories of biopolitics, from Foucault to Agamben, that focus on the nation-state.

Feminist scholars therefore accuse Cuarón's film of enacting "the same sort of discursive violence against Third World women that it critiques on a wider scale" and argue that the film reflects the "infertility anxiety" prompted by falling birthrates in the West (DasGupta 2010, 179; see also Celik 2015, 29). Kee's reproductive and symbolic role redefines her as a "walking womb" without history (DasGupta 2010, 187). Because Theo rescues Kee from Luke, who is also a person of color, DasGupta (2010, 190) points out that the film enacts Gayatri Spivak's (1988) paradigm of "white men saving brown women from brown men." DasGupta relates the film to the use of women from developing countries, particularly India, as gestational surrogates for infertile couples without according them agency (192). She suggests that the convention of omitting a surrogate mother's name from the child's birth certificate continues the history of poor women of color as wet nurses whose economic circumstances force them to leave behind their own children in order to care for those of white mothers (193). She explains how "phenotypic dissimilarity" deemphasizes the relation between surrogate mothers and the infants they deliver in order to create surrogacy as an identity that is fundamentally separate from the infant (195). As Kee names her baby Dylan after Julian and Theo's lost male white child, she occupies the position of a surrogate mother.

These new forms of kinship reflect the way cloning has transformed gender and biology. Its creation of the sheep Dolly in 1996 as "a newly viable form of genetic capital" moved the means of production into a laboratory technique (Franklin 2003, 96, 98). Sarah Franklin describes how "nuclear transfer makes it possible for any animal, male or female, wild or domesticated or even extinct, to become a perpetual germ-line repository, a pure gene bank, because the gametes—the eggs and sperm—are no longer necessary to reproduction" (99). Such a process compresses "genealogical time" and offers "genetic purity, in perpetuity and under patent" (100). The patent protects the original creator as innovator, which distributes Dolly's maternity, as she is "multiply divisible" (102). By removing reproduction from the animal and patenting it, technology recalibrates biology (105–106).

The DVD extra material, entitled *Delivering a Baby the Framestore CFC Way*, celebrates the work of the company responsible for creating the "digital infant." The cinematic apparatus displaces women's reproductive labor, similar to the role of biotechnology in relation to the female body and its reproductive labor. The short documentary demonstrates the way in which the company CFC (Computer Film Company) computer-generated baby Dylan in Theo and Kee's live-action birthing scene. Computer generation "delivered the baby," appropriating the language of reproductive labor for the technological process. Through this short documentary, which replays the birthing scene, the expanded

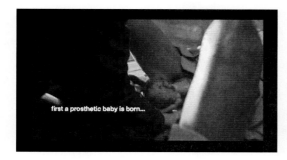

FIGURE 6.2. *Delivering a Baby the Framestore CFC Way.* Bonus materials. *Children of Men* (Alfonso Cuarón, 2006)

film text of *Children of Men* integrates Kee's natural process of giving birth with the technological process of virtual baby (re)production.

In the documentary, the sentence "first a prosthetic baby is born" appears on-screen written over the scene of Kee giving birth. The genre expectation of the intratext of the extra material would be to demystify the technological processes that create the filmic illusion. Instead, the short documentary celebrates the magical quality of technology. In contrast to when the action occurs in the plot, in the extra material the "Alleluia" from Tavener's "Fragments of a Prayer" accompanies the entire scene for its brief duration and with much higher volume. The music's crescendo occurs at the moment when the text on the screen informs us that the birth of the prosthetic baby occurs. As information about the computer generation fades in and out on top of the image of Kee, the short documentary mythologizes technological abilities, similar to biotechnology, and displaces women's reproductive labor. In conclusion, the film apparatus reproduces the structure of biotechnology, which denounces women's reproductive labor and replaces it with technology, celebrating its abilities to produce (virtual) life instead.

Anthropomorphizing Cloning

Never Let Me Go, also based on a novel, moves beyond organ transplants and infertility to narrate its dystopian vision from the perspective of a human clone. The book's author, Kazuo Ishiguro (2005), became famous with his 1988 novel, *The Remains of the Day*, which won the Man Booker Prize. He also won the Nobel Prize for Literature in 2017. Mark Romanek directed *Never Let Me Go*, and Alex Garland, author of *The Beach* (1997) and the screenplay of *28 Days Later* (UK; Danny Boyle, 2002), wrote the script. The film includes two of the most recognizable British actresses, Carey Mulligan and Keira Knightley, who acted together in *Pride & Prejudice* (UK, United States, France; Joe Wright, 2005). Mulligan is associated with other British films, such as *An Education* (UK, United States; Lone Scherfig, 2009), *Far from the Madding Crowd* (UK, United States; Thomas Vinterberg, 2015), and *Suffragette* (UK; Sarah Gavron, 2015), and Knightley acted in *Love Actually* (UK, United States, France; Richard Curtis, 2003) and *Bend It Like Beckham* (UK, Germany, United States; Gurinder Chadha, 2002), among others.

The film tells the story of three clones, Kathy, Ruth, and Tommy, who grew up in a boarding school in the English countryside called Hailsham. They are raised to donate their organs once they have come of age to humans who live to be one hundred. Kathy narrates in a melancholic voice-over, fondly remembering their childhood past and their youth and then recounting their slow decay. As young adults, they live with other clones in the cottages in the countryside, and Tommy and Ruth become a couple. Kathy decides to work as a carer and moves to London to accompany clones while they donate their organs and die slowly. She meets Ruth in a hospital after her second donation, and when the three friends reunite, Ruth confesses that she seduced Tommy because she was jealous of his and Kathy's love. Kathy and Tommy remember that they had heard a rumor that if a couple could demonstrate their mutual love, they would escape their fate as donors. In an attempt to do so, they take art pieces Tommy created at Hailsham to their former headmistress, who explains that they cannot escape their fate. Ruth dies, and Kathy watches Tommy undergo his last operation.

Kathy's work looks indistinguishable from her leisure activities. The film opens with a medium long shot of Kathy from behind looking into a hospital's operating room. After a cut, a reverse medium shot of Kathy allows us to see doctors and nurses reflected in the glass that mirrors the action inside where the professionals work. Kathy watches and remembers. Her memory takes her

FIGURE 6.3. *Never Let Me Go* (Mark Romanek, 2010)

back to Hailsham. Later, when she works as a carer, she sits beside the beds of the donors and reads a book, something she does throughout the entire film. As society has outsourced medical risks to the clones, they constitute a surplus and need not perform productive labor. Thus, Kathy's work looks like leisure activities in her free time.

The narrative claims that the bioeconomy reflects the economic disparity of class, but visually the film associates the clones with a middle class simultaneously defined as white. They sit around watching television, eating, reading, and going for walks. When they live together in the cottages, they take a trip to town to look for the person from whom Ruth has been cloned. Ruth becomes upset because she knows that a woman who looks like her and who works in a travel agency is not her original. She yells at her friends: "We all know it, we just never say it. We are modeled on trash. Junkies, prostitutes, winos, tramps. Convicts, maybe, as long as they aren't psychos." The film suggests that a biotechnologically advanced society would continue the economic disparity that reduces those with limited access to decent work to give blood, tissue, and organs or carry babies. Despite Ruth's outburst, which articulates the discriminatory undergirding of the economy of organ harvesting, *Never Let Me Go* only includes white characters with middle-class accoutrements. The boarding school, the British countryside, the cottages, and the fish-and-chips shops in the seaside village make up a familiar national imaginary. The clones' anthropomorphic embodiment serves as a humanist response to biotechnology and mobilizes English heritage iconography. The nation appears as visual culture of idealized images of Great Britain, without references to politics or economics beyond the limited purview of the clones. The mise-en-scène of the boarding school, with school uniforms, games, and songs, and the countryside of a small town on the seaside evoke nostalgic England.

The notion of universal values mobilized for an antibiotechnological discourse brings with it the clones' embodied middle-class whiteness—even though they are supposedly modeled on those in the economic margins of society. Electronic monitoring devices at cottages hint at an absent state without references to a government or a company with a financial interest. The Donor Company has no location or representatives. An unnamed character delivers vegetables to the cottages, and Kathy informs him when she wants to become a carer, but that is the extent of his role.[8] The disciplinarian boarding school, the massive program, and the absence of financial processes align biotechnology with an invisible state that advances a eugenicist program.

While the characters articulate an economic critique of the classist biomarket, the casting skirts the issues of how class in Great Britain is also racialized and ethnicized. The film depicts the nation through a British iconography but does not investigate the loosely implied connection among the state, biopolitics, technology, and eugenics. *Never Let Me Go* shows the continuation of feminized labor from caretaking of the sick to the dystopian fantasy of cloned carers and donors. The figure of Kathy as simultaneous clone and caretaker advances a dystopian vision of care work in the age of biotechnology. When the film opens, Kathy's voice-over accompanies a medium close-up of her: "I've been a carer for nine years. Carers and donors have achieved so much. That said, we aren't machines. In the end, it wears you down. I suppose that's why I now spend most of my time not looking forwards but looking back, to the cottages and Hailsham, and what happened there." This opening monologue could have been spoken by a nurse in the contemporary health-care system who takes care of donors. The familiar vocabulary remains vague regarding when the narrative takes place. Her reflections resignify the contemporary gift economy in an imaginary society, which suggests a continuity from contemporary caretaking professions to the dystopian fantasy of clones created solely as organ banks. The film's temporal setting reinforces the ambivalence about past, present, and future. It begins in the early to mid-1990s and looks back first to 1978 (Hailsham) and then to 1985 (the cottages). Each moment appears outdated, evoking Bloch's notion of simultaneity of nonsynchronism.

In contrast to films that accompany mechanical labor with rhythmic music and industrial labor with a metallic soundscape, *Never Let Me Go*'s elegiac soundtrack expands the sense of time. The 2.35:1 aspect ratio, the current wide-screen standard historically used by CinemaScope, and the slow editing reinforce the pace, which captures the sense of expansive time. Repeated shots of inanimate objects seem to arrest the forward movement of chronology and evoke the outdated aesthetics of still lives. For example, an out-of-focus close-up of papers with handwritten notes next to a glass of pens in darkish colors is reminiscent of paintings, while the pages' subtle and slow rustle in the wind evokes early cinema.

The film's temporality criticizes the fantasies of limitless futurity that biotechnology promises. The fact that all the clones are of one generation allegorizes the collapse of genealogical time. *Never Let Me Go*'s editing, pacing, and soundtrack create a temporality that moves in the opposite direction of Cooper's (2008) claims that the endless possibilities of biotechnology and neoliberal capitalism produce a sense of limitless futurity. Because the clones are going to die, the film revisits the past from a moment of anticipating Tommy's death until we arrive at the present, reflecting on the gradual vanishing of the clones' remaining lifetime. *Never Let Me Go* decelerates the experience of duration through its elegiac music, pensive voice-over, still lives, long takes, and slow-paced editing, in contrast to the speeding up of the music in the industrial and mechanical heritage cinema and contrapuntal soundtrack in the Italian thrillers that cast suspicion on migrant domestic workers. Contemporary political movements of slow film, food, and scholarship counter industrial and neoliberal temporality of speed (see Gorfinkel 2012b; Jaffe 2014; Koepnick 2014; Berg and Seeber 2016). *Never Let Me Go* evokes the emotional states of the clones, who move toward expiration despite their desperate desire to extend their lifetime, and counters biotechnology's supposed potential of limitless futurity.

Never Let Me Go takes the promise of biotechnology at its face value and presents it as a conflict between the larger good—humans can live longer—and the sacrifice of individuals. Such a humanistic critique differs from Cooper's (2008) and Foucault's (2008) accounts of integrated biopolitics and neoliberalism, the feminist critique of biotechnology, as well as *Dirty Pretty Things* and *Children of Men*. In *Never Let Me Go* complete human bodies, not tissue engineering or biomedical experiments, represent reproductive technology. The biotechnological ability of cloning assumes the form of indivisible humans, not cells, organs, or genetic codes. In addition, while the narrative pivots on the question of whether clones have souls, Kathy and Tommy's love story and her melancholy subjectivity assert their humanity. If the technology exists to grow clones, so would the possibility to clone individual organs. The notion of human clones thus does not reflect a futuristic thinking but instead a failure to imagine already-existing technological possibilities. It falls back on the notion of the anthropomorphic, biologically complete body as the representational form of humanity in the profilmic world on the screen.

Never Let Me Go expresses the limitations of the cultural imagination of biotechnology. Its humanist vision avoids an economic critique, which only comes into view in the form of recycled toys that the children receive for their plastic tokens. Within the narrative, the fantasy that true love, a classic trope, could rescue the clones is an ideological fantasy. But Kathy and Tommy are in love. This identifies them as human beings with the ability to transcend their function for reproduction. The film's commentary on biotechnology eerily reflects Lemke's critique of Foucault's concept of biopolitics, namely, that it "remains bound to the notion of an integral body" (2011, 94). The film's conventional humanism portrays Kathy as authentically concerned about Ruth and Tommy beyond her mandated function as carer for donors. In order to make an ethical and humanist argument against the dangers of biotechnological development, the film imports caring femininity, a white nation with its cultural heritage, and an unseen eugenicist state, ignoring dynamics of class, race, globalization, and the biomarket. Such a humanist approach responds to biotechnology with melancholia for a lost past but does not imagine resistance in the present for a different future.

Conclusion

In sum, *Dirty Pretty Things*, *Children of Men*, and *Never Let Me Go* offer dystopias that lay bare the societal changes resulting from biotechnology. All three films refuse to depict the fragmentation of their characters' bodies by projecting physical integrity. They emphasize camera work but employ it in different ways. *Dirty Pretty Things* uses confusing close-ups to reveal a horrific subterranean reality; *Children of Men* relies on a tension between foreground and background to advance its political claim; and *Never Let Me Go* mobilizes long takes to counter biotechnology's boundless futurity.

Despite the fact that the films take on reproduction in the context of biopolitics and biotechnology, they are beholden to the imaginary of life and the body of the Fordist period. Class, gender, and race shape depictions of reproductive labor in the context of biotechnology. *Dirty Pretty Things* and *Children of Men* foreground the ways in which biopolitics harnesses class, race, and gender for reproductive labor. *Dirty Pretty Things* presents the continuum from service work to the "open-access" body for organ harvesting for women of color. The film clarifies that for those on the national and global economic margins, selling body parts can be a rational choice on the biomarket. *Children of Men* shares the emphasis on biopolitics, charting the state's attempt to capture and control population flows. Its religious iconography of an immaculate conception empties giving birth of its labor, presuming women's natural ability to reproduce. Instead, the DVD extra material celebrates computer-generated imaging. *Children of Men* and *Never Let Me Go* share the humanist approach in their criticism of biotechnology. Thus both films mobilize women's presumed inherent maternal nature.

Whereas *Dirty Pretty Things* and *Children of Men* situate biopolitics in a context of multicultural societies, *Never Let Me Go* imagines a racially pure Great Britain consisting of lush landscapes and an old-fashioned mise-en-scène in which biotechnology advances a eugenicist agenda. It shows the feminization of reproductive labor, but in order to make its humanist argument against bioengineering, it authenticates Kathy's care work as love for her friends. Her reproductive labor remains invisible as she sits reading books at bedsides, an anachronistic activity that defines cultured women.

Biotechnology has transformed the understanding of life, reproductive labor, and kinship, but it also continues the traditions of outsourcing care work to poor women of color, now on a global scale. To different degrees, the films critique, illustrate, or ignore these continuities. They do not investigate, however, how biotechnological processes allow companies and institutions to use patenting to make profit, and they do not link biopolitics and biotechnology to neoliberalism, as do Foucault (2008) and Cooper (2008), respectively. The dystopian nature of their narratives creates distance from the contemporary moment. The final chapter continues with examples of global art cinema, in this case, primarily from Greece, Portugal, and Spain, but also from Germany and the Netherlands. In their attempts to capture the invisible processes of financialization and pervasive debt, the films move beyond anthropomorphic embodiment and search for a new cinematic language in order to visualize the disappearance of work.

CHAPTER 7

Crisis Cinema

> I think time is against us.
> —Karolos Papoulias, Greek president (2005–2015),
> quoted in "The Greek Crisis"

> We can't yet confirm that this will be the full extent and length
> of the global financial crisis.
> —Angela Merkel, German chancellor (2005–), quoted in "Quotes"

> Solving a debt problem with more debt has not
> solved the underlying problem.
> —Alan Brazil, Goldman Sachs strategist,
> quoted in Stephen Foley, "Goldman's Memo"

After six chapters that discuss the presence of working women on twenty-first-century European screens, this final chapter turns to films about the 2008 economic crisis and its aftermath. The challenge to the European welfare states ruptured not only cinema's conventional depictions of labor but also coherent aesthetics across films that coalesced around the crisis and the resulting austerity. The financial crash created economic downturns, underemployment and unemployment, and national retrenchments. More importantly for cinematic representation, it compelled filmmakers to confront the question of how to imagine and represent the economy that exists in transnational virtual spaces, which the global financial crisis exposed. Such understanding in the wake of the eurocrisis radically decentered productive and reproductive labor as engines for social good. Processes of immaterial financialization came to the fore and posed a challenge for media that relies on visual representation.

Filmmakers responded with diverse strategies that this chapter subsumes under the term "weird." They reacted to the eurocrisis—a manifestation of the global financial downturn and the result of relations among the member states of the EU—with extreme, strange, and unusual films. Financialization, the selling of risk and debt, displaces productive and reproductive labor from its central function for the economy. In response, the filmic discourse about the aftereffects of the crisis includes strange or invisible work: labor appears as a ruse for violent patriarchs, occurs off-screen, or turns into a meaningless performance.

Crisis cinema embraces allegory and symbolism, magical realism and dance, absurdity and farce. In other words, films forcefully reject realism in favor of antimimetic styles that do not name the collapse of the vision of an integrated Europe directly. The heterogeneous filmic responses leave behind established conventions of social or socialist realism or genres such as melodrama, science fiction, thriller, and romantic comedy. Part of global art cinema, the films discussed in this chapter integrate diverse aesthetic features. "Weird" thus encompasses a range of aesthetic strategies, some with origins in high art, such as modern dance, others more closely related to art film, such as minimalism, and some that borrow from political discourse in the form of the farce or with roots in the folkloric, such as magical realism. Self-reflexively, the filmmakers have insisted on art's contributions to the public discourse about the financial meltdown. The diversely weird cinema provides insight into a fundamentally transformed understanding of the economy and of representation.

This chapter also demonstrates, however, that these films about the crisis do not share coherent gender politics. Such an observation does not undo the overarching argument that twenty-first-century European cinema advances an explicitly feminist engagement with women's work in the context of migration and the new economy. It does not propose a historical trajectory in which feminism comes to the fore at the beginning of the twenty-first century only for the 2008 crisis to stop its advancements in its tracks. The paradigm shift that this book charts from the twentieth-century cinematic representation of masculine physical labor in industrial settings to the twenty-first-century accounts of feminized work in precarious employment does not develop in a linear fashion to an endpoint when female characters embody neoliberal labor regimes.

The global financial crisis derailed this development in multiple ways. First, the crisis initially left men unemployed and shifted concern back to their roles as breadwinners when the early sectors affected by the downturn included construction and manufacturing. The attention to men's unemployment and economic insecurity sidelined feminist concerns regarding female employment on the European level (see the introduction). Second, the banking crisis highlighted a sector dominated by men and a masculine habitus. Third, as jobs became more scarce, work became elusive but simultaneously desperately desired. Fourth, as the downturn resulted from banks trading in risks and debts, Fordist labor did not promise a path out of the crisis. Subsequently, in austerity cinema, filmmakers have moved away from work as the economic motor. Instead, they have attempted to find a language to capture elusive financial processes. As such filmic discourse turned away from the topic of women and work, this chapter calls for retaining feminist pressure in moments of economic, political, and aesthetic transformation.

The term "Greek weird wave" responds to globally successful Greek art films that emerged at the height of the country's national crash and that exploded familiar forms of cinematic representation. The notion of "weird" extends to films from other European countries that attend to debt and austerity. If other chapters emphasize genres such as romantic comedy, thriller, science fiction, and documentary, this chapter focuses on the vernacular of the globally circulating art cinema from Greece, Spain, and Portugal, three of the hardest-hit countries, in addition to Ireland and Italy. Importantly, national film industries also produce an internal cinema that offers formulaic responses to the country's problems that take the form of popular genres, for example, Spanish comedies about the intercultural adventures of young men migrating to Germany in search of work. The chapter does not limit the weird wave to the countries in the grip of the eurocrisis. Instead, the representational strategy extends to depicting processes of financialization in German and Dutch films about managers and bankers as well.

The term "weird" traces to Greek director Yorgos Lanthimos's *Kynodontas* (*Dogtooth*, 2009). Despite scholarly controversies about the accuracy of the term, it links the new global art cinema to Greece's austerity. The chapter's treatment of the Greek weird wave provides historical context for the Mediterranean countries most severely affected by austerity. *Dogtooth*'s symbolic language does not refer to the crisis, despite the fact that it coincided with it. However, the film also serves as a case in point for the ambivalence vis-à-vis gender that the economic freefall brought forth: paradoxically, the film offers a trenchant critique of the violent structures that organize patriarchy and disavows women's agency through the return to the figure of the housewife.

The character of the housewife—who seems not to work—reappears as bourgeois status symbol in the Greek weird wave. In *Dogtooth*, this much-maligned character serves as an assault on patriarchy but indicates an antifeminist undercurrent. Attention to gender and work produces a reading that departs from film studies' general celebration of *Dogtooth* (e.g., Celik 2013) as an innovative symbolic commentary on patriarchal society in times of retrenchment.

The brief discussion of *Dogtooth* also serves as backdrop for a reading of Athina Rachel Tsangari's 2010 *Attenberg* (Greece). Sharing the aesthetic characteristics of the Greek weird wave, the film offers a subtle account of gendered biopolitics in times of austerity. Equally rejecting realism, it nevertheless echoes social science findings about women's increased workload as a result of the shrinking social welfare states and the latter's effect on declining health and rising death rates. The main characters, young women of the generation that came of age during the lack of opportunities, physically embody weirdness. Their strange gestural performances, when they contort their bodies in a choreographed walk toward the camera, emphasize the ways in which economic limitations affect people at experiential, intimate, and physical levels.

One of the most ambitious cinematic projects that responded to the eurocrisis, Miguel Gomes's epic six-hour Portuguese compilation *As mil e uma noites* (*Arabian Nights*; Portugal, France, Germany, Switzerland, 2015), espouses absurd narratives and magical realism. As a whole, it marginalizes women's work in its meandering collection of tales that combine a range of representational forms. Documentary footage and first-person narratives by unemployed workers, for example, from a shipyard, align masculine labor with national identity. The three volumes weave in and out of documentation of ethnographic studies of unemployment, costumed reenactments of *One Thousand and One Nights*, and Orientalist stagings of European bailout negotiations. The literary figure Scheherazade as icon for modernist storytelling symbolizes the role of the filmmaker-cum-artist as commentator on social relations. Even though she is threatened and exhausted, Scheherazade continues to invent stories and thus functions as a "revitalizing force that comes often from the 'peripheral' regions of Western culture," such as Latin America and Eastern Europe (Faris 1995, 164–165). By likening himself to the famous fictitious storyteller, Gomes accords artists the role of enabling survival. The radical combination of aesthetics, modes, and styles relates the abstract financial forces to their concrete manifestations in the lives of those affected by the eurocrisis. Focusing on one of the film's episodes that centers on a female professional, this chapter explains how it illuminates the ways in which financialization influences gendered sexual and social contracts globally and locally.

The global financial crisis catapulted the financial sector into the limelight. Its professions, in which white men dominate and a masculine habitus pervades, include only a limited number of women, who adapt to the ruthless accumulation of profit based on competition and risk-taking. Public debates about gender and the financial sector question whether higher numbers of female investment bankers and traders could have averted the financial crisis (Prügl 2016). Subsequently, films cast a critical gaze onto the profession of finance. Films such as the German *Zeit der Kannibalen* (*Age of Cannibals*; Johannes Naber, 2014) reflect on a masculinist work culture that demands of women that they simultaneously perform and denounce femininity. Similarly, the figure of the successful businesswoman appropriates the discourse of feminism. The film's farcical exaggeration presents a profession that produces and reproduces inequality to make a profit.

Departing from mimesis to capture the essence of the financial professions, Clara van Gool's 2015 project *Voices of Finance* (Netherlands, UK) turns to dance. In *Voices of Finance* world-renowned choreographers perform interviews with international bankers and traders. While seemingly differing from *Arabian Nights* (*Voices of Finance* runs thirty-five minutes, in contrast to *Arabian Nights*' six hours and twenty-one minutes), it shares the integration of otherwise radically incongruent discourses: modern dance and ethnographic interviews with workers from the financial sector.

As some of the films of the weird wave marginalize women's work, their representation contrasts to the findings of social scientists that women work more in paid and unpaid labor during economic downturns and when states reduce social services. Primarily female and feminist directors investigate the gendered effects of austerity, in contrast to the general trend in the twenty-first century of both male and female directors making films about women's work. For example, the main female character of Spanish filmmaker Isabel Coixet's 2013 *Ayer no termina nunca* (*Yesterday Never Ends*), called C., is unemployed and homeless. The male character accesses the mobility associated with transnational Europe, while C. remains trapped in a nation enveloped by the recession. The film traces the ways in which the effects of the national financial breakdown erode the intimate relations of a couple.

Crisis Case Study: Greek Weird Cinema

On Friday, April 23, 2010, Greek households watched as their prime minister, Yorgos Papandreou, announced on live television the magnitude of the country's debt crisis, the conditions of the EU bailout, its required structural reforms, and the upcoming austerity measures. On the same day, Lanthimos's absurd film *Dogtooth* premiered in London (Mademli 2015). *New York Times* film critic Anthony Oliver Scott (2010) imagined the conversation between two moviegoers after having watched the film: "'What was *that*?' 'I don't know. Weird.' 'Yeah.' [shudder]. 'Weird.'" The dialogue's recourse to the label "weird" would soon become "Weird Greek Cinema," or the operative term for this chapter, "Greek weird wave." Not long after, this coinage expanded to other Greek films that fit the description and then to a wave of art films, even though filmmakers repeatedly denied the existence of a movement (on global art cinema, see Galt and Schoonover 2010). "Are the brilliantly strange films of Yorgos Lanthimos and Athina Rachel Tsangari a product of Greece's economic turmoil?" asked Steve Rose in the *Guardian* (2011). The question initiated a reading of the art films coming out of Greece, Spain, and Portugal as parables for the eurocrisis.[1]

Film scholars, however, disagree about the term "weird." Some propose that it obscures the diversity among the films gathered under its heading. Others claim that the films do not address the financial crisis but instead reveal deeper concerns about values (Chalkou 2012, 245; Papadimitriou 2014, 2). A third group connects the "creative manifestations" of "crisis cinemas" from Portugal, Greece, and Spain to their three bailouts (Kourelou, Liz, and Vidal 2014, 134). Scholars also put forth alternative terms, for example, the "new cinema of 'emancipation'" and "Greek Absurdism," and point out that the Greek press uses other labels, such as "New Elleniko Reuma" (new Greek current) and "Young Greek Cinema" (Chalkou 2012, 244–245; Papadimitriou 2014). Critics complicate the cinema's genealogy as they view the sudden output as a product of "years of prosperity in the Greek audio-visual sector" prior to the economic downturn, which allowed filmmakers to acquire skills in television (Papadimitriou 2012, 247–248). Lanthimos, for example, worked for an advertising company that would later cofinance his film. No matter what term and origins, a striking new art cinema coincided with the eurocrisis in the countries most affected by it.

The discussion around the term "weird" illustrates the symptomatic lack of critical vocabulary in response to the films' aesthetics, which eschews familiar conventions. The coinage also signals difficulty determining whether the films appeared because of or despite the crisis: Were they made in response to the economic collapse or read by spectators as allegories even though filmmakers developed the aesthetics and narratives earlier? Weirdness in its different instantiations signals attempts to visualize immaterial processes of financialization and global flows of risk and debt. In other words, the diverse unconventional aesthetics responds to the challenge of representing the link between the invisible processes of global financial transactions, on the one hand, and the material loss of work, homes, income, and social services, on the other.

Europe: Crisis and Austerity

As young modern democracies, Greece, Portugal, and Spain entered the EU late. After the end of the military dictatorship in 1974, Greece joined the European Economic Community in 1981. Portugal and Spain followed in 1986. After Greece adopted the euro in 2001, the 2000s saw a period of intense economic growth based on external borrowing (Papadimitriou 2014, 4). Dissatisfaction with the national economy became public when in December 2008 young people of the "generation of 700 euro," the minimum wage in Greece before the recession, took to the streets to demonstrate against their government (Chalkou 2012, 257).

Globally, the crisis originated from a financial market that traded in risks, debts, and mortgages. At its center was securitization—the "process of bundling up loans that had income streams and risks, re-dividing them and selling them" (Walby 2015, 43). Deregulation caused the banking, credit, and financial crisis of 2007 and 2009 and the fall of real estate prices (38). The looming bankruptcy of the American company Lehman Brothers turned the crisis into a catastrophe (38). Spreading outward, the systemic failure affected the economy, including production and employment, created governmental budget deficits, led to a recession, and finally encroached into the sphere of politics. Even though scholars consider it a "transmuted and well-camouflaged banking crisis" (Blyth 2013, 5), it affected people's ability to make payments on their homes and their debts (Vrasti 2016, 249). After the recession, the recovery affected output but not wages or living standards (Walby 2015, 2). The sudden attention to the financial sector exposed an almost exclusively white male profession.

In October 2009 a "scandal-ridden" Greek government had to confront "a debt that could not be paid," "bankruptcy was imminent," and by the end of the year Greece was mired in a deep recession (Papadimitriou 2014, 4). Young people who were well educated, often in European universities, faced rising unemployment, limited job prospects, and low income (Chalkou 2012, 257). The bailouts by the troika (the European Commission, the European Central Bank, and the International Monetary Fund) occurred in Greece in the spring of 2010 and in Portugal in April 2011; the rescue of Spanish banks with Eurozone funds took place at the end of 2012 (Kourelou, Liz, and Vidal 2014, 134). The troika's loans to Greece required the country to reduce welfare spending and protections of workers, raise taxes, revise collective bargaining arrangements, and privatize state assets, in short, institutionalize an austerity program that led to high unemployment, particularly among young people (Walby 2015, 136). In 2010 in Greece 77 percent of the average income went to loan repayments, which integrated households into the financialization of everyday activities, such that debt sustained the economy (Agathangelou 2016, 218).

Austerity measures limit governmental social expenditure to reduce budget deficits (Walby 2015, 86, 18). These measures were "supposed to provide stability to the Eurozone countries," particularly Portugal, Ireland, Italy, Greece, and Spain (Blyth 2013, 3). Mark Blyth points out that Greece "saw its debt to GDP [ratio] rise from 106 percent in 2007 to 170 percent in 2012 despite successive rounds of austerity cuts" (4). Ultimately, the measures failed to reduce the debt and promote growth (5).

Women's workload increases under conditions of decreasing welfare services when domestic needs expand. Women also remain in the labor market, which further increases their workload (Walby 2015, 85). Additionally, processes of financialization, debt, and taxes are gendered. Mortgages, pensions invested in financial markets, credit cards, and other debt constitute everyday forms of financialization, the risky speculative investment in assets. The requirements for women to receive loans are typically more stringent than for men, and it is more difficult for women to pay debts than for men (46). Women are overrepresented among those who lose homes to foreclosures and who are targeted for aggressive debt collection practices (Roberts 2016, 68). Women have borne the brunt of the economic collapse, when their unemployment levels rose more than men's following cuts in public expenditure, in contrast to men who lost their jobs at the onset of the recession in sectors such as construction (Walby 2015, 76–78).

Coinciding with the financial crisis, the "inwards, nationally obsessed cinema" of Greece and Portugal developed a transnational outlook (Kourelou, Liz, and Vidal 2014, 138). Contemporary films reference international arthouse cinema (Mademli 2015). As young filmmakers study abroad, they claim a European identity. Producers train as audiovisual entrepreneurs in Europe, travel to festivals, and participate in international networks to attract foreign investment. Tsangari worked with American independent filmmaker Richard Linklater while she held a Fulbright fellowship in the United States. Transnational connections contrast to Greece's previous suspicion of "European institutions and the European Union in general," which characterized the period from the end of the dictatorship to the early 1980s (Chalkou 2012, 252–253).

Filmmakers create internationally successful titles but have to rely on strategies of collaboration to save money in the process of production. Lanthimos and Tsangari produce each other's films and work for free on each other's sets, including as actors (Rose 2011). Directors in Greece and Portugal make movies with unpaid crews "in the houses of friends" and "public spaces" (Kourelou,

Liz, and Vidal 2014, 145). Despite their fame with global audiences, the films are not as successful in their domestic markets (Chalkou 2012, 253; Kourelou, Liz, and Vidal 2014, 136). In their 2010 reevaluation of the previously considered "retrograde" category of art cinema, Rosalind Galt and Karl Schoonover explain that "art cinema provides the only institutional context in which films can find audiences abroad" and that this "international identity constructs art cinema as cosmopolitan" while it also plays "a major role in creating canonical national cinemas" (2010, 7). As such, the films discussed in this chapter can rely on an institutional-economic framework to circulate in the global context of international film festivals and in that process define a national cinema for a transnational audience.

This chapter questions the extent to which the films of the Greek weird wave expose "the misogyny, racism, homophobia and oppressive patriarchy that existed even before the economic meltdown," as many other scholars claim (Kourelou, Liz, and Vidal 2014, 141). While it proposes that the global financial crisis and austerity measures have ruptured the imagination about gender and work, it offers a differentiated account of the weird films that have emerged from the crisis. In contrast to widespread academic celebration, the argument proposes that the films instead demonstrate the renewed importance of feminist analysis that attends to the gendered effects of the economic downturn.

The Return of the Housewife in Times of Crisis

Dogtooth famously initiated the Greek weird wave with unusual acting, mise-en-scène, narrative, camera work, and editing. The film portrays a family living inside a compound, which only the father leaves for his white-collar job in a factory. The children's stiff movements, which characterize their affectless acting, disable identification. With stilted body language, the teenagers engage in ritualistic but nonsensical activities. The characters do not break the filmic frame, enhancing the feeling of being trapped. Scholars read the children's restriction of movement and the lack of the presence of others in their house as an allegory for the borders constituting Greece and Europe (Celik 2013). The father controls the children through ritualizing all aspects of their intimate lives, "from sex to language to the use of mouthwash" (Fisher 2011, 23). The parents teach them a made-up language by replacing some words with random other words. Violence underwrites the parents' authority, and a direct camera captures its sudden eruptions with explicit images, clinical distance, and attention to detail. This is the case, for example, when the father murders a female security guard from his workplace whom he has brought to the home to have sex with his son.

The bourgeois family follows conventional, albeit exaggerated, gender roles. The sole breadwinner, the paterfamilias has at his side his wife, a housewife and mother. He wields absolute control with absurd commands over his children. The bourgeois wife, as the symbol of the middle class, engages in neither domestic chores nor paid work. Shots frame her sitting on the sofa or on a chair, standing only in staged compositions of family scenes, for example, saying good-bye to the father as he leaves for work. Since she also controls the children, in one instance commanding her son to keep mouthwash in his mouth, the film leaves open whether she is a victim or a coconspirator (see also Fisher 2011, 22). She is exempt from the father's violence in this middle-class world with its undercurrent of sex and violence.

The figure of the housewife (discussed in chapter 1) reappears on-screen at the moment of crisis. Feminists have long revealed the idle middle-class woman to be an ideological construction that serves to disavow her labor. Women's productive and reproductive labor disappears at the moment when women's work increases inside and outside the home. *Dogtooth* abstracts from material reality as much as from geographic and temporal specificity to advance a critique anchored in symbolism. By obscuring and denying the labor that inheres in housework, the film affirms one of patriarchy's central myths, namely, that femininity and work are mutually exclusive, which serves to exclude working-class, ethnic, and racialized women from the understanding of femininity. A reading of *Dogtooth* with a focus on gendered work reveals that a film celebrated for its innovative aesthetics, critique of patriarchal values, and allegory of crisis reifies an anachronistic negation of women's reproductive and productive labor, which limits its political import.

Death and the Crisis

Attenberg's focus on a young Greek woman as the main character differentiates it from *Dogtooth*, even though they share the shot compositions, camera work, acting, and mise-en-scène of the weird Greek wave. The film depicts twenty-three-year-old Marina caring for her terminally ill father. Death rates under austerity increase as a result of the deterioration of emergency health care, decrease in preventive services, and lack of food (see Basu and Stuckler 2013). Repeatedly, Marina and her father watch Sir David Frederick Attenborough's BBC television show *Life,* about nature, while they engage in language games (similar to *Dogtooth*). Marina spends time with her friend Bella, and when a stranger comes to town she has sex with him. Toward the film's conclusion her father dies, and the two young women scatter his ashes in the sea.

The film's setting of Aspra Spitia in Greece references the backdrop of industrial labor, as the town grew around an aluminum factory, which repeatedly dominates the shot. In addition to caring for her father, Marina drives a car for a company. Her daily activities capture the normalcy of part-time and gender-transgressive precarious employment. *Attenberg* repeatedly interrupts its narrative when Marina and Bella approach the camera with distorting body movements, reminiscent of the same pattern in Rainer Werner Fassbinder's *Katzelmacher* (West Germany, 1969). The West German director's early film depicts a group of young people who aimlessly hang out in Bavaria and turn against a Greek migrant worker. *Attenberg* faintly echoes the topic of labor migration but focuses on its opposite: entrapment and apathy. In *Katzelmacher*, in intervals a pair of characters walks slowly toward the camera in a refrain that breaks the film's flow but shares its general emphasis on poses that arrest the action. In *Attenberg*, however, the girls contort their bodies as they move, breaking filmic realism and subverting notions of beauty. Their body contortions echo the intermittent segments in *The Drifters* (see chapter 2), when three characters in an empty landscape engage in contact improvisation, an interactive dance form. The young women's walk is unproductive and without any use value, but it is kinetically pleasurable, creative, and dynamic. It strongly contrasts to the internalized repression of the children's generation in *Dogtooth*, as well as the repertoire of runway poses that women inhabit in the aim of seduction and self-representation.[2] Breaking codes of respectability, spectacle, and labor, the absurd gestural language refuses standards of femininity, meaning making, and submission to the discipline of work rhythm, born as it is out of unstructured time.

The father's philosophical metacommentary melancholically refers to the crisis but differs from the next generation's somatic and less intellectual way to live with its effects. When he and Marina sit atop a house in two chairs looking

FIGURE 7.1. *Attenberg* (Anthina Rachel Tsangari, 2010)

across the city, he says, "It is as if we are designing ruins, as if to calculate the final collapse with mathematical precision. Bourgeois arrogance ... especially for a country that has skipped the industrial age altogether." He relates the economic tightening to Greek history rather than to global banking, criticizing those who profited from credit before the financial collapse. *Attenberg*'s younger generation is anarchic and mobile, capturing absurd activity in the absence of regimented labor, reflecting the reality of youth unemployment, which reached an all-time high of 60 percent in March 2013. The film captures neither the despair of the unemployed, which portrays labor as a means of survival, nor the hapless youth and unproductive wives under patriarchal control, as in *Dogtooth*.

The film does not chart individual paths out of the conditions of the recession for Marina or Bella. Marina engages in emotional care, contrasting to the affectless acting style of the Greek weird wave. Without sentimentality or melodrama, the film brings to the fore the ways in which subjects not only become accustomed to but also internalize austerity, unemployment, and precarious jobs, as well as, in the absence of sustained work, mutually engaging play. Marina combines the part-time work as a driver for the factory that ignores conventions of femininity with the deeply gendered expectation of care work in the face of reduced social services. Beyond eccentricity and linguistic play, the film acknowledges the way gender shapes life during the extended downturn.

The Greek weird wave's formal aesthetic features do not constitute a political position. The absurdist language, body rituals, violent outbreaks, long takes, static camera, limited space, and linguistic games offer an allegorical representation that the film leaves open to interpretation. *Dogtooth* compromises its critique by reproducing the traditional image of the bourgeois family. *Attenberg* shares the formal aesthetic characteristics but advances fundamentally different gender politics. Both films—representative of many more from Greece at the time—engage in the search for a new aesthetic language and testify to the need to attend to women and work in times of crisis, even when labor seems to be disappearing.

Narrating Debt

Without question, Gomes's epic film *Arabian Nights* is one of the most unusual films that explicitly responded to the eurocrisis. Gomes's "magnum opus" addresses the global financial crisis in three two-hour films that the Portuguese director wants audiences to view separately, preferably across three days (Rayns 2016). The opus includes material that Gomes gathered when he "operated a newsroom that he described as 'a little factory for making stories'" in 2013–2014

(Hoberman 2015). *Arabian Nights* explodes filmic conventions regarding length, organization, narrative content, and style. It adapts *One Thousand and One Nights'* profusion of narratives, fabulism, and sense of injustice (Rayns 2016). Critics have questioned its political insight, based on the "mishmash of storytelling forms and styles" and "baroque" quality that combines "the factual and the fantastic" and that integrates "magic realism with oblique social reportage" (Hoberman 2015). Despite the limitations of its political analysis, it is nevertheless representative of artists' self-conscious insistence on contributing to life under austerity.

Arabian Nights tells different stories that do not cohere into a single plot. Each tale relates to the eurocrisis and its subsequent austerity measures. Their style varies from fantasy to documentary realism. Individual segments integrate different narrative modes with each other: the fantastic with the documentary and the political with the folkloric. People recount stories of love found in the past, of labor lost, of neighbors, dogs, and roosters, of birds singing and bees dying. Storytelling takes place in the form of song, reenactment, and costumed performance. Absurd imaginary encounters among bankers, ministers, and magical figures transform bailout negotiations into fantastical enactments of Orientalist fairy tales and epic costume dramas. *Arabian Nights* poses a challenge to spectators with its sheer magnitude of material and its meandering text.

The film opens with a documentary vignette that replays a discourse familiar from the early moments of the crisis. The loss of labor initially affected especially such sectors as construction. A panicked public response emphasized the importance of work for men as breadwinners. The film's first sequence similarly documents the closing of the Viana shipyard, aligning labor with heavy industry. Male voice-overs tell stories of entering the shipyard at a young age and reminiscences about their work in the 1980s. These unemployed workers mourn the decline of the national industry and their own livelihood with their memory of building the last ship in 2009. Self-reflective interludes about the work of a film director in times of austerity interrupt these memories. Only one tale, "The Tale of the Tears of the Judge," centers on a female professional, a judge in a surreal court proceeding that offers a symbolic account of financialization as a process that connects people with each other. The judge routes individual stories so that a network emerges among those in her court that makes visible how debt shapes social relations in times of austerity. The shared acts of storytelling and the expression of empathy create community.

The fifty-minute episode occurs in part 2, *As mil a uma noites: Volume 2, O desolado* (*Arabian Nights: Volume 2, The Desolate One*). It opens with a close-up of a male sexual organ in a small pool of blood. A nude woman gets up and walks into the kitchen to call her mother, the judge. They discuss the daughter's loss of her virginity. After the mother begins reciting a recipe, a shot shows an amphitheater at night with a diverse audience as the setting of a fantastic court proceeding. For the remaining sequence the action consists of one of the people or a group standing up and delivering an account of an event that occurred in the past, and then the next person revealing him- or herself to be a subject of the previous story, similar to Scheherazade's embedded narratives. The collective contributions portray relations of theft, debt, violence, and sharing.

The judge moderates the narratives of accusations and explanations of petty crimes, traumatic events, and witness accounts of increasingly absurd stories. A mother and son sold furniture that did not belong to them, illustrating the dynamics of securitization with material objects of the everyday. The son had incurred debt and raped his wife, for which the mother pays restitution, depicting familial violence and amends that circulate in gendered relationships. The daughter-in-law conveys that the landlord called an ambulance, even though there was no emergency. When the judge admonishes him for abusing a public service, his argument turns fantastic, as he demands to be tried by a genie who is present and dressed in an Orientalist costume. The latter's story integrates mythical references with accounts of banking institutions that reformed health care in order to raise the cost of insurance, allowing the pharmaceutical industry to make profits.

Solidarity collapses as stealing and debt define the relations among the characters as a result of the breakdown of the welfare state and the paucity of available jobs. The absurdity increases with a talking cow, a group in folkloric costumes, a deaf woman whose wallet was stolen, an old man who claims to be a manager for social services, and a group of Chinese women, among others. The judge calls the intersecting stories an "endless list of misery and guilt." In this network that pits individuals against each other, women in the audience appear as mothers, wives, and lovers. The lack of working women flies in the face of scholarly findings that labor by women continues and increases in times of crisis and austerity.

This scene employs magical realism, which gives voice to periods of transformation as it offers a "metamorphosis in perception and the things perceived" (Jameson 1986, 302). Magical realism in global art cinema (see also chapter 2) departs from the cinematic vernacular familiar in the depiction of labor, including social realism or genre cinema. The version of magical realism does not beautify horrific historical events into pretty imaginary. Instead of reifying the text for an international market, the use of magic, such as a speaking cow, challenges spectators. When people in costume obviously perform as a speaking

FIGURE 7.2. *Arabian Nights: Volume 2, The Desolate One* (Miguel Gomes, 2015)

cow, the scene reveals its roots in folkloric and carnivalistic practices. Because magical realism offers a "certain poetic transfiguration of the object world itself," it provides a language for what appears to be unrepresentable (301). By referring to the epic and integrating European politics with local customs, the film also relies on the understanding of magical realism as narrative "raw material derived from peasant society" (302). The eurocrisis, so the film implies, demands excessive, extensive responses to acknowledge its weight and impact.

The judge expresses the affective response to the stories that the other characters miss: outrage, surprise, shock, concern, and sadness. The court attendees lack the expected emotional or melodramatic tone appropriate for their tales. The focus on story over emotion brings forth the network instead of highlighting individual fates. The ancient setting, the ivy, the old books, and the judge's robe evoke the tradition of the law, which is at a loss vis-à-vis the collective narration. When the judge declares that "despair is in anguish because it muddles the reasoning that guides me," her emotions overwhelm her in response to the interrelated debt and theft.

The story concludes when the narrative cuts back to the sequence's opening scene, where a nude black woman has taken the place of the daughter baking a cake in the kitchen. When she leaves the frame, the sequence concludes. The three women—the judge, her daughter, and her black replacement—contrast to the many men in other segments who mourn the loss of their jobs at the shipyard, who compete with singing birds, and who tell stories about their unemployment. "The Tale of the Tears of the Judge" links the judge's daughter's private sex life to the public network of theft and debt. The daughter's desire to bake a cake for the man to whom she lost her virginity references the sexual contract of the private sphere as one of exchange. The two women—one white and one black—also appear exchangeable. The loss of her virginity references the virgins whom the original Scheherazade protected and who symbolize male control over reproduction. The framing narrative provides another private dimension to the public stories. Together, they illuminate different forms of social and sexual debt. In the face of the loss of solidarity, the scene presents us with narratives of understanding and empathy among citizens, noncitizens, and animals, self-reflexively staging the power of narrative as a form of survival.

Crisis's Chamber Play

The farcical chamber play *Age of Cannibals* depicts global managers who export financial precarity into the Global South. It relates the meltdown in the metropolis to the outbreak of violence elsewhere turned against German managers who manipulate international clients and compete with each other. Instead of focusing on the precarious underemployed and unemployed, the film caricatures the foot soldiers of global capitalism, the middle managers who find themselves unexpectedly vulnerable to the same kind of precarious conditions that allowed them to turn a profit in the first place. The film connects violence in an unnamed Nigerian city to bankruptcy in the virtual business world and contrasts the virtual network with the extreme spatial limitation of hotel rooms, as it never ventures outside of the business hotel.

Bianca März joins business consultants Kai Niederländer and Frank Öllers in a mise-en-scène that shows them only in their generic hotel rooms, first in India and then in Nigeria. While they exploit their clients in the Global South, Niederländer neurotically obsesses about perfecting travel, and Öllers fights with his wife back home. März has to evaluate the two men. When their new superior, Scherschneider, offers partnerships to Niederländer and Öllers, both eagerly sign their contracts. März joins their celebration and has sex with Öllers, whose wife is divorcing him. Gunfire outside increases, and the hotel loses electricity. When Niederländer attempts to book flights to leave, he realizes that the company is being sued, and because he and Öllers are now partners, their assets are frozen, and they have access neither to credit cards nor to company security. All three become incapacitated by panic, and the film ends with the invisible violent forces preparing to enter their room.

The film uses exaggeration to advance a critique of the global financial class that conducts business with partners who do not share their mobility. It details the minute actions and consequences of the export of capitalism via private companies and transnational political institutions such as the IMF. At the end, in the midst of the crisis, the managers invoke their national belonging by desperately trying to contact the German Embassy. In the privileged and hermetically sealed work environment of global business travel, the managers rely on

FIGURE 7.3. *Age of Cannibals*
(Johannes Naber, 2014)

the affective labor that people of color perform in hotels, including massage, prostitution, and protection from the outside world. Absurd demands, particularly by Niederländer, highlight their presence. The three main characters negotiate their company bankruptcy via their cell phones, Skype conferences, and fax machines while ignoring their immediate and physical surroundings. Niederländer and Öllers are oblivious to the outside world yet deeply cynical about it.

März embodies "global business feminism" in the form of the "Davos woman," who, according to Juanita Elias, provides a "'human face' of globalization in ways that do not alter the underlying structures of capital accumulation" and who advocates for individual success but not gender equality (2016, 115). März participates in cutthroat business negotiations but encounters sexual harassment within her company. In addition, the subtle sexism of her two male colleagues reveals itself early when Niederländer expresses surprise that she will evaluate them. He can imagine her as a colleague but not in a supervisory role. The film depicts the limitations of female advancement in the global business world without idealizing women. Instead, März's attempts to connect with the inhabitants of the Nigerian city appear as a naive counterpart to the men's arrogance. Her superficiality, with which she feigns interest in other cultures while she is part of the economic exploitation of those cultures, exposes self-interested faux feminism and false liberalism.

Age of Cannibals advances a biting farce of the transnational business class that works in the service of the Global North. The film's specific depiction of managers and a financial meltdown differs from the strangeness of the other films. The crisis is immaterial in the West, as the financial processes appear invisible until they affect the managers themselves. The film's weirdness lies in its extreme spatial limitation, antirealist acting, and hyperbolic narrative. The acting evokes no empathy for the film's characters; they are functionaries within a system that has turned them equally neurotic as delirious with fantasies of power.

Through the depiction of the characters' total breakdown at the conclusion, *Age of Cannibals* exposes the fallacy of the illusion of ruthless masculinity and individualism. Yet the film also portrays how women and locals are imbricated in the structures of financial capitalism by revealing März's performance of care as naïveté and the native business partners' desperate desire to escape. This thoroughly cynical representation advances a systemic critique without individualizing psychology. The film suggests that the global dynamics of financialization for profit are thoroughly imbricated with a cultural attitude of superiority toward ethnic others and women. It exposes the ideology that the advancement of individual female European professionals means progress for women as part and parcel of ideologies that sustain structural inequality and produce instability elsewhere.

Dancing through the Landscape of Finance's Architecture

The crisis raised a sudden awareness of the global financial industry that turned attention to the sector's inner workings, including the limited presence of women (see also Fisher 2012). Dutch journalist Joris Luyendijk's banking blog "Voices of Finance," published in the *Guardian* from September 15, 2011, to October 1, 2013, conducted interviews with those working in the business. Clara van Gool's *Voices of Finance*, a thirty-five-minute docudance film, has ten internationally renowned dancers perform their own choreographies while they deliver monologues from Luyendijk's blog in the mise-en-scène of London's financial district. The texts are excerpts from the interviews with a bank equity analyst, a programmer of algorithms, a broker, a human resource manager, and a former treasurer at a collapsed bank, among others.

The monologues cover a range of affects and modes: they are descriptive and self-reflexive, narcissistic and self-possessed, pensive and informative. Some chart unexpected territory, as one compares moving shares to ocean waves, while others support conventional assumptions, as when a young trader recounts making millions at age twenty-five. Repeatedly, narrators grasp for metaphors to give form to the immaterial dynamics, declaring financial processes to be like opera and investment bankers like magicians.

Architectural shots of high-rise buildings with slick glass exteriors alternate with the clean lines of the interior design in meeting rooms, cubicles, elevators, and the entry halls of financial institutions. The dancers inhabit the in-between of buildings and columns with precise movements and athletic dynamism.

Early performances are reminiscent of parkour, the athletic negotiation of the urban environment. A dancer integrates the financial sector's standard black suits in absurd movements, for example, undressing and shoving his shirt into his mouth in a board room. The mise-en-scène becomes part of the symbolic landscape. A dealmaker discusses his desire to be in a company that produces something tangible while he falls in an elevator that is moving up. During his contrapuntal composition, he divulges that he can be fired at any moment. The moving body turns the account of precarious risk-taking into a kinetic experience enhanced by the elevator's movement.

As women are significantly underrepresented in the financial sector, the episode "Human Resource Manager" is one of only two performances by women. She is also the only dancer in the film who dances on pointe; her performance emphasizes discipline. Her classical movements do not intersect with the office workers in the background of her choreography. While she elegantly flows through their work space, she expounds on the firing process, translating her narration into an estranged yet aestheticized process. The scene implies the institutionalized precarity of the workplace.

The film captures and exposes the habitus, architecture, and design that define the workplace of finance as a site of symbolic power. Like the other examples discussed so far, the film attempts to find a new visual language to capture the particularity of finance. The film's intermediality relies on the journalistic blogs but mobilizes the dancing body to translate immaterial processes into physical form. Different from the other films, *Voices of Finance* aestheticizes the processes of financialization. Beauty inheres in the athleticism in the exterior urban landscape, in the self-referential contortions, and in the compositions of detached and controlled movements. *Voices of Finance* shares the attempts at making visible financial processes and self-referentially poses the question about the role of art in times of economic crisis. The narratives cover a range of self-reflective, insightful, pensive, self-centered, and alienated attitudes, reflecting the original blog's ethnographic undertaking. *Voices of Finance* connects the financial characteristic of the twenty-first-century economy and the immediacy of a blog and its ethnographic mode to the documentary gaze of a camera and the high culture of modern dance and classical ballet. What emerges is less a political indictment of masculinist and First World ruthless capitalism, as in *Age of Cannibals,* or the playful drifting and caring in times of austerity, as in *Attenberg*; instead, the film is a multimedia reflection of individuals who make sole profit their goal in a post-Fordist economy and the institutions in which they operate.

Postromance in Postcrisis

If the other films discussed in this chapter cover a range of weird aesthetics, including talking cows and dancing bankers, Coixet's *Yesterday Never Ends* takes minimalism to its extreme. The film explicitly takes place in Spain under austerity, even though it shares with the other films the absence of a realist depiction of the eurocrisis. Instead, it traces its destructive effects on the intimate relation of a couple. The film includes only two characters in one location with sparse action: a divorced couple who have lost their young child. A woman, C. (after the first letter of the actress's first name, Candela Peña), and her former husband, J. (the first letter of actor Javier Cámara's name), meet at a building that appears unfinished and a ruin, as many buildings were abandoned during construction when the crisis hit. This is, however, also the location where their son, Dani, is buried. Their only child died of meningitis because, as a result of the contraction of social services, he did not receive medical attention in time while the father was away at a conference. The couple broke up when the husband left for Germany, where he is now a remarried professor with a pregnant German wife. In addition to waiting for the divorce papers that never arrive, the former couple meet to consider what should happen to the tomb of their deceased son, as a rumor suggests that a casino will open at the site of the cemetery. After they exchange accusations about their shared past, they nostalgically remember its good moments and extend tenderness to each other. The film ends with J. crying at his son's tomb and C. comforting him.

The mise-en-scène consists of a bare building with dilapidated walls of untreated concrete in a monochromatic color scheme of blue and gray. The narrative time is the future of 2017. Their dialogue unfolds in the empty space, interspersed by black-and-white sequences that refer to an unspecified past

FIGURE 7.4. *Yesterday Never Ends* (Isabel Coixet, 2013)

in an indeterminate landscape. In those shots the characters articulate their memories and express their feelings. A third narrative plane captures their shared memory of when they were happy together. Bathed in warm colors with soft lighting, these shots appear sparingly and only make sense retroactively, when the narrative reveals that they depict the moment in the past when the couple conceived Dani. The slow-moving dialogue offers a poetic and painful account of the effects of crisis-ridden Spain.

The film fulfills the demands of feminist economists to include individual well-being in an account of the economic downturn. The opening crosscuts J.'s arrival at the international airport and the global car rental company, Sixt, with C. living in her car. She awakens after a night parked under a rusted ball that advertises a European balloon festival. The radio delivers news about the lower house of the German parliament opposing a third bailout for Spain, proclaiming, "Spaniards just woke up a bit poorer." While J. drives to his destination, people in the background search for food in dumpsters, and prostitutes approach him.

The couple's intimate history of loss reveals the deep, personal effects of the global financial crisis. C. lost her husband, her work, and her home, in addition to her child. Both are cultural workers. While J. is advancing as a professor, she is an unemployed translator whose career has stalled because those who need literary work have left the country. C. sees her own catastrophic situation in the political context of the downturn. She describes the many empty houses in Spain. The casino indicates the shifts toward short-term employment in the service industry and changes to labor laws. In one of the black-and-white scenes that interrupt their conversation, C. says, "And people working. Badly paid. With slave shifts that fifteen years ago would have been forbidden. People will come to gamble away their wages. And people many miles away will get rich exploiting their employees and the punters." C.'s individual despair attunes her to the collective pain.

Scholarship pays attention to cultural producers because they embody hope for a new immaterial economy, most pronounced in Richard Florida's (2011) celebration of the creative class for the reinvigoration of postindustrial cities, and are key to the debate about neoliberalism's demand for flexible labor (see, e.g., Nathanson 2014). J. finding a secure position in Germany and C. being unemployed and homeless in Spain capture the growing income gap between men and women during the economic crisis. While he can afford to participate in the biological, social, and cultural reproduction of transnational Europe, she remains trapped in the crisis-ridden Spanish nation. Consequently, J. repeatedly accuses her of being unproductive.

The film invites cinephilic appreciation of its cinematography, which mirrors the depth of the characters' emotions. The camera varies among long shots, medium long shots, medium close-ups, and many close-ups that emphasize the film's concern with affect. The main setting's mise-en-scène of abstract architecture that emphasizes form, light, and shadow and the beautiful black-and-white shots that provide privileged access to the characters' feelings evoke cinephilia. C. displays a range of emotion throughout, while J. only expresses his loss at the end of the film. She voices her anger at her former husband, sadness at the loss of her child, and a general sense of abandonment from the world.

The film offers a model of human subjectivity produced by austerity that is different from the "cruel optimism" that Lauren Berlant (2011) diagnoses for neoliberal European economy and culture. *Yesterday Never Ends* presents the man putting forth the pragmatism of individual survival based on male privilege versus the woman's emotional and political despair, insight, and refusal. The film aligns itself with the latter over the former. While J.'s success in the EU exposes mobility for all Europeans as an illusion, C.'s entrapment in Spain allegorizes the individual nation in the throngs of austerity. This gendering advances a critique of the way in which European cosmopolitanism has not been equally accessible to all, a process that the crisis has exacerbated.

Rewriting the romance genre in times of austerity, the film traces the aftereffects of the financial collapse and projects them into the future. When J. reproduces himself in the stronger northern country espousing European values, he does not emerge as self-centered and profit-driven as the characters of *Age of Cannibals*. But he benefits from his male privilege, which allows him to prosper in a transnational job market. Such a critique captures the structural inequality of simultaneous transnational European and national Spanish frames that determine the possibilities and limitations of those living in Europe. *Yesterday Never Ends* presents a strong female character who articulates why she cannot access productive and reproductive labor in the age of austerity and how this lack is imbricated in her identity, which endows her with insights from the margins of society.

Conclusion

This chapter attends to films that emerged in conjunction with the global financial crisis, which strongly affected the Mediterranean countries in the form of the eurocrisis and subsequent austerity measures. As a key film of the Greek weird wave, *Dogtooth* depicts a bourgeois family with a violent and controlling father and passive but complicit wife who embodies class status through nonwork. It thus marginalizes women's labor. *Attenberg* indirectly comments on the diminished welfare state by representing familial care for a dying loved one. "The Tale of the Tears of the Judge" from *Arabian Nights* offers a fantastic tale that traces how debt defines social relationships in the absence of work. While *Age of Cannibals* offers a farce on the global business class, *Voices of Finance* gives kinetic expression to the narratives of financial professionals. *Yesterday Never Ends* paints the slow unraveling of a couple's intimacy under the pressures of austerity.

Yesterday Never Ends mobilizes its female character to articulate a forceful critique of gender dynamics, which become pronounced in the crisis. It genders the simultaneous international and national frames, aligning the man with the economic possibilities of the transnational economic union and the woman with being trapped in a crisis-ridden nation. In other words, as a self-reflexive film by a woman director about a female cultural worker, *Yesterday Never Ends* not only analyzes the dynamics of labor in the shadow of the crisis but also transcends the character's limitations. As all films ask the question—to different degrees—about the role of art in times of austerity, *Yesterday Never Ends* forcefully rewrites the slogan "the private is political" as an understanding of the economy as political, which, in turn, shapes the private.

These films share weirdness on the levels of aesthetics and narrative across national cinemas that accompany different degrees of violence, disease, loss, and death, all of which come to prominence during crises and austerity measures. "Weird" remains an ambivalent term in the scholarly vocabulary and as a criterion of analysis with its proximity to the strange, gross, and bizarre. The weird art films assert European cultural production from its crisis-ridden margins, while the biting satire of the masculine managers emerges from the supposedly strong North. The shift from Fordist to post-Fordist labor in the context of financialization leads directors in search of a new cinematic language that remains weird—for now.

Conclusion

This book explores the cinematic representation of work in the twenty-first century. Demonstrating the prevalence of female figures, the book examines the historical imbrication of labor management and visual culture, on the one hand, and the theoretical paradigms that emerged out of second-wave feminism, on the other. Early advocates of efficiency used the medium of film to calculate physical movements in the service of industrial productivity. The figure of the masculine factory worker embodied the concept of labor, denying the effort that was taking place in the domestic sphere. Second-wave feminism's claim that the housewife undertook work was central to its theoretical apparatus, which this book takes as its point of departure. Feminist theory of the 1970s adapted Marxist categories of productive and reproductive labor, as well as Hannah Arendt's understanding of private and public spheres. Most importantly, however, feminists argued that notions of femininity and love obscure domestic and care work and the economic value they produce.

Since the 1970s, work has undergone significant changes that are interconnected with economic, political, and social transformations of family and gender. The collapse of the Eastern Bloc, deindustrialization and the rise of service work, computerization, globalization and Europeanization, the rise of neoliberalism, and the eurocrisis have shaped the organization of work in twenty-first-century Europe, emphasizing outsourcing, flexibility, and short-term contracts. Migration into and mobility within the EU increases paid domestic labor, while biotechnological progress reconfigures life and reproductive work. The primary model of the patriarchal family, with the paterfamilias as the breadwinner, has given way to dual-income and single-headed households. Even though the housewife has become an anachronistic figure in twenty-first-century European cinema about work, films aestheticize reproductive labor and imply the potential for an alternative vision of a market economy based on the ethics of care. At the same time, domesticity persists, haunting films about women who assumed professions coded as masculine.

Films capture the transformation of the cultural imaginary about work with diverse aesthetics. Historically, cinema articulated collective labor through the language of social realism in the West and socialist realism in the East. The collapse of the Eastern Bloc and the explosion of the cultural imagination of labor, however, expanded cinematic vocabulary to depict work. Films from the former Eastern Bloc critique both the past fetishization of the proletariat and the role capitalism accords to women as commodity. Genres have come to the fore. Romantic comedies, biopics, thrillers, and science fiction lay bare stories about working women. Social concerns infuse these generic conventions, enabling multiple readings of individual films. In contrast to Hollywood, independent art cinema in Europe maintains the possibility to escape the pressures of mainstreaming. It imports and, in the process, revises generic conventions, for example, of the comedy.

Increasingly extreme cinematic strategies respond to the global financial crisis and the immateriality of financialization and debt, which shape the global economy. The label of the "weird" wave illuminates the extraordinary range of diverse and unconventional aesthetics that characterize films about the global financial downturn. The strange narratives, affectless acting, language games, excessive length, and hyperbolic farces address debt, financialization, and death as effects of the collapse of social welfare systems without depicting the crisis mimetically. Crisis cinema reflects the displacement of labor from its past centrality in leftist and feminist imaginary. Some of the films, however, resurrect the figure of the housewife, who does not work. Despite the fact that films about the economic downturn criticize patriarchal structures, many ignore women's increasing work responsibility in an age of austerity.

The film analyses rely on contemporary feminist theories about neoliberalism and its emphasis on flexibility, encapsulated in the term "feminization." In the social sciences, scholars attend to the postindustrial rise of the service sector, which advances forms of intimate and emotional labor, whereas academics in film studies observe a postfeminist discourse that dominates in television makeover shows and blockbusters. While advancing these rich theoretical contributions to interdisciplinary feminist theory, this book explores films that offer alternative visions to a totalizing view of neoliberalism, which supposedly has captured economic, political, and social life.

Instead, the book argues that the cinematic representations of labor reflect recent transformations, as well as the histories of racial, ethnic, class, and gender lines. Contemporary social scientists rework the feminist theoretical principles that emerged out of the second women's movement and adapt them for the analysis of neoliberal capitalism. A diverse feminist and independent art cinema in Europe focuses on women's precarious work experience. In contrast to the cinefeminism that emerged in the 1970s, these films also offer a strident critique of Western European women who participate in neoliberal capitalism and benefit from cheap labor elsewhere. Thus, the multiple forms of feminisms demonstrate that singular attention to gender does not suffice for a critical analysis of the contemporary economy.

European feminist films signify a materialist turn that has escaped attention because they do not adhere to traditional Marxist conventions of social or socialist realism. These films are less concerned with the cinematic apparatus, the destruction of the pleasure of the image, or individual psychological studies of subjectivity. Instead, they comment on local, regional, national, and transnational economic processes in which female characters function and assert agency. Such films refuse to participate in the performance of femininity. In this transformation of feminist cinema, the number of working female figures has increased, but their function has expanded beyond the concerns about women as victims of patriarchy. These films reflect on the ways that gender, race, class, ethnicity, and nationality are imbricated in the contemporary political economy. The economic turn, therefore, does not propose a reductive understanding of feminism in which gender is the sole category of oppression or only women are in need of liberation. On the contrary, several films reflect an awareness of how women have made strides to participate in the economies of exploitation. This cinema explores the everyday and isolated moments of resistance, gestures of solidarity, and hope for transformation, and they reflect on the collaborative forms of production of the films themselves.

In contrast, a popular cinema rewrites past feminist and labor paradigms for a faux feminism that offers commodified emotional histories of working-class women who have overcome challenges. The heritage cinema of industrial labor, for example, occurs as a response to the disappearance of industrial production of certain sectors in the West and the rise of information and service work. Postfeminist films nostalgically rehabilitate industrial labor to claim it as heritage. The cinematic image depicts a white labor force, while the soundtrack circulates the transnational sounds of postcolonial music. As these films revise working-class solidarity, they nevertheless indicate the continuing importance of industrial labor for the cultural imagination of work. Their revisionist politics regarding race and class and the centrality of white working-class women for Western European heritage speaks to the ways in which films can harness the affect surrounding gender to exclude the contributions by migrants and minorities.

Paradoxically, significant numbers of films attend to the growing importance of migration for work and family in Europe. Gendered migration influences reproductive labor and family formation. Female labor migrants into and within Europe reconfigure the domestic sphere as they increasingly perform paid housework and care for children and the elderly. Films use voice to project migrants' melancholic memories of a lost homeland for the character to emerge from a timeless past into the present on-screen, where labor transports them into modernity. Narratives of containment in the romantic comedy and phobia in the thriller situate domestic migrant workers in the family home, which is constitutive of the nation. In these contexts, gestures of care work open up ambivalent readings of character motivation. Feminized labor by migrants, lower-class racialized women, and ethnic women continues in the gift economy of donating eggs and surrogacy. Narratives of organ harvesting, infertility, and cloning in dystopian films expand the filmic treatment of biopolitics to include reproductive labor in the context of biotechnology.

Under the neoliberal labor regime, women—associated with care and flexibility—embody work on-screen. The malleability of time associated with housework and naturalized care work appears to make women a flexible workforce. In response, political filmmakers in the tradition of left-wing social realism turn the solitary woman in precarious working conditions into their heroine. Gestures of solidarity continue political ethics. Acknowledging the loss of utopia, feminist films demarcate the limitations of the vision of equality within a reorganized capitalism. The proliferation of diverse feminisms responds to capitalisms that incorporate feminism's key concepts, such as choice and self-actualization. Yet films also confront the difficulty of advocating for an ethics of care without reproducing essentialist notions of femininity.

The work that feminism is called upon to do has changed. New narratives and aesthetics signal the participation of women in the neoliberal workplace, acknowledge women's different access to the labor market, and confront the flexibility that isolates workers. Films' diverse feminist aesthetics creates austere images of the crisis, invokes feminine tactility, endorses negative affect, and reproduces the kinesthetic attachment to the precarious worker moving through cinematic landscapes. Crisis cinema engages in a self-reflexive metadiscourse about the role of art in times of austerity. Films work through the trauma induced by the economic downturn, model storytelling to create networks of empathy, and perform dance to embody abstract processes of financial capitalism.

The varied European films respond to neoliberal capitalisms with flexibility about aesthetics and political strategies. Importing generic conventions, caricaturing capitalism's games, and advancing incongruous metaphors, they expose financial processes and counter with aesthetic gestures. As popular film has appropriated a feminist vocabulary naturalizing neoliberal structures, projecting them into the past, translating them into phobic accounts of migrants, or containing women's work in the romance, they challenge feminist filmmakers to engage in multiple vernaculars, from the absurd and the fantastic to the documentary and the minimalist. In sum, the cinematic landscape of multiple feminisms with diverse aesthetics responds to the political economies of labor under neoliberalism.

Notes

Introduction

1. Scholars differ in their translation of the original German essay, "Ungleichzeitigkeit und Pflicht zu ihrer Dialektik." I follow Mark Ritter's translation, "Nonsynchronism and the Obligation to Its Dialectics" (Bloch 1977). Neville Plaice and Stephen Plaice translate the title as "Non-contemporaneity and Obligation to Its Dialectic" (Bloch 1991). There are subtle differences between their texts as well.

2. One defining difference between feature film and industrial film lies in the fact that for the latter, audience members do not pay to watch. Workers at a company often recognize themselves in an industrial film, related to the "star effect" of the participants in Gilbreths' experiments (Zimmermann 2009, 109–110).

3. An intriguing case study regarding tropes and narrative conventions in films about labor would be the amateur films about work in the GDR and their similarity to and differences from DEFA films. See, for example, the program "Amateur Film I: At Work," curated by Ralf Forster at the Fifty-Ninth International Leipzig Festival for Documentary and Animated Film 2016 (Forster 2016). The films included *Weißes Gold* (*White Gold*; GDR; Alfred Dorn, 1967), *Montage mit DM-SPE* (*Construction with DM-SPE*; GDR; Reimar Rockstroh, 1963), *Zwei Kapitel aus: Der Mensch und seine Arbeit* (*Two Chapters from: Humans at Work*; GDR; Herbert Illgen and Dieter Weigend, 1972), *Damit wir glücklich leben* (*So We Can All Live Happily*; GDR; W.-K. Krekow and Konrad Hildebrand, 1971), *Sechzig Minuten nach Zwölf* (*Sixty Minutes Past Twelve*; GDR; Emil Jurkowski, 1979/1980), *Präsent* (*Present*; GDR; Hubert Andörfer, 1983), *Bumerang* (*Boomerang*; GDR; Heinz Drigalla and Klaus Hessel, 1975), *Faßroller* (*Barrel Roller*; GDR; Gerhard Langer, 1972),

Eine Nummer größer (*One Size Bigger*; GDR; Frank Dietrich, 1981), *Meine Arbeit* (*My Work*; GDR; Peter Gallasch, 1977/1978), and *Ist der Ofen aus?* (*Has the Fire Gone Out?*; GDR; Rainer Hässelbarth, 1988).

    4. Ewa Mazierska's (2015) scholarship constitutes an important exception. Her books regularly include Eastern European, often Polish, films as representative of European cinema.

    5. Both the Routledge series on national cinemas and the Wallflower series 24 Frames, which also covers national cinemas, published fourteen titles each, the former between 1996 and 2008 and the latter between 2004 and 2012.

    6. *Stellar Encounters: Stardom in Popular European Cinema*, edited by Tytti Soila (2009), presents an exception to this survey. While the book's title and the introduction do not focus specifically on gender, women, or sexuality as categories of analysis, the book includes a relatively high number of essays that focus on female stars or the function of gender and sexuality in modernity and advertising, presumably because the topic of "stardom" lends itself to discussions of gender and sexuality, often, but not exclusively, in relationship to women (see Hayward 2009; Kalha 2009; Koivunen 2009; Spazzini 2009; Girelli 2009; Kuhn 2009; Olsson 2009; Laine 2009).

    7. See the website for the Council of Europe and Creative Europe Deutschland.

Chapter 1. The Specter of Domesticity

The title of this chapter references the opening statement of Karl Marx and Friedrich Engels's *Communist Manifesto* (1848): "A specter is haunting Europe—the specter of communism." Jacques Derrida took up the notion in *Specters of Marx: The State of the Debt, the Work of Mourning and the New International* (2006); Joseph Vogl reworked it to address the global financial crisis in *The Specter of Capital* (2005).

    1. This is a play on Sherry B. Ortner's feminist anthropology essay "Is Female to Male as Nature Is to Culture?" (1974).

    2. Margunn Bjørnholt and Ailsa McKay refer to feminist economists who met at the Twenty-First Annual Conference of the International Association for Feminist Economics (IAFFE) and quote from the manifesto signed at the meeting in Barcelona on June 28, 2012 (2014, 7).

    3. The film is "based on the reminiscences of Major Oman, Maria Larsson's daughter, as told to Troell's wife (and Larsson's great-niece), Agneta Ulfsäter-Troell" (White 2008, n.p.).

Chapter 2. Precarious Work in Feminist Film

The original German text for the epigraph from Tatjana Turanskyj's "Vom Leben in der Scheinemanzipation" reads as follows: "Der flexibilisierte globalisierte Kapitalismus schließt 'die Frauen' also nicht mehr aus oder diskriminiert sie offen wie das noch im letzten Jahrhundert der Fall war. Das kann er sich auch nicht leisten, denn er braucht sie als (flexible) Arbeitskräfte und als treue, kaufkräftige Konsumentinnen."

1. McRobbie is aware that the use of the term evokes Pateman's *The Sexual Contract* but claims to use "the phrase quite differently" (90n2).

2. Ken Loach later returns to the classic male hero in *I, Daniel Blake* (2016), which imports a host of conventional signifiers, beginning with Daniel Blake's profession as a carpenter.

3. The Dardenne brothers won the Palme d'Or at Cannes for *Rosetta* (France, Belgium; 1999) in 1999 and for *The Child* (*L'enfant*; France, Belgium; 2005) in 2005, best screenplay for *The Silence of Lorna* (*Le silence de Lorna*; Belgium, France, Italy, Germany; 2008) in 2008, and the Grand Prix for *The Kid with a Bike* (*Le gamin au vélo*; Belgium, France, Italy; 2011) in 2011.

4. Aga Skrodzka points out that the films that she discusses in her volume *Magic Realist Cinema in East Central Europe* do not sell well, even though they are "critically acclaimed on the international film-festival circuit" (2012, xi). Skrodzka's formulation is helpful, as critical acclaim at the international film festival circuit does not imply that individual films are screened in movie houses or distributed on DVDs. *I Am from Titov Veles* is distributed on DVD as part of the Global Film Initiative.

5. Scholars propose different geographic frameworks to discuss films such as *I Am from Titov Veles*. Jennifer Suchland (2011) proposes "Eurasia," Dina Iordanova (2001) values Balkan cinema, Aga Skrodzka (2012) uses East-Central European cinema. Lars Kristensen (2012) and Anikó Imre (2005) emphasize transnational perspectives. Surveys of national cinemas still dominate the field (see Cunningham 2004; Hames 2009; Coates 2005; Werner 2010).

6. Michael Glawogger died on April 23, 2014, of malaria in Monravia, Liberia, while shooting.

7. The title is the infinitive "to fall," but the word also means "traps." The film has received mixed reviews, a reaction that might be gendered. While Derek Elley in *Variety* (2006) calls it a "well-played, cleanly shot but spectacularly empty tale," Nicole Armour in *Film Comment* suggests that the film "deals with the fragmentation of a group" and offers a story "of people disappointed by their own fallibility but still capable of bit ambitions." She continues, "The women in *Falling* have lost touch with their friends and idealism to avoid feeling defeated," and concludes that the film, like others that she reviews, "celebrate[s] humanity . . . by pointing out what's lost or missed when you give up a sense of connection with other" (2006, 69).

Chapter 3. Heritage Cinema of Industrial Labor

1. Heritage conservation relies on national institutions such as Great Britain's National Trust and transnational programs such as UNESCO and the COSME Program. The UNESCO World Heritage Convention defines a group of environmental treaties, while the UNESCO World Heritage Center (founded in 1992) manages the program (see European Commission; The Genius Loci Project).

2. All translations from the German original are mine.

3. According to the press kit, producers Elizabeth Karlsen and Stephen Woolley and costume designer Louise Stjernsward wanted to combine the feeling of the 1960s

210 • Notes to Chapters 3 and 4

with the fact that Dagenham is not the "Carnaby Street cliché of the 1960s" (*Made in Dagenham* 2010, 10). They made a conscious choice "to reflect the women's brightly colored view of the world, and not the grimness of their reality" (10). The dialogue differs from the original script, which exposed Barbara Castle's choice of outfit as a strategic decision:

> BARBARA CASTLE: That's Biba . . . I saw it in a magazine—Rita nods to Mrs Castle's outfit.
> RITA: And that's C and A. I've got one at home . . . Seems we all dressed up . . . And you dressed down . . . Who did that put at an advantage do you think?
> Mrs Castle laughs. (Ivory 2006, 113)

4. The nine different segments of archival footage include advertisements by Ford Motor Company, industrial films, and news reports.

5. The crossing of the factory gate either into or out of the factory is an iconic scene in films about labor, from *Workers Leaving the Lumière Factory in Lyon* (Auguste and Louis Lumière; France; 1895) to Harun Farocki's film and video installations *Workers Leaving the Factory* (*Arbeiter verlassen die Fabrik*; Germany; 1995) and *Workers Leaving the Factory in Eleven Decades* (*Arbeiler verlassen die Fabrik in elf Jahrzehnten*; Germany; 2006).

6. The pen, celebrating Pope John Paul II's trip to Poland in 1979, is exhibited at the Europejskie Centrum Solidarności museum in Gdańsk.

7. For famous examples of this convention, see *Europa Europa* (Germany, France, Poland; Agnieszka Holland, 1990) and *Schindler's List* (US; Steven Spielberg, 1993).

8. See also the Typewriter Database and "ozTypewriter."

9. The French company Japy famously developed technology for typewriters and watches.

10. For a history of women's office work, see Davies (1982); for the turn of the century, see Gardey (2001). Biebl, Mund, and Volkening (2007) discuss the economy of love and labor in literature, film, and theory. For a reading of the figure of women typists in film, literature, and advertising in the Weimar Republic, see Kurash (2015). I thank Jaclyn Kurash for sharing her dissertation and scholarly references with me.

11. See Wershler-Herny (2005). Leroy Anderson's "The Typewriter" (1950), performed by a symphonic orchestra and a manipulated typewriter, was made famous by Jerry Lewis in *Who's Minding the Store?* (US; 1963). *Populaire* includes Gilbert Bécaud's "La machine à écrire" (1957) in its final credit sequence. See the video at https://www.youtube.com/watch?v=op7ofWpNhEc.

12. Pepe Luis recorded a famous version as "The Secretary's Cha Cha Cha (Las Secretarias)" with his Mambo Royal Orchestra (1956).

13. According to Eve Sedgwick (2015), the woman shared between two men cements the homosexual bond.

Chapter 4. Voice in the Cinema of Labor Migration

1. For example, Valie Export's multiscreen installation *Glottis* in (2007) shows an extreme close-up of her vocal cords, expressing her belief that they provide access

to an authentic female identity. Export stated the latter at the event "Conversation Women in Art/Artists" at ArtBasel in Miami, Florida, on December 8, 2007. Personal transcript.

2. Gayatri Spivak's 1988 classic essay accuses theorists of reproducing the hegemony of the Western intellectual by speaking for the subaltern. Spivak argues that the problem of the mute subaltern woman cannot be solved by an essentialist search for her origin in light of the intersection of imperialism and sexism. She illustrates the paradigm of white men saving brown women from brown men with an extensive account of the British abolition of widow sacrifice in 1829, which she contrasts to classical and Vedic texts about Hindu India (1988, 295–297). British imperialism claimed to protect women from their religious and political contexts while neither understanding nor translating such circumstances accurately (206). Spivak's conclusion that the subaltern woman cannot speak results from Western mistranslation that cannot be countered with an essentialist account of authentic origins.

3. "The prefix 'post' does not signal the end of migration, but describes societal negotiation processes that take place after the migration" (Foroutan 2015, my translation). Shermin Langhoff coined the term "postmigrant theatre" (see Foroutan 2015). All translations of Heidenreich (2015) are mine.

4. In contrast, William Brown, Dina Iordanova, and Leshu Torchin (2010) have dedicated a book-length study to films about human trafficking, suggesting that films can play a central role in educating about trafficking.

5. For example, *Coffee-Colored Children* (UK; Ngozi Onwurah, 1988), *Kush* (UK; Pratibha Parmar, 1991), *Looking for Langston* (UK; Isaac Julien, 1989), *Sari Red* (UK; Pratibha Parmar, 1988), and *The Body Beautiful* (UK; Ngozi Onwurah, 1991).

6. The suffering female migrant is a stock character in "the paradigmatic 'problem film' of the 1980s" (Heidenreich 2015, 107).

7. Brick Lane got its name from the brick fields that were dug in 1574 (Newland 2008, 165). Paul Newland points out that the novel *Brick Lane* was "hugely successful with a predominantly white middle-class readership" but nevertheless was "roundly criticized by Bangladeshis living in east London, who suggested that it offered an inauthentic portrayal of their community" (235).

8. Both Sarah-Jeanne Labrosse and Tatiana Maslany are Canadian actresses. Maslany has since become famous for playing clones in the series *Orphan Black*, including one with a Russian accent.

9. Anja Salomonowitz explains in the extra materials of the DVD that these are real people and that the bartender works in a brothel in Vienna.

Chapter 5. Care Work and the Suspicious Gesture

1. Mamaco Yoneyama created the performance *Tango of a Housewife* for the International Women's Conference in Beijing in 1995. See http://makoidemitsu.com/work/at-any-place-4-from-the-tango-of-a-housewife-by-yoneyama-mamako/?lang=en.

2. See, for example, the filmic study *Some Time and Motion Studies: An Analysis of the Gilbreth's Law of Simultaneity* (A. Langsner, n.d.), https://www.youtube.com/watch?v=7vLvFy32h5Y.

3. For example, the German study "Setting the Course for Sharing of Chores in Family and Profession: Research Report of a Representative Questionnaire of Parenting Couples on Behalf of the Federal Ministry for Family, Seniors, Women, and Youth" notes that the combination of a full-time husband and a stay-at-home wife occurs in 8 percent of the interviewed couples before the birth of the first child and in 17 percent of the couples after the birth of the first child. The findings, however, show a strong drop from full-time dual-income households before the birth of the first child (71 percent) to after the birth of the first child (15 percent). In the majority of cases, the father works full time and the mother part time or hourly after the birth of the first child. See http://www.ifd-allensbach.de/uploads/tx_studies/Weichenstellungen.pdf (2015), 6. All translations from the German study are mine.

4. According to the Allensbach study, in Germany mothers performed 70–80 percent of the childcare. The range is the results from different perceptions by fathers and mothers. Fathers perceive mothers to perform 70 percent, and mothers perceive themselves taking care of 80 percent. See http://www.ifd-allensbach.de/uploads/tx_studies/Weichenstellungen.pdf (2015), 11.

5. An exception occurs in *North Country* (United States; Niki Caro, 2005), in which a scene shows several male workers shaking and turning over a portable bathroom, threatening and harassing the main female character, who is trapped inside. The scene invites viewers to identify with the terror of the ambushed woman against the joke that unites the men.

6. Ksenia Rappoport was classically trained in Russia, where she performed onstage and in film. Since her international breakthrough with *The Unknown Woman*, she has garnered several awards. Anca Parvulescu calls her "the only unknown name among the cast," but her fame has since increased (2014, 73). Her performance in the two thematically similar films creates an eerie subtext, as it echoes the uncanny doubling that occurs in both films. In both films she plays a suspicious Eastern European female migrant but not a Russian in the tradition of casting Eastern European actors. For example, Peter Lorre, born László Loewenstein in Austro-Hungary, played different ethnic characters in Hollywood. His portrayal of the character Joel Cairo in *The Maltese Falcon* (John Huston, 1941) coded gayness through his "queer" gestural language.

7. Anca Parvulescu describes the character as "Georgia, who is Ukrainian and whose real name is Irina but whose 'Italian name' is Irena" (2014, 71).

Chapter 6. Reproductive Labor in the Age of Biotechnology

1. Even though this chapter includes a critique of the language of donation, harvesting, and gifting that defines the markets of eggs, tissue, organs, and surrogacy, I use the terms to simplify matters of writing and reading.

2. For example, according to Donna Dickenson, in France, Belgium, and the Netherlands tissue is considered abandoned once it has been removed from the body. She covers the case studies in which individuals felt robbed of their genetic material, including John Moore and Henrietta Lacks (2007, 2008).

3. Both Dickenson (2007, 2008) and Cooper (2008) refer to Richard M. Titmuss's volume ([1970] 1997). Dickenson claims that his scholarship is out of vogue, but in the current debate on biopolitics and biotechnology, his work has reemerged as a reference point for the language of gift and donation in the economics of eggs, tissues, organs, and babies. Titmuss was the father of Ann Oakley, whose study on housework features centrally in chapter 1. She has also authored an academic memoir about her relationship to her father (2014).

4. France refused to endorse the 1998 European biotechnology directive, opposing the notion of turning "life into a commodity." Subsequently, the country received a "formal censure from the European commission" in 2004 (Dickenson 2008, 109).

5. Eckart Voigts views "dystopian and post-apocalyptic narrative" as "subgenres of science fiction" with two key features: "speculation and extrapolation... of a place or society significantly worse than its contextual present" (2015, 1). Dystopian narratives emerged in the twentieth century, with science "as a source of human suppression and control" (2). He links the narratives of "future societal collapse or crisis" to "urgent challenges" that include inequality, migration, and displacement, the social and economic disasters of global capitalism, unchecked scientific dynamics in biotechnology, cloning and "reprogenetics," and viral pandemics (2). He acknowledges that not all dystopian narratives belong to science fiction.

6. A dystopian worldview connects these films. *Dirty Pretty Things* is not a science fiction film. *Children of Men* is set in the future, but London looks contemporary, and there are references to early twenty-first-century events. *Never Let Me Go* is science fiction, but it situates the technological discoveries in the past, and the main character, Kathy, remembers the contemporary period. The topics of the films are typical for science fiction, and several articles address *Children of Men* and *Never Let Me Go* in terms of science fiction. Per Schelde notes a particular concern with "natural versus scientific reproduction" in science fiction (1993, 77).

7. The many references to Senay's Turkish Moslem upbringing imply a cultural argument about rape as shame. Rape, however, is a long-standing trope in Turkish Marxist cinema as an allegory for class exploitation. See, for example, Yilmaz Güney's *Yol* (*The Road*; Turkey, Switzerland, France; 1982) and *Baba* (*The Father*; Turkey; 1971).

8. He is named Keffers in the script, but he only appears to deliver food at the cottages and is not introduced by name in the film.

Chapter 7. Crisis Cinema

1. *Dogtooth* won the Prix Un certain regard at the 2009 Cannes film festival and also earned an Oscar nomination. *Attenberg*'s actress Ariane Labed won the Coppa Volpi

(the Volpi Cup for best actress) at the Venice Film Festival in 2010. Scholars and critics include the following diverse films among the Greek weird wave: *Wasted Youth* (Greece; Argyris Papadimitropoulos and Jan Vogel, 2011), *Hora proelefsis* (*Homeland*; Greece; Syllas Tzoumerkas, 2010), *Macherovgaetis* (*Knifer*; Cyprus, Greece; Yannis Economides, 2010), *Strella* (*A Woman's Way*; Greece; Panos H. Kontras, 2009), *I epithesi tou gigantiaiou mousaka* (*The Attack of the Giant Mousaka*; Greece; Panos H. Koutras, 1999).

2. Carlo Comanducci (2017) reads gesture in *Attenberg* in the context of Agamben's political-philosophical treatise (see also chapter 5).

References

Adkins, Lisa. 2016. "Contingent Labor and the Rewriting of the Sexual Contract." In *The Post-Fordist Sexual Contract: Working and Living in Contingency*, edited by Lisa Adkins and Maryanne Dever, 1–28. London: Palgrave Macmillan.
Adkins, Lisa, and Maryanne Dever, eds. 2016. *The Post-Fordist Sexual Contract: Working and Living in Contingency*. London: Palgrave Macmillan.
Agamben, Giorgio. 1998. *Homo Sacer: Sovereign Power and Bare Life*. Stanford, CA: Stanford University Press.
———. 2000. "Notes on Gesture." In *Means without End: Notes on Politics*, 49–60. Minneapolis: University of Minnesota Press.
Agathangelou, Anna M. 2016. "Global Raciality of Capitalism and 'Primitive' Accumulation: (Un)Making the Death Limit?" In *Scandalous Economics: Gender and the Politics of Financial Crises*, 205–230. Oxford: Oxford University Press.
Agustín, Laura María. 2007. *Sex at the Margins: Migration, Labor, Markets and the Rescue Industry*. London: Zed Books.
Aitken, Ian. 2001. *European Film Theory and Cinema: A Critical Introduction*. Bloomington: Indiana University Press.
Ali, Monica. 2004. *Brick Lane*. New York: Scribner.
Anderson, Bridget. 1999. "Overseas Domestic Workers in the European Union." In *Gender, Migration and Domestic Service*, edited by Janet Henshall Momsen, 117–133. New York: Routledge.
Appiah, Kwame Anthony. 1993. "'No Bad Nigger': Blacks as the Ethical Principle in the Movies." In *Media Spectacles*, edited by Marjorie Garber, Jann Matlock, and Rebecca L. Walkowitz, 81–90. New York: Routledge.

Arendt, Hannah. 1998. *The Human Condition*. Chicago: University of Chicago Press.
Armour, Nicole. 2006. "Getting Real: In Search of the Authentic Self across a Half-Dozen Selection." *Film Comment* 42:68–69.
Artaud, Antonin. (1947) 2001. "Van Gogh, the Man Suicided by Society." In *Surrealist Painters and Poets: An Anthology*, edited by Mary Ann Caws, 103–110. Cambridge, MA: MIT Press.
Aslaksen, Julie, Torunn Bragstad, and Berit Ås. 2014. "Feminist Economics in Times of Economic Crisis." In *Counting on Marilyn Waring: New Advances in Feminist Economics*, edited by Margunn Bjørnholt and Ailsa McKay, 21–36. Bradford, ON: Demeter Press.
Aslaksen, Julie, and Charlotte Koren. 2014. "Reflections on Unpaid Household Work, Economic Growth, and Consumption Possibilities." In *Counting on Marilyn Waring: New Advances in Feminist Economics*, edited by Margunn Bjørnholt and Ailsa McKay, 55–69. Bradford, ON: Demeter Press.
Austin, Guy. 1996. *Contemporary French Cinema: An Introduction*. Manchester: Manchester University Press.
Babington, Bruce. 2014. *The Sports Film: Games People Play*. London: Wallflower.
Bacon, Terryl, and Govinda Dickman. 2009. "'Who's the Daddy?': The Aesthetics and Politics of Representation of Alfonso Cuarón's Adaptation of P. D. James's *Children of Men*." In *Adaptation in Contemporary Culture: Textual Infidelities*, edited by Rachel Carroll, 147–162. London: Continuum.
Baer, Hester. 2017. "Disorganizing Comedy: Genre, Normativity, and Neoliberalism in Maren Ade's *Toni Erdmann*." Unpublished talk, University of Florida, September 20.
Ballesteros, Isolina. 2015. *Immigration Cinema in the New Europe*. Bristol: Intellect.
Bardan, Alice. 2013. "The New European Cinema of Precarity: A Transnational Perspective." In *Work in Cinema: Labor and the Human Condition*, edited by Ewa Mazierska, 69–90. New York: Palgrave.
Barthes, Roland. 2010. *Camera Lucida: Reflections of Photography*. New York: Hill and Wang.
Basu, Sanjay, and David Stuckler. 2013. *The Body Economic: Why Austerity Kills; Eight Experiments in Economic Recovery, from Iceland to Greece*. London: Allen Lane.
Beck, Ulrich. 2000. *What Is Globalization?* Cambridge: Polity.
Beck, Ulrich, and Elisabeth Beck-Gernsheim. 2014. *Distant Love: Personal Life in the Global Age*. Cambridge: Polity.
Benjamin, Orly. 2016. "Negotiating Job Quality in Contracted-Out Services: An Israeli Institutional Ethnography." In *The Post-Fordist Sexual Contract: Working and Living in Contingency*, edited by Lisa Adkins and Maryanne Dever, 149–169. London: Palgrave Macmillan.
Berebitsky, Julie. 2012. *Sex and the Office: A History of Gender, Power, and Desire*. New Haven, CT: Yale University Press.
Berg, Maggie, and Barbara K. Seeber. 2016. *The Slow Professor: Challenging the Culture of Speed in the Academy*. Toronto: University of Toronto Press.

Berghahn, Daniela, and Claudia Sternberg, eds. 2010. *European Cinema in Motion: Migrant and Diasporic Film in Contemporary Europe.* New York: Palgrave.
Berlant, Lauren. 2011. *Cruel Optimism.* Durham, NC: Duke University Press.
Betz, Mark. 2009. *Beyond the Subtitle: Remapping European Art Cinema.* Minneapolis: Minnesota University Press.
Bhabha, Jacqueline. 2009. "The 'Mere Fortuity of Birth'? Children, Mothers, Borders, and the Meaning of Citizenship." In *Migrations and Mobilities: Citizenship, Borders, and Gender*, edited by Seyla Benhabib and Judith Resnik, 187–227. New York: New York University Press.
Biebl, Sabine, Verena Mund, and Heide Volkening, eds. 2007. *Working Girls: Zur Ökonomie von Liebe und Arbeit.* Berlin: Kadmos.
Bingham, Dennis. 2010. *Whose Lives Are They Anyway? The Biopic as Contemporary Film Genre.* New Brunswick, NJ: Rutgers University Press.
Bjørnholt, Margunn, and Ailsa McKay, eds. 2014. *Counting on Marilyn Waring: New Advances in Feminist Economics.* Bradford, ON: Demeter Press.
Bloch, Ernst. 1977. "Nonsynchronism and the Obligation to Its Dialectics." Translated by Mark Ritter. *New German Critique* 11 (Spring): 22–38.
———. 1991. "Non-contemporaneity and Obligation to Its Dialectic." In *Heritage of Our Times*, translated by Neville Plaice and Stephen Plaice, 97–149. Cambridge: Polity Press.
Blyth, Mark. 2013. *Austerity: The History of a Dangerous Idea.* Oxford: Oxford University Press.
Bohle, Dorothee, and Béla Greskovits. 2012. *Capitalist Diversity on Europe's Periphery.* Ithaca, NY: Cornell University Press.
Borda, Jennifer L. 2011. *Women Labor Activists in the Movies: Nine Depictions of Workplace Organizers, 1954–2005.* Jefferson, NC: McFarland & Company.
Boris, Eileen, and Rhacel Salazar Parreñas, eds. 2010. *Intimate Labors: Cultures, Technologies, and the Politics of Care.* Stanford, CA: Stanford University Press.
Boyle, Kirk. 2009. "*Children of Men* and *I am Legend*: The Disaster-Capitalism Complex Hits Hollywood." *Jump Cut: A Review of Contemporary Media* 51. https://www.ejumpcut.org/archive/jc51.2009/ChildrenMenLegend/.
Bronfen, Elisabeth. 1992. *Over Her Dead Body: Configurations of Femininity, Death and the Aesthetic.* New York: Routledge.
Brown, Elspeth. 2005. *The Corporate Eye: Photography and the Rationalization of American Commercial Culture 1884–1929.* Baltimore, MD: Johns Hopkins University Press.
Brown, Wendy. 2015. *Undoing the Demos: Neoliberalism's Stealth Revolution.* New York City: Zone Books.
Brown, William, Dina Iordanova, and Leshu Torchin. 2010. *Moving People, Moving Images: Cinema and Trafficking in the New Europe.* St. Andrews: St. Andrews Film Studies.
Butler, Cornelia, and Lisa Gabrielle Mark. 2007. *WACK! Art and the Feminist Revolution.* Cambridge, MA: MIT Press.

Camper, Fred. 1985. "Sound and Silence in Narrative and Nonnarrative Cinema." In *Film Sound: Theory and Practice*, edited by Elisabeth Weis and John Belton, 369–381. New York: Columbia University Press.

Carter, Erica. 1997. *How German Is She? Postwar West German Reconstructions and the Consuming Woman*. Ann Arbor: University of Michigan Press.

Celik, Ipek A. 2013. "Family as Internal Border in *Dogtooth*." In *Frontiers of Screen History: Imagining European Border in Cinema, 1945–2010*, edited by Raita Merivirta, Kimmo Ahonene, Heta Mulari, and Rami Mahkä, 219–233. Bristol: Intellect.

———. 2015. *In Permanent Crisis: Ethnicity in Contemporary European Media and Cinema*. Ann Arbor: University of Michigan Press.

Chakrabarty, Dipesh. 2000. *Provincializing Europe: Postcolonial Thought and Historical Difference*. Princeton, NJ: Princeton University Press.

Chalkou, Maria. 2012. "A New Cinema of 'Emancipation': Tendencies of Independence in Greek Cinema of the 2000s." *Interactions: Studies in Communication & Culture* 3(2): 243–261.

Chare, Nicholas, and Liz Watkins. 2015. "Introduction: Gesture in Film." *Journal for Cultural Research* 19 (1): 1–5.

Chaudhary, Zahid R. 2009. "Humanity Adrift: Race, Materiality, and Allegory in Alfonso Cuarón's *Children of Men*." *Camera Obscura* 24 (3): 73–109.

Chilcoat, Michelle. 2008. "Queering the Family in François Ozon's *Sitcom*." In *Queer Cinema in Europe*, edited by Robin Griffiths, 23–33. Bristol: Intellect.

Chion, Michel. 1999. *The Voice in the Cinema*. New York: Columbia University Press.

Coates, Paul. 2005. *The Red & the White: The Cinema of People's Poland*. London: Wallflower.

Cobble, Dorothy Sue. 2004. *The Other Women's Movement: Workplace Justice and Social Rights in Modern America*. Princeton, NJ: Princeton University Press.

Cockett, Richard. 1994. *Thinking the Unthinkable: Think-Tanks and the Economic Counterrevolution, 1931–83*. New York: HarperCollins.

Cohen, Sheila. 2012. "Equal Pay—or What? Economics, Politics and the 1968 Ford Sewing Machinists' Strike." *Labor History* 53 (1): 51–68.

———. 2013. *Notoriously Militant: The Story of a Union Branch*. London: Merlin Press.

Coontz, Stephanie. 2011. *A Strange Stirring: "The Feminine Mystique" and American Women at the Dawn of the 1960s*. New York: Basic Books.

Cooper, Melinda. 2008. *Life as Surplus: Biotechnology & Capitalism in the Neoliberal Era*. Seattle: University of Washington Press.

Cooper, Sarah. 2007. "Mortal Ethics: Reading Levinas with the Dardenne Brothers." *Film-Philosophy* 11 (2): 66–87.

Corea, Gena. 1985. *The Mother Machine: Reproductive Technologies from Artificial Insemination to Artificial Wombs*. New York: Harpercollins.

Comanducci, Carlo. 2017. "Empty Gestures: Mimesis and Subjection in the Cinema of Yorgos Lanthimos." *Apparatus: Film, Media, and Digital Cultures in Central and Eastern Europe* 5: n.p. http://www.apparatusjournal.net/index.php/apparatus.

Council of Europe: Eurimages—European Cinema Support Fund. http://www.coe.int/t/dg4/eurimages/.

Cowie, Elizabeth. 2015. "The Time of Gesture in Cinema and Its Ethics." *Journal for Cultural Research* 19(1): 82–95.

Cox, Rosie. 1999. "The Role of Ethnicity in Shaping the Domestic Employment Section in Britain." In *Gender, Migration and Domestic Service*, edited by Janet Henshall Momsen, 134–147. New York: Routledge.

Creative Europe Deutschland. http://www.creative-europe-desk.de/.

Cunningham, John. 2004. *Hungarian Cinema from Coffee House to Multiplex*. London: Wallflower.

Curtis, Scott. 2009. "Images of Efficiency: The Films of Frank B. Gilbreth." In *Films That Work: Industrial Film and the Productivity of Media*, edited by Vinzenz Hediger and Patrick Vonderau, 85–99. Amsterdam: Amsterdam University Press.

DasGupta, Sayantani. 2010. "(Re)conceiving the Surrogate: Maternity, Race, and Reproductive Technologies in Alfonso Cuarón's *Children of Men*." In *Gender Scripts in Medicine and Narrative*, edited by Marcelline Block and Angela Laflin, 178–211. Newcastle upon Thyme: Cambridge Scholars Publishing.

Dave, Paul. 2006. *Visions of England: Class and Culture in Contemporary Cinema*. Oxford: Berg.

Davies, Margery W. 1982. *Woman's Place Is at the Typewriter: Office Work and Office Workers 1870–1930*. Philadelphia: Temple University Press.

Derrida, Jacques. 2006. *Specters of Marx: The State of the Debt, the Work of Mourning and the New International*. New York: Routledge.

Dickenson, Donna. 2007. *Property in the Body: Feminist Perspectives*. Cambridge: Cambridge University Press.

———. 2008. *Body Shopping: Converting Body Parts to Profit*. Oxford: Oneworld.

Dinerstein, Joel. 2003. *Swinging the Machine: Modernity, Technology, and African American Culture between the World Wars*. Amherst: University of Massachusetts Press.

Doane, Mary Ann. 1985. "The Voice in the Cinema: The Articulation of Body and Space." In *Film Sound: Theory and Practice*, edited by Elisabeth Weis and John Belton, 162–176. New York: Columbia University Press.

Dolar, Mladen. 2006. *A Voice and Nothing More*. Cambridge, MA: MIT Press.

Duffy, Enda. 2009. *The Speed Handbook: Velocity, Pleasure, Modernism*. Durham, NC: Duke University Press.

Dyer, Richard. 2001. "Nice Young Men Who Sell Antiques: Gay Men in Heritage Cinema." In *Film/Literature/Heritage: A Sight and Sound Reader*, edited by Ginette Vincendeau, 43–48. London: BFI.

Dyer, Richard, and Ginette Vincendeau, eds. 1992. *Popular European Cinema*. London: Routledge.

Efron, David. (1941) 1972. *Gesture and Environment: A Tentative Study of Some of the Spatiotemporal and "Linguistic" Aspects of the Gestural Behavior of Eastern Jews and Southern Italians in New York City, Living under Similar as Well as Different Environmental Conditions*. The Hague: Mouton.

Elias, Juanita. 2016. "Whose Crisis? Whose Recovery? Lessons Learned (and Not) from the Asian Crisis." In *Scandalous Economics: Gender and the Politics of Financial Crises*, edited by Aida A. Hozić and Jacqui True, 109–125. Oxford: Oxford University Press.

Elley, Derek. 2006. "*Falling*." *Variety*. http://variety.com/2006/film/reviews/falling-3-1200513746/.

Elsaesser, Thomas. 2005. *European Cinema: Face to Face with Hollywood*. Amsterdam: Amsterdam University Press.

Enstad, Nan. 1999. *Ladies of Labor, Girls of Adventure: Working Women, Popular Culture, and Labor Politics at the Turn of the Twentieth Century*. New York: Columbia University Press.

European Commission. COSME. Europe's Programme for Small and Medium-Sized Enterprises. https://ec.europa.eu/growth/smes/cosme_en.

Ezra, Elizabeth, ed. 2004. *European Cinema*. Oxford: Oxford University Press.

Fainde, Omolara, ed. 2010. *Mobility & Inclusion: Managing Labor Migration in Europe: Dossier*. Berlin: Heinrich-Böll-Stiftung. https://heimatkunde.boell.de/sites/default/files/dossier_mobility_and_inclusion.pdf.

Falser, Michael. 2001. "Is Industrial Heritage Under-Represented on the World Heritage List?" In *Global Strategy Studies: Under-Represented Categories (Industrial Heritage)*. Paris: World Heritage Centre UNESCO. http://whc.unesco.org/archive/indstudy01.pdf.

Faris, Wendy B. 1995. "Scheherazade's Children: Magical Realism and Postmodern Fiction." In *Magical Realism: Theory, History, Community*, edited by Lois Parkinson Zamora and Wendy B. Faris, 163–190. Durham, NC: Duke University Press.

Farocki, Harun. 2004. "Workers Leaving the Factory." In *Working on the Sightlines*, edited by Thomas Elsaesser, 237–243. Amsterdam: Amsterdam University Press.

Federici, Silvia. 2012a. *Revolution at Point Zero: Housework, Reproduction, and Feminist Struggle*. Oakland, CA: PM Press.

Federici, Silvia. 2012b. "Wages against Housework (1975)." In *Revolution at Point Zero: Housework, Reproduction, and Feminist Struggle*, 15–22. Oakland, CA: PM Press.

FEMEN: Official Blog. http://femen.org/?attempt=1.

Ferris, Suzanne, and Mallory Young, eds. 2007. *Chick Flicks: Contemporary Women at the Movies*. New York: Routledge.

"Fertility Clinics Abroad: Your Choice, Your Family, Your Life." La Coruña. https://www.fertilityclinicsabroad.com/cities/la-coruna/.

Firestone, Shulamith. (1970) 2003. *The Dialectic of Sex: The Case for Feminist Revolution*. New York: Farrar, Straus and Giroux.

Fisher, Mark. 2011. "*Dogtooth*: The Family Syndrome." *Film Quarterly* 64(4): 22–27.

Fisher, Melissa S. 2012. *Wall Street Women*. Durham, NC: Duke University Press.

Flitterman-Lewis, Sandy. 1996. *To Desire Differently: Feminism and the French Cinema*. New York: Columbia University Press.

Florida, Richard. 2011. *The Rise of the Creative Class*. New York: Basic Books.

Foley, Stephen. 2011. "Goldman's Memo on How to Cash In on the Europe Crisis." *Independent*. https://www.independent.co.uk/news/business/news/goldmans-memo-on-how-to-cash-in-on-euro-crisis-2347796.html.

Forbes, Jill, and Sarah Street. 2000. *European Cinema: An Introduction*. New York: Palgrave.
Foroutan, Naika. 2015. "Die postmigrantische Gesellschaft." In *Kurzdossiers: Bundeszentrale für politische Bildung: Zuwanderung, Flucht und Asyl. Aktuelle Themen*. http://www.bpb.de/gesellschaft/migration/kurzdossiers/205190/die%20 postmigrantische-gesellschaft.
Forster, Ralf. 2016. "Amateur Film I: At Work." In *Program: 59th International Leipzig Festival for Documentary and Animated Film*, 218.
Foucault, Michel. 2008. *The Birth of Biopolitics: Lectures at the Collège de France 1978–1979*. New York: Palgrave.
Fowler, Catherine, ed. 2002. *The European Cinema Reader*. London: Routledge.
Franklin, Sarah. 2003. "Kinship, Genes, and Cloning: Life after Dolly." In *Genetic Nature / Culture: Anthropology and Science beyond the Two-Culture Divide*, edited by Alan H. Goodman, Deborah Heath, and M. Susan Lindee, 95–110. Berkeley: University of California Press.
Fraser, Ian. 2013. "Affective Labor and Alienation in *Up in the Air*." In *Work in Cinema: Labor and the Human Condition*, edited by Ewa Mazierska, 29–48. New York: Palgrave.
Fraser, Nancy. 2013a. *Fortunes of Feminism: From State-Managed Capitalism to Neoliberal Crisis*. London: Verso.
———. 2013b. "How Feminism Became Capitalism's Handmaiden—and How to Reclaim It." *Guardian*, October 13. https://www.theguardian.com/commentisfree/ 2013/oct/14/feminism-capitalist-handmaiden-neoliberal.
Friedan, Betty. (1963) 2013. *The Feminine Mystique*. New York: W. W. Norton.
Frieden, Sandra, Richard W. McCormick, Vibeke R. Petersen, and Laurie Melissa Vogelsang, eds. 1993a. *Gender and German Cinema*. Vol. 1, *Gender and Representation in New German Cinema*. Oxford: Berg.
———. 1993b. *Gender and German Cinema*. Vol. 2, *German Film History / German History on Film*. Oxford: Berg.
Frölich, Margrit. 2011. "Tauschgeschäfte: Die Filme *Le silence de Lorna* und *L'enfant* von Jean-Pierre und Luc Dardenne" [Bartering transactions: The films *The Silence of Lorna* and *The Child* by Jean-Pierre and Luc Dardenne]. In *Geld und Kino* [Money and cinema], edited by Margrit Frölich and Rembert Hüser, 219–234. Marburg: Schüren.
Galt, Rosalind. 2006. *The New European Cinema: Redrawing the Map*. New York: Columbia University Press.
———. 2011. *Pretty: Film and the Decorative Image*. New York: Columbia University Press.
Galt, Rosalind, and Karl Schoonover. 2010. *Global Art Cinema: New Theories and Histories*. Oxford: Oxford University Press.
Gardey, Delphine. 2001. "Mechanizing Writing and Photographing the Word: Utopias, Office Work, and the Histories of Gender and Technology." *History and Technology* 17:319–352.
Garland, Alex. 1997. *The Beach*. New York: Riverhead Books.
The Genius Loci Project. http://www.europeangeniusloci.eu/.

Giftlife Egg Bank. "I Want to Become a Surrogate Mother!" http://www.giftlife.in/index.php?option=com_content&view=article&id=459:sm0310417&catid=11&Itemid=486.

Gill, Rosalind, and Christina Scharff. 2011. *New Femininities: Postfeminism, Neoliberalism and Subjectivity*. New York: Palgrave Macmillan.

Girelli, Elisabetta. 2009. "Stardom, Italianness, and Britishness in Post-war Britain." In *Stellar Encounters: Stardom in Popular European Cinema*, edited by Tytti Soila, 171–179. Herts: John Libbey Publishing.

Göktürk, Deniz. 1999. "Turkish Delight—German Fright: Migrant Identities in Transnational Cinema." *Transnational Communities Working Paper Series*, 1–14.

Goodwin, Michele. 2006. *Black Markets: The Supply and Demand of Body Parts*. Cambridge: Cambridge University Press.

Gorfinkel, Elena. 2012a. "Introduction: Dossier: The Work of the Image; Cinema, Labor, Aesthetics." *Framework* 53 (1): 43–46.

———. 2012b. "Weariness, Waiting: Endurance and Art Cinema's Tired Bodies." *Discourse* 34 (2–3): 311–347.

"The Greek Crisis: In Quotes." 2012. *Telegraph*. May 15. https://www.telegraph.co.uk/finance/financialcrisis/9267333/The-Greek-crisis-in-quotes.html.

Gregg, Melissa. 2011. *Work's Intimacy*. Malden, MA: Polity Press.

Griffiths, Robin, ed. 2008. *Queer Cinema in Europe*. Bristol: Intellect.

Gutiérrez-Rodríguez, Encarnación. 2010. *Migration, Domestic Work and Affect: A Decolonial Approach on Value and the Feminization of Labor*. London: Routledge.

Halle, Randall. 2008. *German Film after Germany: Toward a Transnational Aesthetic*. Urbana: University of Illinois Press.

———. 2013. "Großstadtfilm and Gentrification Debates: Localism and Social Imaginary in *Soul Kitchen* and *Eine flexible Frau*." *New German Critique* 40:171–191.

———. 2014. *The Europeanization of Cinema: Interzones and Imaginative Communities*. Urbana: University of Illinois Press.

Hames, Peter. 2009. *Czech and Slovak Cinema: Theme and Tradition*. Edinburgh: University of Edinburgh Press.

Haraway, Donna J. 1991. "A Cyborg Manifesto: Science, Technology, and Socialist-Feminism in the Late Twentieth Century." In *Simians, Cyborgs, and Women: The Reinvention of Nature*, 149–182. New York: Routledge.

Hardy, Jane. 2010. "'Brain Drain,' 'Brain Gain' or 'Brain Waster': East–West Migration after Enlargement." In *Mobility & Inclusion: Managing Labor Migration in Europe: Dossier*, edited by Omolara Fainde, 48–54. Berlin: Heinrich-Böll-Stiftung. https://heimatkunde.boell.de/sites/default/files/dossier_mobility_and_inclusion.pdf.

Harper, Graeme, and Jonathan Rayner, eds. 2010. *Cinema and Landscape*. Bristol: Intellect.

Harrod, Mary. 2015. *From France with Love: Gender and Identity in French Romantic Comedy*. London: I. B. Tauris.

Harvey, David. 1990. *The Condition of Postmodernity*. Cambridge, MA: Blackwell.
Hatzfeld, Nicolas, Gwenaële Rot, and Alain P. Michel. "Filming Work on Behalf of the Automobile Firm: The Case of Renault (1950–2002)." In *Films That Work: Industrial Film and the Productivity of Media*, edited by Vinzenz Hediger and Patrick Vonderau, 187–209. Amsterdam: Amsterdam University Press.
Hayes, Lydia. 2016. "Sex, Class and CCTV: The Covert Surveillance of Paid Home Care Workers." In *The Post-Fordist Sexual Contract: Working and Living in Contingency*, edited by Lisa Adkins and Maryanne Dever, 171–193. New York: Palgrave.
Hayward, Susan. 2009. "Simone Signoret: Costume Drama and the Star Text—a Case Study: *Casque d'or*." In *Stellar Encounters: Stardom in Popular European Cinema*, edited by Tytti Soila, 121–131. Herts: John Libbey Publishing.
Hediger, Vinzenz. 2009. "Thermodynamic Kitsch: Computing in German Industrial Films, 1928–1963." In *Films That Work: Industrial Film and the Productivity of Media*, edited by Vinzenz Hediger and Patrick Vonderau, 127–149. Amsterdam: Amsterdam University Press.
Hediger, Vinzenz, and Patrick Vonderau, eds. 2009a. *Films That Work: Industrial Film and the Productivity of Media*. Amsterdam: Amsterdam University Press.
———. 2009b. "Record, Rhetoric, Rationalization: Industrial Organization and Film." In *Films That Work: Industrial Film and the Productivity of Media*, edited by Vinzenz Hediger and Patrick Vonderau, 35–49. Amsterdam: Amsterdam University Press.
Heidenreich, Nanna. 2015. *V/Erkennungsdienste, das Kino und die Perspektive der Migration*. Bielefeld: transcript.
Held, Virginia. 2006. *The Ethics of Care: Personal, Political, and Global*. Oxford: Oxford University Press.
Hewison, Robert. 1987. *The Heritage Industry: Britain in a Climate of Decline*. London: Methuen.
Hicks, Heather J. 2003. "Hoodoo Economics: White Men's Work and Black Men's Magic in Contemporary American Film." *Camera Obscura* 18 (2): 27–55.
Higson, Andrew. 1993. "Re-presenting the National Past: Nostalgia and Pastiche in the Heritage Film." In *British Cinema and Thatcherism: Fires Were Started*, edited by Lester Friedman, 109–129. London: UCL Press.
Hjort, Mette, and Duncan Petrie, eds. 2007. *The Cinema of Small Nations*. Bloomington: Indiana University Press.
Hoberman, Jim. 2015. "Miguel Gomes Blends Fantasy and Real Life 'Arabian Nights.'" *New York Times*, November 25. https://www.nytimes.com/2015/11/29/movies/miguel-gomes-blends-fantasy-and-real-life-arabian-nights.html.
Hochschild, Arlie Russell. 2012. *The Managed Heart: Commercialization of Human Feeling*. Berkeley: University of California Press.
Hozić, Aida A., and Jacqui True, eds. 2016. *Scandalous Economics: Gender and the Politics of Financial Crises*. Oxford: Oxford University Press.
Hughes, Alex, and James S. Williams, eds. 2001. *Gender and French Cinema*. Oxford: Berg.
Imre, Anikó, ed. 2005. *East European Cinemas*. New York: Routledge.

———. 2009. *Identity Games: Globalization and the Transformation of Media Cultures in the New Europe*. Cambridge, MA: MIT Press.
Indian Egg Donors. "International Surrogacy in 4 Easy Steps." http://www.indianeggdonors.com/.
Iordanova, Dina. 2001. *Cinema of Flames: Balkan Film, Culture and the Media*. London: BFI.
Ishiguro, Kazuo. 2005. *Never Let Me Go*. New York: Vintage.
Ivory, William. 2006. "Dagenham Girls" (working title). London: UK Film Council. http://downloads.bbc.co.uk/writersroom/scripts/Made-in-Dagenham.pdf.
Jäckel, Anne. 2003. *European Film Industries*. London: British Film Institute.
Jaffe, Ira. 2014. *Slow Movies: Countering the Cinema of Action*. London: Wallflower Press.
Jameson, Fredric. 1986. "On Magical Realism in Film." *Critical Inquiry* 12 (2): 301–325.
Kalha, Harri. 2009. "The Case of Theodor Tugai: The Filmstar and the Factitious Body." In *Stellar Encounters: Stardom in Popular European Cinema*, edited by Tytti Soila, 132–142. Herts: John Libbey Publishing.
Kallio, Kalle, and Nick Mansfield. 2013. "Labor and Landscape: Editorial." *International Journal of Heritage Studies* 19 (5): 401–407.
Kang, Miliann. 2010. *The Managed Hand: Race, Gender, and the Body in Beauty Service Work*. Berkeley: University of California Press.
Karamessini, Maria, and Jill Rubery. 2014. *Women and Austerity: The Economic Crisis and the Future for Gender Equality*. New York: Routledge.
Kempadoo, Kamala, ed. 2005. *Trafficking and Prostitution Reconsidered: New Perspectives on Migration, Sex Work, and Human Rights*. Boulder, CO: Paradigm Publishers.
Kerber, Linda K. 2009. "The Stateless as the Citizen's Other: A View from the United States." In *Migrations and Mobilities: Citizenship, Borders, and Gender*, edited by Seyla Benhabib and Judith Resnick, 76–123. New York: New York University Press.
Kessler-Harris, Alice. 2007. *Gendering Labor History*. Urbana: University of Illinois Press.
Klein, Naomi. 2007. *The Shock Doctrine: The Rise of Disaster Capitalism*. New York: Picador.
Knight, Deborah. 1997. "Naturalism, Narration and Critical Perspective: Ken Loach and the Experimental Method." In *Agent of Challenge and Defiance: The Films of Ken Loach*, edited by George McKnight, 60–81. Westport, CT: Praeger.
Koepnick, Lutz. 2002. "Reframing the Past: Heritage Cinema and Holocaust in the 1990s." *New German Critique* 87:47–82.
———. 2014. *On Slowness: Toward an Aesthetic of the Contemporary*. New York: Columbia University Press.
Kofman, Eleonore, Annie Phizacklea, Parvati Raghuram, and Rosemary Sales. 2000. *Gender and International Migration in Europe: Employment, Welfare and Politics*. London: Routledge.
Köhn, Steffen. 2016. Migrantische Medien—der Migration." *Frauen und Film* 67:53–66.
Koivunen, Anu. 2009. "Soulfulness, Sichtbarkeit and the Sexual Politics of National Cinema." In *Stellar Encounters: Stardom in Popular European Cinema*, edited by Tytti Soila, 143–160. Herts: John Libbey Publishing.

Konstantarakos, Myrto, ed. 2000. *Spaces in European Cinema*. Exeter: Intellect.
Kourelou, Olga, Mariana Liz, and Belén Vidal. 2014. "Crisis and Creativity: The New Cinemas of Portugal, Greece and Spain." *New Cinemas: Journal of Contemporary Film* 12 (1 and 2): 133–151.
Kovács, András Bálint. 2007. *Screening Modernism: European Art Cinema, 1950–1980*. Chicago: University of Chicago Press.
Kristensen, Lars, ed. 2012. *Postcommunist Film—Russia, Eastern Europe and World Culture: Moving Images of Postcommunism*. New York: Routledge.
Kuhn, Annette. 2002. *Dreaming of Fred and Ginger: Cinema and Cultural Memory*. New York: New York University Press.
———. 2009. "Film Stars in 1930s Britain: A Case Study in Modernity and Femininity." In *Stellar Encounters: Stardom in Popular European Cinema*, edited by Tytti Soila, 180–194. Herts: John Libbey Publishing.
Kurash, Jaclyn. 2015. "Mechanical Women and Sexy Machines: Typewriting in Mass-Media Culture of the Weimar Republic, 1918–1933." Ph.D. diss., Ohio State University.
Lai, Larissa. 2010. "Neither Hand, nor Foot, nor Kidney: Biopower, Body Parts, and Human Flows in Stephen Frears' *Dirty Pretty Things*." *CineAction* 80:68–72.
Laine, Kimmo. 2009. "Celebrity Culture and the Preconditions for Finnish Film Stardom in the 1920s and 30s." In *Stellar Encounters: Stardom in Popular European Cinema*, edited by Tytti Soila, 245–253. Herts: John Libbey Publishing.
Laing, Stuart. 1997. "Ken Loach: Histories and Context." In *Agent of Challenge and Defiance: The Films of Ken Loach*, edited by George McKnight, 11–27. Westport, CT: Praeger.
Landsberg, Alison. 2004. *Prosthetic Memory: The Transformation of American Remembrance in the Age of Mass Culture*. New York: Columbia University Press.
Lemke, Thomas. 2011. *Biopolitics: An Advanced Introduction*. New York: New York University Press.
Levitt, Deborah. 2008. "Notes on Media and Biopolitics: 'Notes on Gesture.'" In *The Work of Giorgio Agamben: Law, Literature, Life*, edited by Justin Clemens, Nicholas Heron, and Alex Murray, 193–211. Edinburgh: Edinburgh University Press.
Lim, Bliss Cua. 2009. *Translating Time: Cinema, the Fantastic, and Temporal Critique*. Durham, NC: Duke University Press.
Loiperdinger, Martin. 2009. "Early Industrial Moving Pictures in Germany." In *Films That Work: Industrial Film and the Productivity of Media*, edited by Vinzenz Hediger and Patrick Vonderau, 65–73. Amsterdam: Amsterdam University Press.
Loshitzky, Yosefa. 2010. *Screening Strangers: Migration and Diaspora in Contemporary European Cinema*. Bloomington: Indiana University Press.
Made in Dagenham: A Sony Pictures Classics Release. 2010. Press Kit. http://www.sonyclassics.com/madeindagenham/madeindagenham_presskit.pdf.
Mademli, Geli. 2015. "On the Importance of Being Weird: On Language Games in Contemporary Greek Films." *Filmicon: Journal of Greek Film Studies*, April 23. http://filmiconjournal.com/blog/post/41/the-importance-of-being-weird.

Mai, Joseph. 2010. *Jean-Pierre and Luc Dardenne*. Urbana: University of Illinois Press.
Malik, Sarita. 1996. "Beyond 'The Cinema of Duty'? The Pleasures of Hybridity: Black British Film of the 1980s and 1990s." In *Dissolving Views: Key Writings on British Cinema*, edited by Andrew Higson, 202–215. London: Bloomsbury.
Marçal, Katrine. 2016. *Who Cooked Adam Smith's Dinner? A Story of Women and Economics*. New York: Pegasus.
Marsh, Steven, and Parvati Nair, eds. 2004. *Gender and Spanish Cinema*. Oxford: Berg.
Marx, Karl, and Friedrich Engels. 1848. *Manifesto of the Communist Party*. https://www.marxists.org/archive/marx/works/1848/communist-manifesto/ch01.htm.
Mazierska, Ewa, ed. 2013. *Work in Cinema: Labor and the Human Condition*. New York: Palgrave.
——. 2015. *From Self-Fulfilment to Survival of the Fittest: Work in European Cinema from the 1960s to the Present*. New York: Berghahn.
Mazierska, Ewa, and Laura Rascaroli. 2006. *Crossing New Europe: Postmodern Travel and the European Road Movie*. London: Wallflower.
McHugh, Kathleen Anne. 1999. *American Domesticity: From How-to Manual to Hollywood Melodrama*. New York: Oxford University Press.
McKnight, George. 1997. Introduction to *Agent of Challenge and Defiance: The Films of Ken Loach*, edited by George McKnight, 1–10. Westport, CT: Praeger.
McLean, Adrienne L. 2004. *Being Rita Hayworth: Labor, Identity, and Hollywood Stardom*. New Brunswick, NJ: Rutgers University Press.
McNeill, David. 2015. "Speech-Gesture Mimicry in Performance: An Actor → Audience, Author → Actor, Audience → Actor Triangle." *Journal for Cultural Research* 19 (1): 15–29.
McRobbie, Angela. 2009. *The Aftermath of Feminism: Gender, Culture and Social Change*. Washington, DC: Sage.
Moitra, Stefan. 2009. "'Reality Is There, but It's Manipulated': West German Trade Unions and Film after 1945." In *Films That Work: Industrial Film and the Productivity of Media*, edited by Vinzenz Hediger and Patrick Vonderau, 329–345. Amsterdam: Amsterdam University Press.
Montoya, Celeste. 2016. "Exploits and Exploitations: A Micro and Macro Analysis of the 'DSK Affair.'" In *Scandalous Economics: Gender and the Politics of Financial Crisis*, edited by Aida Hozić and Jacqui True, 145–164. Oxford: Oxford University Press.
Mortimer, Claire. 2010. *Romantic Comedy*. London: Routledge.
Mosley, Philip. 2013. *The Cinema of the Dardenne Brothers: Responsible Realism*. London: Wallflower.
Mulvey, Laura. (1975) 1988. "Visual Pleasure and Narrative Cinema." In *Feminism and Film Theory*, edited by Constance Penley, 57–68. London: Routledge.
——. 2015. "Cinematic Gesture: The Ghost in the Machine." *Journal for Cultural Research* 19 (1): 6–14.
Musser, Charles. 2004. "At the Beginning: Motion Picture Production, Representation and Ideology at the Edison and Lumière Companies." In *The Silent Cinema Reader*, edited by Lee Grieveson and Peter Krämer, 15–30. New York: Routledge.

Naficy, Hamid. 2001. *An Accented Cinema: Exilic and Diasporic Filmmaking*. Princeton, NJ: Princeton University Press.

Nathanson, Elizabeth. 2013. *Television and Postfeminist Housekeeping*. New York: Routledge.

———. 2014. "Dressed for Economic Distress: Blogging and the 'New' Pleasures of Fashion." In *Gendering the Recession: Media and Culture in an Age of Austerity*, edited by Diane Negra and Yvonne Tasker, 136–160. Durham, NC: Duke University Press.

Neale, Steve. 1986. "Melodrama and Tears." *Screen* 27:6–22.

Negra, Diane. 2009. *What a Girl Wants? Fantasizing the Reclamation of Self in Postfeminism*. New York: Routledge.

Negra, Diane, and Yvonne Tasker, eds. 2007. *Interrogating Postfeminism: Gender and the Politics of Popular Culture*. Durham, NC: Duke University Press.

Ness, Sally Ann. 2008. "Conclusion." In *Migrations of Gestures,* edited by Carrie Noland and Sally Ann Ness, 259–279. University of Minnesota Press.

Newland, Paul. 2008. *The Cultural Construction of London's East End: Urban Iconography, Modernity and the Spatialization of Englishness*. Leiden: Brill.

Ngai, Sianne. 2005. *Ugly Feelings*. Cambridge, MA: Harvard University Press.

Noland, Carrie. 2008. Introduction to *Migrations of Gesture*, edited by Carrie Noland and Sally Ann Ness, ix–xxvii. Minneapolis: University of Minnesota Press.

———. 2009. *Agency and Embodiment: Performing Gestures / Producing Culture*. Cambridge, MA: Harvard University Press.

North, Michael. 2009. *Machine-Age Comedy*. Oxford: Oxford University Press.

Nye, David E. 2013. *America's Assembly Line*. Cambridge, MA: MIT Press.

Nystrom, Derek. 2009. *Hard Hats, Rednecks, and Macho Men: Class in 1970s American Cinema*. Oxford: Oxford University Press.

Oakley, Ann. 1974. *The Sociology of Housework*. New York: Pantheon.

———. 2014. *Father and Daughter: Patriarchy, Gender and Social Science*. Bristol: Policy Press.

Ogrodnik, Ben. 2014. "Focalisation Realism and Narrative Symmetry in Alfonso Cuarón's *Children of Men*." *Senses of Cinema* 71. http://sensesofcinema.com/2014/feature-articles/focalization-realism-and-narrative-asymmetry-in-alfonso-cuarons-children-of-men/.

Olsson, Jan. 2009. "'Dear Miss Gagner!': A Star and Her Methods." In *Stellar Encounters: Stardom in Popular European Cinema*, edited by Tytti Soila, 217–229. Herts: John Libbey Publishing.

Ortner, Sherry B. 1974. "Is Female to Male as Nature Is to Culture?" In *Women, Culture, and Society*, edited by Michell Rosaldo and Louise Lamphere, 68–87. Stanford, CA: Stanford University Press.

"ozTypewriter: The Wonderful World of Typewriters." http://oztypewriter.blogspot.de/.

Papadimitriou, Lydia. 2014. "Locating Contemporary Greek Film Cultures: Past, Present, Future and the Crisis." *Filmicon: Journal of Greek Film Studies* 2:1–19.

Parreñas, Rhacel Salazar. 2008. *The Force of Domesticity: Filipina Migrants and Globalization*. New York: New York University Press.

Parvulescu, Anca. 2014. *The Traffic in Women's Work: East European Migration and the Making of Europe*. Chicago: University of Chicago Press.
Pateman, Carole. 1988. *The Sexual Contract*. Stanford, CA: Stanford University Press.
Peranson, Mark. 2016. "A Battle of Humor: Maren Ade on *Toni Erdmann*." *Cinema Scope*. http://cinema-scope.com/spotlight/battle-humour-maren-ade-toni-erdmann/.
Perrons, Diane, and Ania Plomien. 2014. "Gender, Inequality and the Crisis: Towards More Equitable Development." In *Women and Austerity: The Economic Crisis and the Future for Gender Equality*, edited by Maria Karamessini and Jill Rubery, 295–313. London: Routledge.
Petrie, Duncan, ed. 1992. *Screening Europe: Image and Identity in Contemporary European Cinema*. London: British Film Institute.
Plumpe, Werner, and André Steiner. 2016. "Der Mythos von der postindustriellen Welt." In *Der Mythos von der postindustriellen Welt: Wirtschaftlicher Strukturwandel in Deutschland 1960–1990*, edited by Werner Plumpe and André Steiner, 7–14. Göttingen: Wallst ein Verlag.
Polaschek, Bronwyn. 2013. *The Postfeminist Biopic: Narrating the Lives of Plath, Kahlo, Woolf and Austen*. Houndsmills: Palgrave Macmillan.
"*Populaire*: One Absolute Ripper of a Typewriter Movie." http://oztypewriter.blogspot.de/search?q=Populaire.
Powrie, Phil. 1998. "Heritage, History and 'New Realism': French Cinema in the 1990s." *Modern & Contemporary France* 6 (4): 479–491.
Prügl, Elisabeth. 2016. "'Lehman Brothers and Sisters': Revisiting Gender and Myth after the Financial Crisis." In *Scandalous Economics: Gender and the Politics of Financial Crises*, edited by Aida A. Hozić and Jacqui True, 21–40. Oxford: Oxford University Press.
Qayum, Seemin, and Raka Ray. 2010. "Traveling Cultures of Servitude: Loyalty and Betrayal in New York and Kolkata." In *Intimate Labors: Cultures, Technologies, and the Politics of Care*, edited by Eileen Boris and Rhacel Salazar Parreñas, 101–116. Stanford, CA: Stanford University Press.
"Quotes: EU Leaders Talk Financial Crisis." 2008. *Café Babel*. October 28. http://www.cafebabel.co.uk/politics/article/quotes-eu-leaders-talk-financial-crisis.html.
Rabinbach, Anson. 1990. *The Human Motor: Energy, Fatigue, and the Origins of Modernity*. Berkeley: University of California Press.
Radner, Hilary. 2011. *Neo-feminist Cinema: Girly Films, Chick Flicks and Consumer Culture*. New York: Routledge.
Rayns, Tony. 2016. "Film of the Week: *Arabian Nights Volume 1: The Restless One*." *Sight and Sound: The International Film Magazine*, May. http://www.bfi.org.uk/news-opinion/sight-sound-magazine/reviewsrecommendations/film-week-arabian-nights-volume-1-restless.
Rieger, Sophia Charlotte. 2017. "Interview with Barbara Albert: Supporting Women in the Film Industry Means Supporting a More Diverse Cinema." European Women's Audiovisual Network. http://www.ewawomen.com/en/events/interview-with

-barbara-albert:-supporting-women-in-the-film-industry-means-supporting-a-more-diverse-cinema.html.

Rifkin, Jeremy. 2005. *The European Dream: How Europe's Vision of the Future Is Quietly Eclipsing the American Dream*. New York: Penguin.

Roberts, Adrienne. 2016. "Finance, Financialization, and the Production of Gender." In *Scandalous Economics: Gender and the Politics of Financial Crisis*, edited by Aida Hozić and Jacqui True, 57–75. Oxford: Oxford University Press.

Rodriguez Ortega, Vincente. 2011. "Surgical Passports, the EU and *Dirty Pretty Things*: Rethinking European Identity through Popular Cinema." *Studies in European Cinema* 871:21–30.

Rose, Steve. 2011. "*Attenberg, Dogtooth*, and the Weird Wave of Greek Cinema." *Guardian*, August 27. https://www.theguardian.com/film/2011/aug/27/attenberg-dogtooth-greece-cinema.

Ross, Kristin. 1995. *Fast Cars, Clean Bodies: Decolonization and the Reordering of French Culture*. Cambridge, MA: MIT Press.

Rushton, Richard. 2014. "Emphatic Projection in the Films of the Dardenne Brothers." *Screen* 55 (1): 303–316.

Sagall, Sabby (S.S.). 1968. "Rose Boland, Shop Steward at Ford's Dagenham, Talks about the Women Machinists' Struggle for Equal Pay to Sabby Sagall. 'I Don't Know What Wilson's Trying to Do, but I'd Like to Shake the Liver out of Him." *Socialist Worker*, p. 2.

Schelde, Per. 1993. *Androids, Humanoids, and Other Science Fiction Monsters: Science and Soul in Science Fiction Films*. New York: New York University Press.

Schoonover, Karl. 2014. "Histrionic Gestures and Historical Representation: Masina's Cabiria, Bazin's Chaplin, and Fellini's Neorealism." *Cinema Journal* 53:93–116.

Schwartz, Vanessa R. 2007. *It's So French! Hollywood, Paris, and the Making of Cosmopolitan Film Culture*. Chicago: University of Chicago Press.

Scott, Anthony Oliver. 2010. "A Sanctuary and a Prison." *New York Times*, June 24. http://www.nytimes.com/2010/06/25/movies/25dog.html.

Sedgwick, Eve Kosofsky. 2003. *Touching Feeling: Affect, Pedagogy, Performativity*. Durham, NC: Duke University Press.

———. 2015. *Between Men: English Literature and Male Homosocial Desire*. New York: Columbia University Press.

Seltzer, Mark. 1992. *Bodies and Machines*. New York: Routledge.

Shackel, Paul A., Laurajane Smith, and Gary Campbell. 2011. "Labor's Heritage: Editorial." *International Journal of Heritage Studies* 17 (4): 291–300.

Shafi, Monika. 2012. *Housebound: Selfhood and Domestic Space in Contemporary German Fiction*. Rochester, NY: Camden House.

Sharp, Lesley A. 2011. "The Invisible Woman: The Bioaesthetics of Engineered Bodies." *Body & Society* 17 (1): 1–30.

Sieg, Katrin. 2008. *Choreographing the Global in European Cinema and Theater*. New York: Palgrave.

Silverman, Kaja. 1988. *The Acoustic Mirror: The Female Voice in Psychoanalysis and Cinema*. Bloomington: Indiana University Press.

Sklar, Deidre. 2008. "Remembering Kinesthesia: An Inquiry into Embodied Cultural Knowledge." In *Migrations of Gestures*, edited by Carrie Noland and Sally Ann Ness, 85–111. Minneapolis: University of Minnesota Press.

Skrodzka, Aga. 2012. *Magic Realist Cinema in East Central Europe*. Edinburgh: Edinburgh University Press.

Soila, Tytti, ed. 2009. *Stellar Encounters: Stardom in Popular European Cinema*. Herts: John Libbey Publishing.

Sontag, Susan. 2001. "Notes on 'Camp.'" In *Against Interpretation and Other Essays*, 275–292. New York: Picador.

Sorlin, Pierre, ed. 1991. *European Cinemas, European Societies, 1939–1990*. London: Routledge.

Sparling, Nicole R. 2014. "Without a Conceivable Future: Figuring the Mother in Alfonso Cuarón's *Children of Men*." *Frontiers: A Journal of Women's Studies* 35 (1): 160–180.

Spazzini, Maddalena. 2009. "'Italy's New Sophia Loren': Sabrina Ferilli." In *Stellar Encounters: Stardom in Popular European Cinema*, edited by Tytti Soila, 161–168. Herts: John Libbey Publishing.

Spivak, Gayatri. 1988. "Can the Subaltern Speak?" In *Marxism and the Interpretation of Culture*, edited by Cary Nelson and Larry Grossberg, 271–313. Urbana: University of Illinois Press.

Standing, Guy. 2011. *The Precariat: The New Dangerous Class*. London: Bloomsbury Academic.

Stead, Peter. 1989. *Film and the Working Class: The Feature Film in British and American Society*. London: Routledge.

Steiner, André. 2016. "Abschied von der Industries? Wirtschaftlicher Strukturwandel in West- und Ostdeutschland seit den 1960er Jahren." In *Der Mythos von der postindustriellen Welt: Wirtschaftlicher Strukturwandel in Deutschland 1960–1990*, edited by Werner Plumpe and André Steiner, 15–54. Göttingen: Wallstein Verlag.

Stern, Lesley. 2008. "Ghosting: The Performance and Migration of Cinematic Gesture, Focusing on Hou Hsiao-Hsien's *Good Men, Good Women*." In *Migrations of Gestures*, edited by Carrie Noland and Sally Ann Ness, 185–215. Minneapolis: University of Minnesota Press.

Suchland, Jennifer. 2011. "Is Postsocialism Transnational?" *Signs* 36 (4): 837–862.

Tasker, Yvonne. 1998. *Working Girls: Gender and Sexuality in Popular Cinema*. New York: Routledge.

Taylor, Frederick Winslow. (1911) 2014. *The Principles of Scientific Management*. Mansfield Centre, CT: Martino Publishing.

Taylor, Jessica. 2016. "Laptops and Playpens: 'Mommy Bloggers' and Visions of Household Work." In *The Post-Fordist Sexual Contract: Working and Living in Contingency*, edited by Lisa Adkins and Maryanne Dever, 109–128. London: Palgrave Macmillan.

Titmuss, Richard M. (1970) 1997. *The Gift Relationship: From Human Blood to Social Policy*. New York: New Press.

True, Jacqui. 2016. "The Global Financial Crisis' Silver Bullet: Women Leaders and 'Leaning In.'" In *Scandalous Economics: Gender and the Politics of Financial Crisis*, edited by Aida Hozić and Jacqui True, 41–56. Oxford: Oxford University Press.

Turanskyj, Tatjana. 2015. "Vom Leben in der Scheinemanzipation oder die Madonna mit der Kreissäge" [About life under false emancipation or the Madonna with a circular saw]. *What?! Just Another Feminist Blog*. https://turanskyj.wordpress.com/2015/07/15/dies-ist-unsere-zeit-weil-wir-sie-erschaffen/.

The Typewriter Database. http://typewriterdatabase.com/.

Varjonen, Johanna, and Leena M. Kirjavainen. 2014. "Women's Unpaid Work Was Counted but . . ." In *Counting on Marilyn Waring: New Advances in Feminist Economics*, edited by Margunn Bjørnholt and Ailsa McKay, 71–87. Bradford, ON: Demeter Press.

Verstraete, Ginette. 2010. *Tracking Europe: Mobility, Diaspora, and the Politics of Location*. Durham, NC: Duke University Press.

Villa, Paola, and Mark Smith. 2014. "Policy in the Time of Crisis: Employment Policy and Gender Equality in Europe." In *Women and Austerity: The Economic Crisis and the Future for Gender Equality*, edited by Maria Karamessini and Jill Rubery, 273–294. London: Routledge.

Vogl, Joseph. 2015. *The Specter of Capital*. Stanford, CA: Stanford University Press.

Voigts, Eckart. 2015. "Introduction: The Dystopian Imagination—an Overview." In *Dystopia, Science Fiction, Post-Apocalypse: Classics—New Tendencies—Model Interpretations*, edited by Eckart Voigts and Alessandra Boller, 1–11. Trier: WVT Wissenschaftlicher Verlag.

Volkening, Heide. 2007. "Working Girl—eine Einleitung." In *Working Girls: Zur Ökonomie von Liebe und Arbeit*, edited by Sabine Biebl, Verena Mund, and Heide Volkening, 7–22. Berlin: Kadmos.

Vonderau, Patrick. 2009. "Touring as a Cultural Technique: Visitor Films and Autostadt Wolfsburg." In *Films that Work: Industrial Film and the Productivity of Media*, edited by Vinzenz Hediger and Patrick Vonderau, 153–166. Amsterdam: Amsterdam University Press.

Vora, Kalindi. 2010. "The Transmission of Care: Affective Economies and Indian Call Centers." In *Intimate Labors: Cultures, Technologies, and the Politics of Care*, edited by Eileen Boris and Rhacel Salazar Parreñas, 33–48. Stanford, CA: Stanford University Press.

Vrasti, Wanda. 2016. "Self-Reproducing Movements and the Enduring Challenge of Materialist Feminism." In *Scandalous Economics: Gender and the Politics of Financial Crisis*, edited by Aida Hozić and Jacqui True, 248–265. Oxford: Oxford University Press.

Walby, Sylvia. 2015. *Crisis*. Cambridge: Polity.

Waldby, Catherine, and Robert Mitchell. 2006. *Tissue Economies: Blood, Organs, and Cell Lines in Late Capitalism*. Durham, NC: Duke University Press.

Waldman, Diane, and Janet Walker. 1999. Introduction to *Feminism and Documentary*, edited by Diane Waldman and Janet Walker, 1–35. Minneapolis: University of Minnesota Press.

Walentynowicz, Anna. 2012. *Solidarność—eine persönliche Geschichte*. Edited by Tytus Jaskułowski. Göttingen: V&Runipress.

Waring, Marilyn. 1988. *If Women Counted: A New Feminist Economics*. New York: Harper & Row.

Weeks, Kathi. 2011. *The Problem with Work: Feminism, Marxism, Antiwork Politics, and Postwork Imaginaries*. Durham, NC: Duke University Press.

Weiner, Elaine. 2007. *Market Dreams: Gender, Class & Capitalism in the Czech Republic*. Ann Arbor: University of Michigan Press.

Werner, Mateusz, ed. *Polish Cinema Now! Focus on Contemporary Polish Cinema*. London: Adam Mickiewicz Institute.

Wershler-Henry, Darren. 2005. *The Iron Whim: A Fragmented History of Typewriting*. Ithaca, NY: Cornell University Press.

"We Want Sex." https://www.flickr.com/photos/followthethings/10491675236/in/photostream/.

White, Armond. 2008. "Ways of Seeing." In *Everlasting Moments*, booklet accompanying DVD. Criterion.

Williams, Linda. 1988. "Feminist Film Theory: *Mildred Pierce* and the Second World War." In *Female Spectators: Looking at Film and Television*, edited by E. Deidre Pribram, 12–29. London: Verso.

Williams, Linda Ruth. 2005. *The Erotic Thriller in Contemporary Cinema*. Bloomington: Indiana University Press.

Wills, Jenny. 2007. "I's Wide Shut: Examining the Depiction of Female Refugees' Eyes and Hands in Stephen Frears's *Dirty Pretty Things*." *Refuge* 24 (2): 115–124.

Wolff, Charlotte. (1945) 2016. *A Psychology of Gesture*. New York: Routledge.

Yildiz, Yasemin. 2012. *Beyond the Mother Tongue: The Postmonolingual Condition*. New York: Fordham University Press.

Zarnowski, Frank. 2013. *American Work-Sports: A History of Competitions for Cornhuskers, Lumberjacks, Firemen and Others*. Jefferson, NC: McFarland.

Zimmermann, Yvonne. 2009. "'What Hollywood Is to America, the Corporate Film Is to Switzerland': Remarks on Industrial Film as Utility Film." In *Films That Work: Industrial Film and the Productivity of Media*, edited by Vinzenz Hediger and Patrick Vonderau, 101–117. Amsterdam: Amsterdam University Press.

Žižek, Slavoj. 2006. "*Children of Men* Comments." *Children of Men* extra material, DVD.

Film Index

#MyEscape (Elke Sasse, 2016), 109
28 Days Later (Danny Boyle, 2002), 171–72
1,000 Times Good Night (*Tusen ganger god natt*; Erik Poppe, 2013), 47–50
1001 Grams (*1001 Gram*; Bent Hamer, 2014), 45–48, 51
Age of Cannibals (*Zeit der Kannibalen*; Johannes Naber, 2014), 182, 193–95, 196, 199–200
Ali: Fear Eats Soul (*Angst essen Seele auf*; Rainer Werner Fassbinder, 1974), 96
All's Well (*Tout va bien*; Jean-Luc Godard, 1974), 1
All That Heaven Allows (Douglas Sirk, 1955), 96
Another Country (Marek Kanievska, 1984), 79
Arabian Nights (*As mil e uma noites*; Miguel Gomes, 2015), 182
Arabian Nights: Volume 2, The Desolate One (*As mil e uma noites: Volume 2, O desolado*; Miguel Gomes, 2015), 190–192, 200
Attack of the Giant Mousaka, The (*I epithesi tou gigantiaiou mousaka*; Panos H. Koutras, 1999), 214n1
Attenberg (Anthina Rachel Tsangari, 2010), 181, 187–89, 196, 200, 213–14n1

Barrel Roller (*Faßroller*, Gerhard Langer, 1972), 207n3
Bend It Like Beckham (Gurinder Chadha, 2002), 172
Biutiful (Alejandro González Iñárritu, 2010), 40, 42–43, 48, 51, 74
Blacksmithing Scene (Wiliam Kennedy Laurie Dickson, 1893), 9
Body Beautiful, The (Ngozi Onwurah, 1991), 211n5
Boomerang (*Bumerang*; Heinz Drigalla, Klaus Hessel, 1975), 207n3
Brick Lane (Sarah Gavron, 2007), 109–17, 121, 27, 211n7
Bridget Jones's Diary (Sharon Maguire, 2001), 54

Child, The (*Le fils*; Jean-Pierre Dardenne and Luc Dardenne, 2005), 209n3
Children of Men (Alfonso Cuarón, 2006), 155, 161, 166–69, 171, 175–76, 213n6
Class, The (*Entre les murs*; Laurent Cantet, 2008), 61
Cleo from 5–7 (*Cléo de 5 à 7*; Agnès Varda, 1962), 94
Coco before Chanel (*Coco avant Chanel*; Anne Fontaine, 2009), 84

Coffee Colored Children (Ngozi Onwurah, 1988), 211n5
Construction with DM-SPE (*Montage mit DM-SPE*; Reimar Rockstroh, 1963), 207n3
Cyrano de Bergerac (Jean-Paul Rappeneau, 1990), 95

Dirty Pretty Things (Stephen Frears, 2002), 155, 160–66, 175–76, 213n6
Disorientation Is Not a Crime (*Orientierungslosigkeit ist kein Verbrechen*; Tatjana Turanskyj, 2016), 69
Dogtooth (*Kynodontas*, Yorgos Lanthimos, 2009), 180–82, 186–89, 199–200, 213–14n1
Double Hour, The (*La doppia ora*; Giuseppe Capotondi, 2009), 136, 141–42, 144–45, 152–53
Drifters, The (*Eine flexible Frau*; Tatjana Turanskyj, 2010), 69–71, 73, 188

Eastern Promises (David Cronenberg, 2007), 109, 114–17, 121, 127
Education, An (Lone Scherfig, 2009), 172
Esma's Secret—Grbavica (*Grbavica*; Jasmila Zbanic, 2005), 74
Europa Europa (Agnieszka Holland, 1990), 210n7
Everlasting Moments (*Maria Larssons eviga ögonblick*; Jan Troell, 2008), 32–35, 38, 51

Falling (*Fallen*; Barbara Albert, 2006), 73–76, 209n7
Far from Heaven (Todd Haynes, 2002), 96
Far from the Madding Crowd (Thomas Vinterberg, 2015), 172
Father, The (*Baba*; Yilmaz Güney, 1971), 213n7
Florence Foster Jenkins (Stephen Frears, 2016), 161
Fräulein (*Das Fräulein*; Andrea Štaka, 2006), 74
Free Radicals (*Böse Zellen*; Barbara Albert, 2003), 74

Germinal (Claude Berri, 1993), 80, 95
Ghost (Jerry Zucker, 1990), 44

Has the Fire Gone Out? (*Ist der Ofen aus?*; Rainer Hässelbarth, 1988), 208n3
Heading South (*Vers le sud*; Laurent Cantet, 2005), 61
Help, The (Tate Taylor, 2011), 140
Hi Cousin! (*Salut cousin!*; Merzak Allouche, 1996), 101
Hidden Figures (Theodore Melfi, 2016), 140
Home (Ursula Meier, 2008), 38–39
Homeland (*Hora proelefsis*; Syllas Tzoumerkas, 2010), 214n1
Honey (*Miele*; Valeria Golino, 2013), 40–42, 51
Howard's End (James Ivory, 1992), 111
Human Resources (*Ressources humaines*; Laurent Cantet, 1999), 56, 61

I, Daniel Blake (Ken Loach, 2016), 11, 62, 209n2
I Am from Titov Veles (*Jas sum od Titov Veles*; Teona Strugar Mitevska, 2007), 64–69, 76, 209n4
I Love Budapest (Ágnes Incze, 2001), 99–100, 102
Imitation of Life (Douglas Sirk, 1959), 44
Indochine (Regis Wargnier, 1992), 112
In Love with Lou (*Lou Andreas-Salome*; Cordula Kablitz-Post, 2016), 84
Iron Lady, The (Phyllida Lloyd, 2011), 84
It Happened Just Before (*Kurz davor ist es passiert*; Anja Salomonowitz, 2006), 110, 125–26
It's a Free World... (Ken Loach, 2007), 57–60

Kid with a Bike, The (*Le gamin au vélo*; Jean-Pierre Dardenne and Luc Dardenne, 2011), 209n3
Knifer (*Macherovgaltis*; Yannis Economides, 2010), 214n1
Kush (Pratibha Parmar, 1991), 211n5

Le Havre (Aki Kaurismäki, 2011), 109
Léon: The Professional (*Léon*; Luc Besson, 1994), 40
Looking for Langston (Isaac Julien, 1989), 211n5
Lou Andreas-Salome (Cordula Kablitz-Post, 2016), 84

Love Actually (Richard Curtis, 2003), 172

Made in Dagenham (Nigel Cole, 2010), 82–88, 90, 96, 102
Mademoiselle Paradis (*Licht*; Barbara Albert, 2017), 74
Maid, The (*La nana*; Sebastián Silva, 2009), 140
Maltese Falcon, The (John Huston, 1941), 212n6
Marie Curie: The Courage of Knowledge (*Marie Curie*; Marie Noelle, 2016), 84
Maurice (James Ivory, 1987), 79
Metropolis (Fritz Lang, 1927), 1, 46, 137–38
Modern Times (Charlie Chaplin, 1936), 10
My Beautiful Laundrette (Stephen Frears, 1985), 79, 161
My Work (*Meine Arbeit*; Peter Gallasch, 1977/1978), 208n3

Never Let Me Go (Mark Romanek, 2010), 155, 160–61, 171–76, 213n6
Nikita (Luc Besson, 1990), 40
North Country (Niki Caro, 2005), 212n5
Northern Skirts (*Nordrand*; Barbara Albert, 2000), 74

One, Two, Three (Billy Wilder, 1961)
One Size Bigger (*Eine Nummer größer*; Frank Dietrich, 1981), 208n3
Other Side of Hope, The (*Toivon tuolla puolen*; Aki Kaurismäki, 2017), 109

Passage to India, A (David Lean, 1984), 79, 112
Paula (Christian Schwochow, 2016), 84
Philomena (Stephen Frears, 2013), 161
Populaire (Régis Roinsard, 2012), 90–93, 96, 102, 210n11
Potiche (Fraçois Ozon, 2010), 95, 97–98, 102
Present (*Präsent*; Hubert Andörfer, 1983), 207n3
Price of Coal, The (Ken Loach, 1977), 60
Prick Up Your Ears (Stephen Frears, 1987), 161
Pride & Prejudice (Joe Wright, 2005), 111
Promise and Unrest (Alan Grossman and Áine O'Brien, 2010), 109, 117, 119–21, 127

Queen, The (Stephen Frears, 2006), 84

Road, The (*Yol*; Yilmaz Güney, 1982), 213n7
Room with a View, A (James Ivory, 1985), 79
Rosa Luxemburg (Margarethe von Trotta, 1986)
Rosetta (Jean-Pierre Dardenne and Luc Dardenne, 1999), 209n3

Salut Cousin! (Merzak Allouche, 1996), 101
Sammy and Rosie Get Laid (Stephen Frears, 1987), 161
Samouraï, Le (Jean-Pierre Melville, 1967), 40
Sari Red (Pratibha Parmar, 1988), 211n5
Schindler's List (Steven Spielberg, 1993), 210n7
Second Mother, The (*Que horas ela volta?*; Anna Muylaert, 2015), 140–41
Sense and Sensibility (Ang Lee, 1995), 111
Sex and the City (Michael Patrick King, 2008), 54
Silence of Lorna, The (*Le silence de Lorna*; Jean-Pierre Dardenne and Luc Dardenne, 2008), 74
Sixty Minutes Past Twelve (*Sechzig Minuten nach Zwölf*; Emil Jurkowski, 1979/1980), 207n3
Slumming (Michael Glawogger, 2006), 74
Snow (*Snijeg*; Aida Begić, 2008), 35–38
Some Time and Motion Studies: An Analysis of the Gilbreth's Law of Simultaneity (A. Langsner, n.d.), 212n2
So We Can All Live Happily (*Damit wir glücklich leben*; W.-K. Krekow and Konrad Hildebrand, 1971), 207n3
Spiral Staircase, The (Robert Siodmak, 1946), 148–49
Strike (*Stachka*; Sergei M. Eisenstein, 1925), 1, 68, 88
Strike (*Strajk: Die Heldin von Danzig*; Volker Schlöndorff, 2006), 88
Suffragette (Sarah Gavron, 2015), 172

Thelma & Louise (Ridley Scott, 1991), 101
Time Out (*L'emploi du temps*; Laurent Cantet, 2001), 61
Toni Erdmann (Maren Ade, 2016), 11, 14, 71–73

Top Girl (Tatjana Turanskyj, 2014), 69
Two Chapters from: Humans at Work (*Zwei Kapitel aus: "Der Mensch und seine Arbeit"*; Herbert Illgen and Dieter Weigend, 1972), 207n3
Two Days, One Night (*Deux jours, une nuit*; Jean-Pierre Dardenne and Luc Dardenne, 2014), 11, 62

Unknown Girl, The (*Le fille inconnue*; Jean-Pierre Dardenne and Luc Dardenne, 2016), 62
Unknown Woman, The (*La sconosciuta*; Giuseppe Tornatore, 2006), 136, 141, 145–53

Vertigo (Alfred Hitchcock, 1958), 149
Vie en Rose, La (Olivier Dahan, 2007), 84
Voices of Finance (Clara van Gool, 2015), 182, 195–96, 200

Wasted Youth (Argyris Papadimitropoulos and Jan Vogel, 2011), 214n1
We Are Based Down South (*Wir sitzen im Süden*; Martina Priessner, 2010), 109, 121, 123–24, 127
White Gold (*Weißes Gold*; Alfred Dorn, 1967), 207n3
Whores' Glory (Michael Glawogger, 2011), 74
Who's Minding the Store? (Frank Tashlin, 1963), 210n11
Woman's Way, A (*Strella*; Panos H. Kontras, 2009), 214n1
Women on the Sixth Floor, The (*Les femmes du 6e étage*; Philippe Le Guay, 2010), 136–38

Workers Leaving the Factory (*Arbeiter verlassen die Fabrik*; Harun Farocki, 1995), 210n5
Workers Leaving the Lumière Factory in Lyon (*La sortie de l'usine Lumière à Lyon*; Auguste and Louis Lumière, 1895), 9–10, 210n5
Workingman's Death (Michael Glawogger, 2005), 74

Yesterday Never Ends (*Ayer no termina nunca*; Isabel Coixet, 2013), 182, 197–200

Performance Pieces / Video Installations

At Any Place 4: From the Tango of a Housewife (Mako Idemitsu, 1978), 129, 131, 211–12n1
Glottis (Valie Export, 2007), 210–11n1
Workers Leaving the Factory in Eleven Decades (*Arbeiter verlassen die Fabrik in elf Jahrzehnten*; Harun Farocki, 2006), 78, 210n5

Television Series

Clean Sweep (2003–2005, TLC), 54
Downton Abbey (2010–2015, ITV), 138
Orphan Black (2013–2017, BBC America), 211n8
Queer Eye for the Straight Guy (2003–2007, Bravo TV), 54
Upstairs Downstairs (1971–1975, ITV, and 2010–2012, BBC 1), 138
What Not to Wear (2003–2013, TLC), 54

General Index

accents of workers in call centers, 121–24
acting in emotional labor, 131–32
Ade, Maren, 7, 52
Adkins, Lisa, 31
Agamben, Giorgio, 134, 157–58, 164
agency and gestures, 135
Albert, Barbara, 52, 73–74
Ali, Monica, 110
Allouche, Merzak, 101
anachronisms, 39
Anderson, Bridget, 106
Appiah, Kwame Anthony, 44
Arendt, Hannah, 24, 27–28, 201
Artaud, Antonin, 78
artisinal modes of production, 37–38
Attenborough, David, 187
austerity measures, European, 184–86, 205

Baer, Hester, 72
Ballesteros, Isolina, 115, 116
Barillet, Pierre, 95
"Battle of Humor, A," 52
Beach, The, 171
beauty, 112–14
Bedos, Nicolas, 95

Begić, Aida, 35
Benjamin, Walter, 10
Bergman, Ingmar, 35
Berlant, Lauren, 55–56, 147, 199
Betz, Mark, 15, 66
Bhabha, Jacqueline, 103
biopics, 84, 88–89
biopolitics, 156, 157; dystopian motherhood and, 166–71
biotechnology, 154–61, 176–77; cloning, 155, 171–76; cord blood, 160; dystopian motherhood with, 166–71; ethical dimensions of, 157; underground economy of organ harvesting, 161–65
Bizet, Georges, 129
Bloch, Ernst, 6, 19, 82, 121, 156
"body-machine complex," 7
Bohle, Dorothee, 99
Boland, Rosie, 83
Boris, Eileen, 131
Boyle, Kirk, 167
Braune, Wilhelm, 9
Brazil, Alan, 178
Brexit, 105
Brick Lane, 110, 111, 113

Brown, Elspeth, 8
Brown, Wendy, 54

call centers, 121–24
camp, 95–98
Cantet, Laurent, 56
"Can the Subaltern Speak?," 104–5, 211n2
capitalism. *See* neoliberal capitalism
Castle, Barbara, 83
Celik, Ipek A., 107–8
Chakrabarty, Dipesh, 37, 95
chamber play, 193–95
Chaplin, Charlie, 10, 134
Chaudhary, Zahid R., 167
Chion, Michel, 103
cinéma du look, 40–41
"Cinematic Gesture," 129
Cliff, Jimmy, 87
cloning, 155, 171–76
Coixet, Isabel, 182, 197
cold labor, 45–47
Cold War, end of the, 14, 52–53, 98–101
color, use of, 67–68
Communism: industrial ruins of, 64–69
cool labor, 39–42
Cooper, Melinda, 157, 174
cord blood, 160
Corea, Gena, 158
corporate films, 12–13
corporate identity, 12
creative class, 198
Creative Europe, 16
crime and gesturing, 145–52
crisis cinema, 178–82, 199–200, 205; chamber play, 193–95; death in, 187–89; European crisis and austerity in, 184–86; Greek weird cinema as, 178, 182–83; landscape of the financial industry in, 195–96; narrating debt, 189–93; postromance in postcrisis, 197–99; return of the housewife in, 186–87
Cronenberg, David, 109, 114
"cruel optimism," 55–56, 147
Cuarón, Alfonso, 166, 168, 169
Cunningham, John, 99

dangerous work, women in, 47–50
Dardenne brothers, 53, 64, 74

DasGupta, Sayantani, 157, 170
death in crisis cinema, 187–89
debt and theft, 189–93
Dekker, Desmond, 87
Delsarte, François, 134
democratic freedom, 28
Dench, Judi, 161
Deneuve, Catherine, 95, 97
Depardieu, Gérard, 95
Dialectic of Sex: The Case for Feminist Revolution, The, 158
diasporic filmmaking, 107–8
Dickenson, Donna, 157, 159–60, 165
division of labor, 39, 45, 131
Doane, Mary Ann, 108
documentaries, 117–21
domesticity, 24–27, 50–51; crisis cinema return of housewives and, 186–87; dangerous work and the failure of maternity in, 47–50; in European precarity and African maternity, 42–45; female to male as labor to work as private to public, 27–28; gestures in, 129–30, 133, 136–41; maternal failure and, 45–47; migration and, 106, 117–21, 204; portrayed as beautiful drudgery, 32–35; sexualization of migrant workers and, 132, 140–41, 143, 145–48; subsistence labor in the shadow of trauma and, 35–38; suffocating, 38–39; theorizing invisible and unpaid domestic work and, 28–32
Dyer, Richard, 14, 80
dystopian motherhood, 166–71
dystopian science fiction, 3

East Europe, 14
Edison, Thomas, 9, 10
Efron, David, 134
Eisenstein, Sergei M., 1, 68, 88
Elsaesser, Thomas, 37–38
"emergent Euroculture," 3
empowerment, 54–55
entrepreneurialism, 70–71
epistolary voice-over, 110–14; long-distance intimacy and, 117–21
Equal Pay Act, UK, 87
ethics of care, 7, 42. *See also* gestures

Europe 2020, 17
European cinema, twenty-first century: biotechnology in (*see* biotechnology); crisis cinema (*see* crisis cinema); feminist turn in, 2, 4 (*see also* feminism); in film studies after the fall of the Wall, 14–16; genres in, 3, 202, 213n5; heritage cinema (*see* heritage cinema of industrial labor); imagining alternatives and offering commentaries, 5; of migration (*see* migration, labor); national waves in, 15, 186; strong appearance of women's work in, 1–3, 201–2. *See also* film
European Economic Community, 105
European Economic Recovery Plan, 17
European Employment Strategy, 17
Europeanization, 3, 14
exilic filmmaking, 107–8

Falser, Michael, 81
Farocki, Harun, 78
Fassbinder, Rainer Werner, 96, 188
Federici, Silvia, 24, 29, 113
female labor. *See* women's work
Feminine Mystique, The, 18, 85
feminism, 2, 4; beauty and, 112–14; biotechnology of reproductive labor and, 156, 158; Europe's gendered economy and, 16–21; as "handmaiden of neoliberalism," 6–7; "housework" term used in, 25; and labor conjoined in heritage cinema, 91; liberal, 55–56; neoliberalism's appropriation of, 54–55, 202–3; precarious management and legacy of social realism and, 57–61; projected onto the East, 88–90; second-wave, 17–18, 24, 55; theorizing invisible and unpaid domestic work in, 28–32. *See also* postfeminism
film: biopic, 84, 88–89; camp in, 95–98; collapse of the Eastern bloc and studies of European, 14–16; corporate, 12–13; crucial role of, in visualizing work processes, 7; depicting the postindustrial world, 11; depicting the space of work, 9–10; depicting working-class masculinity, 12; documentary, 117–21; early integration of labor and, by Edison, 9; efficiency experts' use of, 8; exilic and diasporic, 107–8; gestures in (*see* gestures); heritage cinema (*see* heritage cinema of industrial labor); magical realism in, 191–92; melodrama in, 43–44, 96–97; mise-en-scène in, 46–47, 88, 120, 129, 135, 193, 197–98; motion studies using, 8–9; music in, 92–94, 171; pacing in, 10; postfeminist analysis of, 18–19; scientific management and, 8; social realism in, 57–61, 101; sound and voice in, 108–10; twenty-first century scholarship on labor in, 11–14; use of color in, 67–68. *See also* European cinema, twenty-first century
Film and the Working Class: The Feature Film in British and American Society, 10–11
Firestone, Shulamith, 18, 158
Fischer, Otto, 9
Fitzgerald, Ella, 94
Florida, Richard, 198
Foley, Stephen, 178
Fordism, 9, 31
Ford strike, 1967, 82–87
Foucault, Michel, 157–58, 159, 175
Franklin, Sarah, 157, 170
Fraser, Nancy, 6, 55, 131
Frears, Stephen, 161–62, 164–65
freelancing, 70–71
French New Wave, 15
Friedan, Betty, 18, 85
friendship, female, 73–76

Galt, Rosalind, 15, 66, 80, 112, 186
Garland, Alex, 171
Garnett, Tony, 11
Gavron, Sarah, 109, 110
gendered labor/economy, 3, 16–21, 106
gender mainstreaming, 30
genres, 3, 202, 213n5
gestures, 129–36, 152–53; agency and, 135; as "agent of the heart," 134; economy of, 136–41; by mental patients, 134; of migrant workers, 141–45; racial and ethnic dimension of, 134; suspicious, 145–52
"Ghosting," 129

Giftlife Egg Bank, 154
Gilbreth, Frank, 8–9, 130
Gilbreth, Lillian, 8–9, 130
Gill, Rosalind, 54
glass ceilings, 71–73
Glawogger, Michael, 74
global art cinema, 3, 179
global financial crisis, 178–82, 205; chamber play, 193–95; Europe's austerity measures and, 184–86; Greek weird cinema and, 178, 182–83; landscape of the financial industry and, 195–96
"Global Financial Crisis's Silver Bullet, The," 1
globalization, 57–58, 104. *See also* migration, labor
Global South, the, 5, 19, 21, 103, 106, 113; biotechnology and, 155, 156–57; domesticity and, 29, 42, 43, 45, 49–50; financial precarity in, 193; voice and migration of women from, 108, 110. *See also* migration, labor
Godard, Jean-Luc, 1
Göktürk, Deniz, 107
Goldberg, Whoopi, 44
"Goldman's Memo," 178
Golino, Valeria, 40
Gomes, Miguel, 189
González Iñarretu, Alejandro, 42, 74
Goodwin, Michele, 159
Gorfinkel, Elena, 7, 12, 135
Grédy, Jean-Pierre, 95
"Greek Crisis, The," 178
Greek weird cinema, 178, 182–83; death in, 187–89
Gregg, Melissa, 59
Greskovits, Béla, 99
Grossman, Alan, 109
Gutiérrez-Rodríguez, Encarnación, 118

Halle, Randall, 16, 66
Hamer, Bent, 45
Haraway, Donna, 44–45
Hard Hats, Rednecks, and Macho Men: Class in 1970s American Cinema, 12
Hardy, Jane, 105
Harvey, David, 120
haunting voice, 114–17

Haynes, Todd, 96
Hediger, Vinzenz, 12–13, 46
Heidenreich, Nanna, 107, 116
heritage cinema of industrial labor, 78–82, 102; capitalist dreams and postcommunist labor in, 98–101; projecting feminism onto the East, 88–90; queer camp and, 95–98; voice and sound in, 111–12; womens' strike in England in, 82–87; work as sport and modernization in, 90–95
Heritage Industry, The, 78, 81
Hewison, Robert, 78, 81
Hicks, Heather J., 44
Higson, Andrew, 15, 79–80, 82
Hochschild, Arlie Russell, 1, 117, 131–32
Holbein, Hans, 167
housework. *See* domesticity
Human Condition, The, 24

Idemitsu, Mako, 129
identity, corporate, 12
If Women Counted, 40
Incze, Ágnes, 99
industrial films, 12–13, 207n2. *See also* heritage cinema of industrial labor
industrialism, 7
industrial mode of production, 38
Industrial Revolution, 28
institutional memory, 12
International Journal of Heritage Studies, 80
"Interview with Barbara Albert," 52
intimacy of work, 59–60
Ishiguro, Kazuo, 171
Islamophobia, 110
Italian neorealism, 15
Ivory, James, 111

Jäckel, Anne, 16
James, P. D., 166–67

Kaurismäki, Aki, 109
Kempadoo, Kamala, 107
Kerber, Linda K., 103
kinetoscopes, 9
Klein, Naomi, 167
Knight, Deborah, 57
Knightley, Keira, 172

labor migration. *See* migration, labor
Labrosse, Sarah-Jeanne, 115
Lai, Larissa, 164
Landsberg, Alison, 80, 84, 95
Lang, Fritz, 1, 46
Lanthimos, Yorgos, 180, 182–83, 185
Laurie, William Kennedy, 9
Lean, David, 112
Lee, Ang, 111
Lemke, Thomas, 156, 157–58
Levinas, Emmanuel, 64
Levitt, Deborah, 134
liberal feminism, 55–56
Linklater, Richard, 185
Loach, Ken, 11, 53, 57, 59
Loiperdinger, Martin, 12–13
long-distance intimacy, 117–21
Lorber, Monika, 67
Lumière, Auguste, 9–10
Lumière, Louis, 9–10
Luyendijk, Joris, 195

"magical negro," 44
magical realism, 191–92
Malik, Sarita, 107
Managed Heart, The, 1
Marçal, Katrine, 36
Marey, Étienne-Jules, 8, 130, 134
Marx, Karl/Marxism, 11, 27–28, 55, 71, 201
masculinized protagonists, 40–41
Maslany, Tatiana, 115
Mazierska, Ewa, 11, 12
McKnight, George, 57, 59
McRobbie, Angela, 19, 54–55, 75
melodrama, 43–44, 96–97
"Mere Fortuity of Birth?," 103
Merkel, Angela, 178
middle-class women, friendships of, 74–76
migration, labor, 26, 29, 58, 60, 103–5, 127–28, 204; affective accents in call centers and, 121–24; epistolary voice-over and, 110–14; European cinema of migration and, 107–8; gestures and, 130–31, 132, 141–45; haunting voice of, 114–17; long-distance intimacy and, 117–21; and mobility defining and challenging Europe, 105–7; sexualization of, 132, 140–41, 143, 145–48; sound and voice in space of the cinema and, 108–10; ventriloquized clandestine voices and, 125–27
Mirren, Helen, 161
mise-en-scène, 46–47, 88, 120, 129; crisis and, 193; gestures and, 135; postromance, 197–98
Mitevska, Labina, 65–66
Mitevska, Teona Strugar, 64–66, 69
Mitevska, Vuc, 66
motherhood, dystopian, 166–71
Mother Machine: Reproductive Technologies from Artificial Insemination to Artificial Wombs, The, 158
motion studies, 8–9
Mulligan, Carey, 172
Mulvey, Laura, 15, 86, 112, 129, 135
music, film, 92–94, 171
Musser, Charles, 9–10
Muybridge, Eadweard, 8, 130, 134

Naficy, Hamid, 109
Nathanson, Elizabeth, 18, 19, 54
National Heritage Acts, UK, 79
national waves in European cinema, 15, 186
Negra, Diane, 18, 19, 54
neoliberal capitalism, 4–5, 52–57, 76–77, 202–3; "cruel optimism" in, 55–56, 147; diversity in, 99–100; empowerment in, 54–55; end of the Cold War and, 14, 52–53; Europe's gendered economy and, 17; financial crisis in (*see* crisis cinema); freelancing and entrepreneurialism in, 69–71; gendered economy of, 3, 16–21, 106; glass ceilings and outsourcing in, 54, 71–73; industrial ruins of Communism and, 64–69; mass infertility as allegory for, 167–68; middle-class women and, 74–76; migrant workers in, 26, 29, 58, 60; postfeminism and, 18; precarious falling and female friendship in, 73–76; precarious labor and elusive solidarity in, 61–64; private sphere in, 31
Ness, Sally Ann, 150
"new British realism," 11
New Europe, 105
New German Cinema, 15, 88

242 • General Index

9/11 terrorist attacks, 110
Noland, Carrie, 135
nonsynchronism, 6, 19, 82, 121, 156, 174
North, Michael, 10
"Notes on Gesture," 134
Nystrom, Derek, 12

Oakley, Ann, 28–29, 32, 36–37
O'Brian, Áine, 109
organ harvesting, 161–65
Orientalist projections, 37
outsourcing, 54, 71–73
Ozon, François, 95, 96–97

pacing, film, 10
Papandreou, Yorgos, 182
Papoulias, Karolos, 178
Parreñas, Rhacel Salazar, 118, 119, 131
Parvulescu, Anca, 14, 147
Pateman, Carole, 17, 24, 30, 32, 140
Peranson, Mark, 52
Perrons, Diane, 16–17
Plomien, Ania, 16–17
Plumpe, Werner, 81
Polaschek, Bronwyn, 82
political economy of labor, 5–6
postcommunist labor, 98–101
postfeminism, 18–19, 85–86
post-Fordism, 17, 25, 31, 53, 90, 135
postindustrial context. *See* neoliberal capitalism
postromance, 197–99
precarious labor and elusive solidarity, 61–64
precarious management, 57–61
Priessner, Martina, 109, 121
Principles of Scientific Management, The, 129
professional-managerial class (PMC), 12
projection of feminism onto the East, 88–90
Pro Quote Film, 69
prostitution, 125–27, 151–52

queer camp, 95–98

racism in biopolitics, 155–56
Radner, Hilary, 54
Rappoport, Ksenia, 145

Remains of the Day, The, 171
reproductive labor, 147–48; biotechnology and, 154–61; dystopian motherhood and, 166–71
Rieger, Sophia Charlotte, 52
Romanek, Mark, 171
Rousseau, Jean-Jacques, 17–18

Salomonowitz, Anja, 109–10, 125–27
Scharff, Christina, 54
Schlöndorff, Volker, 88, 90
Schoonover, Karl, 66, 186
scientific management, 7–8, 129, 134
Scott, Anthony Oliver, 182–83
Scott, Ridley, 101
Screen (journal), 57
second-wave feminism, 17–18, 24, 55
Sedgwick, Eve, 116, 144
self-actualization, 113
Seltzer, Mark, 7
sex-trafficking, 147
sexual contract, 24, 140–41
Sexual Contract, The, 24
sexualization of domestic workers, 132, 140–41, 143, 145–48
Sieg, Katrin, 3, 20
Silverman, Kaja, 108
Sirk, Douglas, 96
Smith, Adam, 26, 36
Smith, Mark, 17
social contract, 18
Socialist Worker, 83
social realism, 101; legacy of, 57–61
solidarity movement in Poland, 88–90
sound. *See* voice
Spivak, Gayatri, 104–5, 170, 211n2
Standing, Guy, 43, 76
"Stateless as the Citizen's Other, The," 103
Stead, Peter, 11
Steiner, André, 81
Stern, Lesley, 129, 135
Streep, Meryl, 161
strikes, labor, 82–87
Strindberg, August, 35
subsistence labor, 35–38
suffocating domesticity, 38–39
suspicious gestures, 145–52

Tasker, Yvonne, 18, 19, 54
Taylor, Frederick Winslow/Taylorism, 8–9, 129, 130, 134
Taylor, Jessica, 32
television makeover shows, 18
temporality, 107–8, 116, 147–48
Thalbach, Katharina, 90
Thatcher, Margaret, 57, 79
Three Sisters, 67
thrillers, gesturing in, 145–52
Titmuss, Richard, 158
Treaty of Rome, 16, 105
Troell, Jan, 32
Trophy Wife, The, 95
True, Jacqui, 1
Tsangari, Athina Rachel, 183, 185
Turanskyj, Tatjana, 52, 69
typewriters, 90–95

UNESCO, 80–81, 209n1
United Nations System of National Accounts (UNSNA), 29–30
upper-class women, gestures of, 140

"Van Gogh, the Man Suicided by Society," 78
Van Gool, Clara, 182, 195
Varda, Agnès, 94
ventriloquized clandestine voices, 125–27
Villa, Paola, 17
Vincendeau, Ginette, 14
Vincent, Gene, 94
"Visual Pleasure and Narrative Cinema," 86
voice, 104–5, 127–28; affective accents in call centers and, 121–24; in documentaries, 117–21; epistolary voice-over, 110–14; epistolary voice-over and long-distance intimacy, 117–21; haunting, 114–17; and sound in the space of the cinema, 108–10; ventriloquized clandestine, 125–27
Voice in the Cinema, The, 103
Volkening, Heide, 1, 13
"Vom Leben in der Scheinemanzipation," 52
Vonderau, Patrick, 12, 46
Vora, Kalinda, 122

"Wages against Housework," 18, 24, 29
Walentynowicz, Anna, 88–89
Wargnier, Regis, 112
Waring, Marilyn, 17, 29–31
Weeks, Kathi, 18, 55
Weiner, Elaine, 99
Wershler-Henry, Darren, 90
Wills, Jenny, 164
Wilson, Harold, 83
Wolff, Charlotte, 134
women's work: in call centers, 121–24; as dangerous, 47–50; division of labor and, 39, 45, 131; domestic (*see* domesticity); empowerment in, 54–55; in Europe's gendered economy, 16–21, 106; female friendship in, 73–76; feminist turn and, 2, 4 (*see also* feminism); film portrayal of, 7–14; in freelancing and entrepreneurialism, 70–71; glass ceilings and outsourcing in, 54, 71–73; in heritage films (*see* heritage cinema of industrial labor); industrial ruins of Communism and, 64–69; intimacy of, 59–60; migration and (*see* migration, labor); modernization and, 90–95; neoliberal capitalism and (*see* neoliberal capitalism); and 1967 strike in England, 82–87; nonsynchronism and, 6; outsourcing and, 54; political economy of labor and, 5–6; in prostitution, 125–27; sexualization of, 132, 140–41, 143, 145–48; strong appearance in twenty-first-century European cinema, 1–3. *See also* neoliberal capitalism
"Workers Leaving the Factory," 78
working-class masculinity, 12
"Working Girl-eine Einleitung," 1
World Heritage Sites, 81, 209n1
Wright, Joe, 111

Yildiz, Yasemin, 109
Yoneyama, Mamako, 129

Zbanic, Jasmila, 74
Žižek, Slavoj, 166–67

BARBARA MENNEL is an associate professor of film studies in the Departments of English and of Languages, Literatures, and Cultures at the University of Florida. Her books include *The Representation of Masochism and Queer Desire in Film and Literature* and *Queer Cinema: Schoolgirls, Vampires, and Gay Cowboys*.

The University of Illinois Press
is a founding member of the
Association of American University Presses.

Composed in 10.25/13 Marat Pro
with Trade Gothic Condensed display
by Kirsten Dennison
at the University of Illinois Press
Cover designed by Jennifer S. Fisher
Cover illustration: Déborah François in *Populaire*, directed by
Régis Roinsard (The Weinstein Company/Photofest)

University of Illinois Press
1325 South Oak Street
Champaign, IL 61820-6903
www.press.uillinois.edu